To Professor G. H. Turnbull

with affectionate regard.

October 1951.

INTERNATIONAL LIBRARY OF SOCIOLOGY
AND SOCIAL RECONSTRUCTION

Editor: Dr. Karl Mannheim

STUDIES
IN THE SOCIAL PSYCHOLOGY
OF ADOLESCENCE

by

J. E. RICHARDSON, J. F. FORRESTER,
J. K. SHUKLA
AND P. J. HIGGINBOTHAM

edited with a foreword by
C. M. FLEMING

ROUTLEDGE & KEGAN PAUL LTD
Broadway House, Carter Lane
London

FOREWORD

THE study of children in their social relationships, the effect of membership of groups, the school as a social therapeutic institution. These are relatively novel phrases and like all such fresh phrases they point to a new emphasis in the observation of human beings and in the formulation of basic hypotheses as to their nature. Much that they denote is very recent in its structure and its procedure. Much that they connote is very old and has its roots in the long history of educational thought.

This book of studies in social psychology, while offering a distinctive contribution, is therefore admittedly in its contents both very old and very new. Much of its language and its interpretation is not to be found prior to the fourth or fifth decade of this century. Certain of the procedures it describes have been in use for many hundreds of years. All had their recent antecedents in the 'play-way', the 'individual work', the 'project methods', the 'group activities', to which educational discussion was devoted in the 1910's and 1920's; but their more immediate origins may be traced in the experimental work of the 1930's and the 1940's conducted in the University of London Institute of Education with the co-operation of the late Professor H. R. Hamley.

In the 1920's and the 1930's a transition was being effected in psychological interpretation from the study of individual children in laboratories and the treatment of individual patients in consulting rooms to some awareness of the significance of the school life and home background of problem pupils and some study of the social environment of juvenile delinquents. This recognition of society as a background to humanity affected teaching methods first through an emphasis on the social relevance of the curriculum—in terms of an arithmetic which led to more intelligent utilisation of public resources and a study of English usage which contributed to better citizenship. The concern of reformers in the middle years was with the child and society—the pupil and his social background. More recently it has passed beyond this to an endeavour to understand the meaning for a child of his membership of groups, the influences of groups upon individuals and of individuals upon groups, the inter-actions and tensions within groups, the social forces which operate in homes and schools and clubs, and the effect of differing types of social climate and group atmosphere upon the behaviour of pupils in classrooms and children in their homes.

The studies here presented deal with group experiences as observable in the teaching of English and of citizenship, with surveys of attitudes, and with enquiries into the accompaniments of friendship. They cover a period of about six years from the time of Forrester's enquiry into the attitude of adolescents towards their own development to the years in which the sociometric techniques of Moreno and his associates were deliberately applied to classroom procedures in the fashion described in the record of experimental work given in Part I. All of them fall into place when seen in the present-day setting of an interpretation in terms of the socialising effect of school membership, the therapy of groups and the admittedly great complexity of a human nature for whose description the earlier individualistic terminology is now believed to be inadequate. Each of the investigations is relatively small in itself—dealing with a few dozen or a few hundred pupils—but in their totality they are highly significant and they are in accord with many other enquiries whose scope is indicated by the bibliographies appended.

Together also they form a contribution to educational research which is of value not merely to teachers but to parents, club-leaders, employers and magistrates. To all such workers they bring evidence not only as to the methods being adopted to foster successful learning in schools, but as to the attitudes held by boys and girls towards their own development. They serve further to confirm the belief that the most effective incentives are not merely materialistic, competitive or individualistic in nature.

Human beings are inescapably social. They have been born into membership of groups and are conditioned to such membership. They are so made that their primary attribute is co-operation and their first need that of receiving appreciation from, and making contributions to the intimate small circle of their closest associates.

FOREWORD

Boys and girls require not only affection and acceptance in their homes, but the opportunity of taking a responsible share in the activities of their companions—in working hours as well as in moments of leisure. The most effective schooling is therefore that which permits some degree of group activity and some measure of classification by friendship, just as the highest morale is found in those industries in which men and women are not only aware of the meaning of the service they render, but are convinced of the appreciative regard in which they are held by those with whom they come in contact.

Co-operation in such working hours is recommended not merely as an aid to more effective output, but as a means by which mental health and wholesome attitudes may be fostered—in individuals as well as in groups. And this finding has a significance which extends beyond the classroom. Racial prejudice and intolerance are more liable to be found in homes or schools in which fears and antipathies have been sown by dictatorial methods motivated by distrust of human nature and by the belief that boys and girls are primarily self-seeking and essentially egocentric. International sympathies and the tolerance which contributes to world peace flower best in human soil in which a sense of security and serenity is consequent on the satisfaction of the basic human needs; and human beings appear to find stability only in some measure of insight into the meaning of their activities, coupled with an opportunity to make an acceptable contribution to the welfare of their fellows.

All this is not explicit in every chapter of this book; but something of this sort is the implication which its findings can justifiably be said to carry; and in this is to be found its significance and its challenge to further enquiry and research.

C. M. FLEMING

London, 1951

CONTENTS

CONTENTS

PART THREE
GROUP WORK AND CLASSROOM ATTITUDES

x

PART ONE

CLASSIFICATION BY FRIENDSHIP: SOCIOMETRIC TECHNIQUES APPLIED TO THE TEACHING OF ENGLISH

CHAPTER ONE

GROUP RELATIONS AND EDUCATION

PSYCHOLOGISTS in many fields have during the last twenty years given increasing attention to interpersonal relationships. From factories, hospitals, schools and clinics researches have been reported which have not only shown the interconnections of these fields but have together provided a fund of information about the behaviour of human beings in groups. In these enquiries a social group is regarded as a unit and the investigator concerns himself with a total situation rather than with an isolated segment of human experience.[1] Groups in factories, homes, clinics, schools, clubs and residential institutions have therefore been studied in functional situations in order to interpret the behaviour both of those groups and of the individuals comprising them. Under Moreno and Lewin in the United States of America[2] two different but related techniques of studying the dynamics of human personality have been developed, which culminated in the foundation of the Sociometric Institute in New York in 1942 and in the setting up of the Research Center for Group Dynamics at the Massachusetts Institute of Technology in 1945. In England evidence of the same spirit is to be seen in the work of the University of London Institute of Education and of the Tavistock Institute of Human Relations.[3] Hoggarth in 1938, for example, reported the results of comparative study of individual and group methods of teaching mathematics.[4] Four methods were used: in the first the boys worked individually without regard to the progress or difficulties of the others; in the second, one boy worked in front of the others at the blackboard; in the third the class co-operated in solving the problems; in the fourth the boys worked in co-operating groups of three, each at its own blackboard. Hoggarth found that the use of group methods led to improvement both in attainment and attitude, that the group-blackboard method was the most popular of the four and that certain individuals became

3

less shy and made new friends after experiencing it. He himself found this method more effective since it enabled him to supervise the work efficiently and deal with mistakes promptly. Horne in 1943 reported an experiment in a Free Topic method of teaching science.[5] The boys in his experimental group were allowed complete freedom to make what use they liked of the books and apparatus provided and were given the master's help only when they asked for it. Whereas in the control group, which continued to be taught by the traditional demonstration method, the usual distribution of interest, toleration and boredom was apparent, the experimental group developed real enthusiasm for the subject and learned to organise their own programmes of work. Although at first the boys worked individually, a desire to co-operate in groups of two or three was showing itself in the second year of the investigation. These attempts at group work were at first unsuccessful, owing to outbursts of quarrelling and jealousy, but by the end of the year all such difficulties had disappeared and the boys were working efficiently in groups. Simpson in 1947 measured the effect of group discussion on the understanding and appreciation of films[6], and found that boys who had discussed films understood them better and were more capable of concentrating on those particular aspects which were relevant for the particular needs of their class. The importance of social incentives in education was also demonstrated experimentally by C. M. Lambert in 1944, when she studied the nature of the interests shown by secondary school children in the various subjects of the curriculum.[7] In comparing eight different trends of interest (utilitarian, humanistic, creative, activity, scientific, vocational, æsthetic and social) she found that, considering all subjects as one, the social interest (defined as 'interest in working and co-operating with others') ranked second for the whole group and either first, second or third for each year level.

These findings suggest that teachers could with advantage give more opportunities for co-operative work than they have done in the past. There still exists among many teachers a tendency to discourage children from helping one another and to promote rivalry rather than co-operation. The result of this is to make many children seek help from one another surreptitiously in the effort to collect marks and thus to lose all sense of personal satisfaction in achievement. This kind of satisfaction can be enhanced by group co-operation, as experimental investigations have shown. It is possible that freedom to co-operate openly at certain times may induce in children a more honest and self-respecting attitude to work than do constant exhortations to work alone and unaided.

The gradual evolution of twentieth-century thought on the nature of the 'group mind' is typical of the changes that have affected psychological theory generally. It is a far cry indeed from Le Bon's conception of the group mind to the views expressed in the writings of Lewin and Moreno. To Le Bon, writing in 1895,[8] the effect of the collective mind was such as to obliterate all individual acquirements and to force each member of the group to yield to instincts which he would normally have restrained. Thus, through the emergence of the racial unconscious, individuals in groups showed always an 'average' character, and even came, under the influence of the group, to exhibit entirely new characteristics. Groups were therefore invariably impulsive and changeable, apt to go from one extreme to another, in need of excessive stimulus and satisfied with mere illusions. To Moreno a group is a constantly changing structure, affecting and being affected by the individuals who enter it. In every group of individuals, brought together by biological or social processes, there exists a pattern of relationships which determines the behaviour both of the individuals and of the group as a whole. These relationships can be described as feelings of attraction, indifference or repulsion; they may or may not be exchanged mutually and they extend beyond the boundaries of single groups to form networks spreading over the large communities in which they operate. Since the behaviour of every individual in a given community is directly affected by his position in that community, it follows that his behaviour may be modified by an improvement or deterioration in his social status. The educator or therapist is therefore in a position both to diagnose his needs (by observing where his spontaneous preferences lie) and to satisfy them by giving him opportunities for association with those chosen companions.

EARLY INVESTIGATIONS INTO GROUP BEHAVIOUR

Scientific investigations into the nature of group behaviour appear to have begun with F. H. Allport in 1920, when he conducted a series of experiments with word association tests, using as his subjects a group of students at Harvard and Radcliffe Colleges.[9] He found that his subjects produced a greater variety of ideas when working together than when working alone, and concluded from the quality of these ideas that there was 'some sort of attitude assumed by the individual in the group' which directed his ideas towards outside objects, and to the actual presence of others, so that he became 'objective rather than egocentric, present rather than retrospective'.

The results of a further experiment, in recording thought processes, suggested that there was in group work a spreading out of thought rather than a strong output of originality, and that group thought was 'extensive' whereas individual thought was to some extent 'intensive'. The experiences of Travis [10] with stutterers, using the same kind of word-association test, appeared to contradict Allport's findings, since the majority of his subjects did better work alone. Here, however, the result was obviously affected by the subjects' inhibitions: the physical defect and the 'social morbidity' arising from it formed a vicious circle from which the neurotic subject could not escape. In the light of later developments in Group Psychotherapy one can imagine these same stutterers, in a different situation, benefiting by the presence of the very companions who had inhibited their efforts in Travis' test situation.

In 1927 and 1928 South and Watson in a similar fashion investigated different aspects of co-operative mental activity. South,[11] using two kinds of tests involving æsthetic and emotional judgments and two involving logical deductions, found that small groups of three were better for the former kind of exercise and larger groups of six for the latter; all groups were more efficient when given a time limit. Watson,[12] using a word-building test, compared individuals and groups and found that the product of group thinking was superior to that of even the best member of the group, but that the quality of the group performance depended mainly on the ability of the best members.

In 1932 an experiment was recorded which not only contributed to this accumulating evidence on the phenomenon of co-operation but also represented a significant advance in methodology. M. E. Shaw [13] was the first in this line of investigators to attempt to record the interactions of the individuals in a group. Her subjects, psychology students at Columbia University, worked first individually and then in groups of four to solve a set of problems which had been so devised as to ensure diversity of opinion and lively discussion and to demand a logical series of decisions. It was found that the groups achieved a larger proportion of correct solutions than the individuals, largely because the subjects when working together rejected incorrect suggestions and checked mistakes and so did not err so soon in the logical thought process as when they worked separately. These conclusions were drawn not only from the number of correct and incorrect solutions submitted but also from detailed notes taken by observers dispersed among the groups. J. F. Dashiell in his survey of these experimental studies referred to Shaw's research as 'a genuine beginning' in the empirical scientific investigation of discussion, and foresaw later developments in such methods of recording: he believed that 'a fruitful avenue' for the refinement and elaboration of the technique of recording was opening up, and that the use of full stenographic notes and detailed schedules for tallying and checking ought to provide 'more and more penetrating analyses'.[14]

Since co-operative group work inevitably involves discussion and necessitates some degree of compromise or modification of individual opinion, research workers next turned their attention to the effect of majority decisions on individual judgment. Wheeler and Jordan[15] found that individuals whose opinions were endorsed by the group were strengthened in their beliefs, while those who found themselves in disagreement with the majority tended to modify their views. Jenness[16] carried out a series of experiments using committees of three and four to determine the number of beans in a sealed bottle; he found that ninety-three per cent of the individual judgments changed after group discussion and that although the accuracy of the group judgment was not improved, the majority of the individual opinions were.[17]

This growing belief in the importance of group behaviour was the driving force behind a number of important researches in the fields of industry, psychotherapy and social science which are relevant to any discussion on educational method. The new spirit was evident in the study of working conditions which was carried out between 1927 and 1933 at the Hawthorne Works of the Western Electric Company, Chicago, a study which was characterised by a genuine interest in the human factor in industry and by a willingness on the part of the investigators to go out in new directions of enquiry whenever unsuspected truths emerged. It inspired at Iowa University a series of investigations under Lewin's direction into the dynamics of group behaviour and the relative merits of authoritarian and democratic control in clubs, factories and housewives' groups. It led to the practice of a new kind of therapeutic treatment of psychoneurotic patients in many different clinics and hospitals in America; and it promoted the rapid spread and development of those sociometric techniques for discovering and modifying group structure which were first used on a large scale in Moreno's study of the New York State Training School for Girls.

THE WESTERN ELECTRIC RESEARCHES [18]

The Western Electric Researches had a dynamic quality which was new in industrial studies. In seeking for clues to the industrial problems of the day, these investigators turned their attention to representative groups of workers and studied not only their attitudes to their jobs and to their employers but also their relations with one another, their home conditions, their extra-vocational interests and any other information which might contribute to an understanding of the total pattern of their existence. A preliminary experiment in the effects of varying lighting conditions had revealed that psychological factors as well as physical factors were contributing to the morale of the workers; the purpose of the subsequent investigations was to discover the nature of these psychological factors. Six girls, working on the assembly of telephone relays, were selected to work in a special room apart from the rest of the department. This group, which was in existence from 1927 to 1933, came to be known as the Relay Assembly Test Room. The girls were told that they would be under observation for research purposes, but were assured that their future would in no way be in danger. They were given certain privileges, such as permission to talk while at work, and were constantly consulted as to the changes which were to be introduced. The findings revealed no correlation between changes in output and changes in working conditions. What they did reveal was a new factor of deeper human interest: the accumulated records of the human activity in that test room became in fact a fascinating record of the social development of a group. Patterns of attraction and repulsion, of leadership and submission, of popularity and isolation took shape as time went on and these proved to be affecting individual output far more closely than any physical conditions such as light, humidity, fatigue or hunger. The group developed cohesion; social customs came into being; leaders emerged and won recognition. It was observed that friends stimulated each other to greater output and that if they were separated by a change in seating arrangements the

8

correlation between their rates of work was destroyed. Similarly, the removal of one personality from the test room had some effect on the psychological atmosphere or social climate of the group.

Struck by the marked contrast between the good morale in the test room and the poor morale in the department, the investigators deliberately shifted their attention from the study of conditions of work to the study of human relations, and organised an extensive interviewing programme. This brought to light facts hitherto unsuspected about the complex inner organisation of many of the workers' groups and unveiled antagonisms towards the management of which supervisors had been dimly aware but which they had been incapable of modifying. The fourth phase of the investigation was then planned with the aim of directly observing a group at work, without radically altering its normal working conditions or changing its existing relationship with the management. In November 1931 the Bank Wiring Observation Room was set up, the personnel consisting of nine wiremen, three soldermen and two inspectors. Whereas the girls in the Relay Assembly Test Room had developed a highly co-operative attitude towards the management, the men in the Bank Wiring Observation Room continued to organise themselves against the management, deliberately keeping their output on a level which was neither noticeably low nor noticeably high. The observers found that the group shared certain sentiments, among which disapproval of 'rate-busters', 'chiselers' and 'squealers' ranked high. There was a good deal of informal helping of one man by another and 'job-trading' was fairly common: records of this kind of social intercourse revealed that the group was divided into two cliques and indicated that special friendships existed between some of the men.

Interpreting all these findings, Roethlisberger and Dickson pointed out the danger of treating men in industry as though they were unrelated by ties of feeling and custom. When, for example, a new machine is introduced into a department its advent is liable to break up established customs and work habits and so disturb social relationships. Such changes with their accompanying emotional disturbances are apt to arouse hostility even if they have been planned to facilitate the workers' tasks.

To the educationist as well as to the industrialist the Hawthorne researches carry an important lesson. In any work situation, whether its purpose be the production of manufactured goods or the acquisition of knowledge and skills, the interpersonal relations both within the working group and between the group and its overseers are of paramount importance. The reward incentive, whether it take the form of workers' wages or of school marks and prizes, is insufficient to ensure good morale. T. N. Whitehead, commenting on the Hawthorne Researches, draws attention to the importance of group integration, which, he says, evidently depends on 'the mutual support of social sentiment and social action' and results from 'routine relations between people developed over a period of time'.[18] Gordon Allport expresses this view in a different way by the term 'participation'. The worker is participant or 'industrially active' when he is 'busily engaged in using his talents, and having pleasant relations with foreman and fellow worker'. He points out that this co-operative satisfaction through group participation can be found in other walks of life—in schools, in administrative departments, in the armed forces, wherever, in fact, groups of people are to be found working together towards a common end.[19]

INVESTIGATIONS INTO THE EFFECT OF DIFFERENT KINDS OF LEADERSHIP

Between 1938 and 1945 experimental evidence of the relationship between certain kinds of leadership and certain kinds of group behaviour was accumulating. It became evident that satisfying group activity was characteristic of democratically organised groups rather than of autocracies and that the behaviour of the same group of individuals might undergo startling modifications as a result of changed leadership policy.

N. C. Kephart,[20] working in Wayne County Training School for high-grade mentally defective children, experimented with democratic methods of organisation in a cottage group in an attempt to produce better social cohesion and to reduce misbehaviour and truancy. A council of five boys was set up with authority to deal with disciplinary cases and responsibility for planning activities. Although at first many of the boys joined in the activities only from selfish motives, the council was eventually able to secure their willing co-operation and baits such as prizes became unnecessary. Sociometric tests* given before the experiment began and after five months of self-government revealed that the group had become better integrated: a powerful, aggressive clique which had been responsible for

* See page 19

much of the earlier trouble had been reduced in size from eight to four, while unconnected small groups had become linked by new bonds of friendship. Records of behaviour and attendance showed a corresponding improvement during the period of the experiment. A similar experience was reported in 1939 by O. H. Mowrer[21] of the Department of Psychology at the Institute of Human Relations, Yale University. The experiment was carried out with a cottage group at the New Haven Children's Center. The children, who had arrived at the cottage suffering from resentment and hostility, were just emerging from a period of recovery, during which they had enjoyed complete freedom. The problem which presented itself was how best to handle the re-educating process and give the necessary training in good social habits. Instead of demanding cleanliness, honesty and respect for property on moral grounds, the Staff inaugurated a system of self-government, and, merely pointing out that the exercise of such habits made living conditions pleasanter for everyone, let the group undertake its own re-education. The effect of this procedure was a remarkable decrease in the infringement of rules and a great improvement in adult-child relations. The children did, in fact, become responsible for their own behaviour and at the same time adopted a friendly attitude to the Staff, whom they had formerly regarded as their natural enemies.

A carefully conducted research into the effect of three different kinds of control was carried out with boys' clubs by Lewin, Lippitt and White between 1939 and 1940.[22] The investigators claimed that their method represented a distinct breakaway from the usual procedure in that they sought to record not merely 'certain predetermined symptoms of behaviour', but 'the total behaviour' of the group. Working with clubs of ten-year-old boys (five in each) they compared the effects of three different kinds of leader-control: authoritarian, in which the leader gave all orders and made all decisions, democratic, in which the leader co-operated with the children, and laissez-faire in which the children were left completely free. In order to take into account such variables as club personnel, leader personality and sequence of club experience each group was observed under both authoritarian and democratic leadership, and two groups were observed under all three types of control; each of the leaders acted the rôles of both authoritarian and democratic leaders at least once. It was therefore possible to study the transition from one atmosphere to another in each group and to compare the behaviour of the four groups under the same kind of control. The records contained quantitative running accounts of the social inter-actions of the children and the leader, analyses of group structure as it became evident in the course of activities, accounts of significant individual actions and changes in group feeling, and continuous records of all conversations. Interviews with the boys and with their parents and teachers also took place, so that the boys' attitudes towards the club leaders might be ascertained and their behaviour patterns in other situations described.

Through these procedures the investigators endeavoured to put into practice Lewin's theories of dynamic field psychology and so build up a more valid picture of social behaviour than the usual limited kind of recording could produce. The different effects of the three types of control were striking: under authoritarian leadership the boys remained in ignorance of the purpose of their activity and became either apathetic and submissive or irritable and rebellious; under democratic leadership they took a full share in planning objec-tives and setting standards and became highly co-operative both with one another and with the leader; under laissez-faire they deteriorated into undisciplined gangs without goals, standards or satisfactions. Perhaps the most significant sign of this difference was that boys under authoritarian rule lost interest in their work as soon as the leader went out of the room, whereas under democratic rule the leader's departure produced no change in behaviour, the boys remain-ing absorbed in their tasks. Under laissez-faire the boys were equally disorganised whether the leader was present or absent. When their opinions on the different leaders were asked for, all the boys but one pronounced the democratic leader the best, but the other two received about equal votes as second choice. These differences in reaction were partly accounted for by the fact that clubs which came back to authoritarian control after experiencing a democratic organisation were no longer prepared to accept dictatorship willingly, whereas after a purposeless laissez-faire club they might welcome a return to stricter discipline. The relations between club members were affected directly by the leader's policy during any period; democratic control was observed to bring about greater social cohesion, shown by the increase in friendly conversation and co-operative work. The investigators attributed the low morale under authoritarianism to restriction of movement, denial of the need for sociability and opposition to or mere detachment from the leader's objectives.

These findings were corroborated in 1942 by A. Bavelas [23] of the Child Welfare Research Station at Iowa University. Working under Lewin's direction, he carried out a programme of training in the principles and techniques of democratic leadership and studied the effects of this training on the morale both of the leaders and of the youth groups which they controlled. Two playground supervisors and four craftwork instructors were selected for the investigation. At the first testing records were made of the number of instances of authoritarian and democratic control; three of the leaders were then given three weeks' training in democratic methods and at the end of the fourth week all six were retested by the same quantitative recording methods. The retest showed that the three trained leaders had practically ceased to use dictatorial methods and were instead giving the responsibility for making decisions to the children and encouraging them to work in groups, while the untrained leaders had become more autocratic and gave few opportunities for co-operative work. The effect of this on the children was marked: whereas before the experiment members had attended the club irregularly and drifted from one group to another, the three groups with democratic leaders now showed constant membership and a new enthusiasm for the tasks they undertook. At the same time the three leaders, who had previously disliked their work, were now aware of a new sense of purpose and achievement. Bavelas emphasised in his report that the training course which had effected these changes of attitude was itself conducted democratically, so that the leaders, through discussion, mutual criticism and a kind of psychodramatic acting out of different situations, were themselves experiencing membership of a democratically organised group.

These indications of people's fitness to make their own decisions were confirmed by an enquiry of a somewhat different nature conducted by Lewin's group of investigators at Iowa. Alex Bavelas, Marian Radke and Dana Klusirich experimented with groups of housewives and factory workers to ascertain whether changes in food consumption habits, care of babies and rate of work output could be effected more easily by lecture methods or by group discussion. In every case the discussion method proved better: housewives could not be persuaded by even the friendliest of lecturers to cook more hearts, sweetbreads and kidneys or to increase their milk consumption, but did so after discussing the matter among themselves under a capable group leader; mothers instructed individually in the use of orange juice and cod liver oil for their babies often remained unconvinced, whereas after group discussion the majority began to use them; workers who fixed their own target far surpassed what had formerly been considered the ceiling, while others who were merely addressed on the subject showed little change in output.[24] Since each discussion was led democratically these findings were closely related to the earlier experiences with boys' clubs, where self-governing methods had improved morale and efficiency.

In 1945 and 1946 the American Association for Applied Psychology published the findings of a well-integrated series of experiments conducted under the leadership of H. H. Anderson.[25] This research gives further evidence of the advantages of democratic methods of teaching and affords an interesting parallel to the two studies of youth clubs reviewed above. Anderson's terms 'dominative' and 'socially integrative' correspond closely to the terms 'authoritarian' and 'democratic' as used by Lewin, Lippitt, White and Bavelas. Anderson defines domination as behaviour which tends to obstruct the spontaneous behaviour of another and is the expression of resistance against change; in contrast, integrative behaviour promotes the interplay of differences and is flexible, adaptive, objective and co-operative. The investigators first set themselves to devise categories of these two types of behaviour on the part of teachers and a second set of categories for the classroom reactions of children. The validity of the categories and the reliability of the recorders were carefully checked and the machinery of recording was set up for the first investigation. In a study of two second-grade teachers and children J. E. Brewer found that in one room, where the teacher used more integrative contacts and tended to promote co-operation rather than competition, the children showed fewer signs of distraction, boredom or resistance and participated more freely in discussion and problem solving, whereas in the other room, where the teacher was more dominating, inattention and conflict occurred frequently. Anderson next studied two fourth-grade and three sixth-grade classrooms to ascertain whether the observational method was applicable to older classes, and found further evidence to support Brewer's earlier belief in a measurable relationship between the classroom behaviour of teachers and children. Two follow-up investigations were then undertaken: M. F. Reed made a study of the two second-grade teachers with new groups of children and of the original second-grade children with their new teachers in the third grade, and

Anderson and Brewer made consecutive studies of two third-grade teachers at the beginning and end of a five-month period. Reed's study revealed that the behaviour patterns of the two teachers persisted even with different sets of children, the one still stifling initiative and creating misunderstanding and conflict, the other still trying to work with the children rather than against them. The third-grade children, on the contrary, did not show the same behaviour patterns as they had done the previous year, but responded to the personalities of their new teachers. These findings were supported by the other follow-up study, which showed that the two third-grade teachers had not changed their methods during the five months intervening between the tests, and that the more dominating one was meeting increased hostility, while the more democratic one was establishing more satisfactory relations with her class. This evidence seemed to show that children between the ages of seven and twelve have, in Reed's words, a high degree of flexibility in meeting their environments.

All these studies in methods of controlling and directing groups appear to indicate that friendliness and satisfaction in work are more frequently to be found under democratic rule than under autocracies, and that the behaviour of the same group may change radically as a result of a change in leadership policy.

GROUP THERAPY: CLINICAL RESEARCH

Belief in the efficacy of group experiences in improving social adjustment was also affecting psychiatric practice during these years. The immediate origins of current methods of group therapy have been traced in two widely separated cities—Boston and Vienna. In 1906 Dr. J. H. Pratt of Boston attempted the treatment of tuberculous patients by mass instruction. This group treatment was begun as an economy measure owing to understaffing and pressure of time, but as the work proceeded it became apparent that the patients benefited from the new order, and found the presence of others in a class both sustaining and helpful. By 1908 Dr. Emerson had followed Pratt's example and was using a class method with a group of undernourished children at the Boston Dispensary. In the meantime, on the other side of the world, Dr. J. L. Moreno was studying the spontaneous play of children's groups in the Vienna Meadow Gardens. In 1911 he published his first records of impromptu drama sessions at the Children's Spontaneity Theatre and was already developing his theories on the rôle of spontaneity in social development; and by 1927 he had opened the first therapeutic impromptu theatre in the United States of America. These examples of this approach to therapy were reported by Dr. J. I. Meiers [26] to the second Round Table Conference of Group Psychotherapy held by the American Psychiatric Association at Philadelphia in 1944. On this occasion Meiers, contrasting the methods used by Pratt and Moreno, expressed his view that the second type of group therapy, in which through 'dramic' methods the group itself became the real therapeutic agent, was gaining momentum over the first 'didactic' method, where the lecturer maintained the rôle of therapist. Reports were also read at this conference by Moreno and others indicating that such psychodramatic methods were also being used for the treatment of psychoneurotic patients, for the training of supervisors in hospitals and factories, for the selection of officers in the armed forces and for the education of feeble-minded children and adults. Moreno, for example, described how his subjects were encouraged to come forward and act out with one another and with 'auxiliary egos' (helpers trained to play supporting rôles) certain of the situations which had given rise to their disorders or problems which they might be required to face on returning to normal life or on taking up new posts as supervisors and foremen. These reports indicated that the method was suitable not merely for the treatment of psychiatric cases, but for the training of normal people in those interpersonal relationships on which an individual's success in any social situation largely depends.

While Moreno and his associates were developing the psycho-dramatic technique in hospitals, civil resettlement units, child guidance clinics and training institutions, another group of workers, mainly under S. R. Slavson of the Jewish Board of Guardians, was engaged in evolving group activity programmes with maladjusted children.[27] Slavson began in 1934 by instituting classes for problem children in New York City. The purpose of these classes was both diagnostic and therapeutic. It was believed that the therapist could, by allowing a child to act as he pleased towards his environment, recognise more easily the symptoms of his disorder, and at the same time allay suspicion and hostility. In a therapy group a child learned to adjust himself to his contemporaries, to the therapist and to the materials provided for his amusement and interest. As time went on

16

Slavson and his associates laid increasing emphasis on the potency of group life in character formation. The therapy classes developed into social clubs to which children were invited by personal letters from the club leader. Children who had formerly been unsociable and hostile became so enthusiastic about club meetings that they went to considerable trouble to attend them regularly. A series of articles published in the American Journal of Orthopsychiatry in 1939 and 1944 gave practical instances of the efficacy of these group activity methods. Durkin, for example, experimented with eight pre-school children from over-privileged homes.[28] For about two months, for five mornings a week, she observed them in a free-play situation, eliminating prohibition as far as possible. She concluded from these observations that many of the problems of young children could be handled through group relationships and that the method might well have significance for normal nursery school groups as well as for clinical cases. In the same year Gabriel reported how she had come, largely by accident, to use the group method with children whom she had formerly treated individually. The opportunity arose by chance as a result of an arrangement she made to use a neighbouring office as her clinic, thus relieving children from the necessity of travelling long distances to see her. Finding that many of the children came in casually, she decided to establish a therapeutic relationship with the group to avoid neglecting some in attending to others. Like Slavson she left the children free at first to behave as they liked, only gradually introducing restraints as they became sufficiently recovered in mental health to accept them. At the meetings she acted chiefly as observer, and although the children knew she made notes on their behaviour they did not resent this, nor were they inhibited by it. She found that clinging, jealous children became more self-reliant, that withdrawn, isolated children began to take part in group activities and to show a more aggressive spirit and that over-dominating, anti-social children acquired a better sense of comradeship and co-opera-tion. She emphasised in her report, however, that group treatment needed to be supplemented by individual treatment. In 1939 she began a series of investigations with six girls, who had been referred to her for social backwardness; with them, too, the group had a definite therapeutic effect.[29]

A comparable experiment was conducted by Axelrod, Cameron and Solomon at the Mount Zion Psychiatry Clinic, San Francisco.[30] Eleven Jewish girls of thirteen to fifteen years of age suffering from similar social defects were selected to take part in weekly meetings of one and a half hours' duration. The record of the first eight months of this project is a study of the evolution of an integrated social group out of a set of unconnected, mutually indifferent individuals. The authors describe how at the first meeting the girls remained aloof from one another, speaking only very occasionally to the leader and each giving her whole attention to the craft material she had selected, how at the second meeting one girl initiated a limited kind of conversation by asking another which school she came from, how by the eighth meeting clusters of two and three were forming within which some interchange of suggestions and borrowing of tools went on, how during the fifth month a feeling of dissatisfaction with individual work began to stir among the girls and how games involving the whole group were introduced, and how eventually, as a result of spontaneous co-operative action, a party was planned, one committee being formed to write and produce a play and another to buy food and serve refreshments. From this point the group developed rapidly, and after holding a fortnight's summer camp the girls announced that they wished to organise themselves as a club. Leaders rapidly emerged to deal with this new venture and an open meeting was held at which plans were made and two new members were voted into the group. By this time the group could no longer be regarded as a therapeutic one. It had in fact become by its own co-operative efforts an autonomous society and its transfer to the supervision of the recreational worker in the regular Centre was accordingly arranged. All these girls, originally referred to the clinic for serious maladjustment, thus became active, happy members of the community centre.

In 1942, in response to complaints from teachers and group workers that the materials provided by psychiatrists did not ease the problem of dealing with neurotic children in their groups, an enterprise was begun which came to be known as the Detroit Group Project.[31] It was believed that in dealing with neurotic cases a group setting had certain advantages over an interview. It was less artificial and therefore less likely to promote resistance and self-consciousness; it gave opportunities for studying a child's behaviour in social situations and for seeing how others reacted to him; and it enabled the leader to modify his own behaviour, to try different groupings, to interpret behaviour on the spot and to judge more accurately the best moment for interfering in any child's activities. The leaders encountered difficulties in placing each child in such a way that he and the group benefited mutually from his inclusion, and they had constantly to guard against helping one child at the expense of another. They had to learn to make decisions over changes in the composition of groups and over the introduction of activity programmes, and to develop, as recorders, what Redl called a group memory, especially in dealing with groups of more than eight.

In reviewing this material it is interesting to note that both Slavson [32] and Redl [31] suggest that group activities need not be confined to clinical situations. Every teacher has to diagnose causes of personality difficulty in his dealings with children and every teacher is, to some extent, a therapist. By encouraging group activity he can more easily discover the causes of conflict and can at the same time create situations which may help to resolve it. Group activity gives children opportunities of educating one another, both emotionally and intellectually, and brings about a more fruitful relationship between the teacher and his pupils than formal teaching alone can effect.

THE ORIGIN AND DEVELOPMENT OF SOCIOMETRY

It was Dr. J. L. Moreno, the instigator of psychodrama, who invented the technique of measuring individual status and group structure which we now know as Sociometry. In 1934 he published an account of a long-term experiment carried on in the New York State Training School for Girls at Hudson, New York.[33] In this he recorded the steps by which he had arrived at this large-scale investigation. First came the observational method of watching children's spontaneous groupings in the Vienna Gardens, then the partnership method of entering into groups and himself experiencing their tensions, and last the experimental method of testing individuals as to their choices of companions, thus gaining insight into the spontaneous group structures underlying any artificial groupings imposed from above. In a previous experiment carried out in Sing-Sing Prison [34] Moreno had discovered how wide were the psychological possibilities of group placement, and had become convinced that the most beneficial groupings were those in which there was a natural affinity between the individuals concerned.

The New York State Training School was an ideal field for such an investigation. It was a closed community, embracing many kinds

19

of human groupings. The girls (sent in from the New York courts because of behaviour disorders, personality problems or unsatisfactory homes) were housed in cottages, each in the charge of a housemother, and it was this circumstance which gave Moreno his first opportunity for a sociometric test. Each girl was asked to write down the names of those with whom she would choose to live and, if she wished, the names of any whom she would reject as companions. This data enabled Moreno and his colleagues to make charts showing the structure of each cottage group and the position of every girl within it and maps showing the patterns of attraction and repulsion existing over the entire community. Certain individuals were observed to attract many choices, others to be isolated or rejected; some formed chain associations, others banded together in groups of three or four. A close relationship was found to exist between the choice-pattern in a cottage group and the efficiency of its organisation: laziness, superficiality or destructiveness might be the result of varying factors, such as friction and jealousy within the group, complete indifference of many of its members towards one another, or networks of hostility and rebellion against the housemother. The most satisfactory cottage groups appeared to be those in which the majority of the girls accepted each other and the housemother and had also some ties of friendship with members of other cottages, and in which the leaders were girls in key positions in the groups and not merely dominating members of exclusive cliques. In order to learn more about the motivation of some of these choices, Moreno followed up the sociometric tests by interviews and spontaneity tests. Since the girls sometimes failed to give the real reasons for their choices, the spontaneity tests were designed to reveal by psychodramatic technique through the acting out of impromptu situations the feelings which they really experienced towards one another. By such measures as these the investigators accumulated much information which enabled them to reorganise some of the cottage groups in the light of the girls' expressed preferences. It soon became obvious, however, that the construction of an ideal community based on sociometric choices was no simple matter, since only a very small number chose each other mutually, while the majority were either rejected or ignored by those to whom they felt attracted. Nevertheless, it was possible to modify groups, to arrange for the placement of new arrivals and to allocate housemothers to cottages in such a way as to ensure for every girl her 'optimum choice', or in other words to give her as many of her preferences as was consistent with the claims of other members of the community. Fanny French Morse, paying tribute to Moreno's psychological beliefs on the occasion of his report on the Sing-Sing prison experiment and speaking of her experiences of these methods at Hudson, endorsed his view that the best grouping must come, not from any consideration of mental or physical uniformity, but from the voluntary choice of one individual for another. This, then, was the principle which governed all Moreno's work with the girls at Hudson, and it has remained one of the strongest characteristics of sociometric work ever since.

In her editorial to the tenth volume of Sociometry, Helen Jennings observes somewhat ironically that 'now, in 1947, it appears merely of historical interest that in 1930 children were not consulted about their own relationships directly nor systematically allowed a voice in their own groupings'. Moreno, she says, was the first to tap the dynamics of children's interrelations in a manner which respected the full stature of the child. Hence has come a new orientation among research workers. An investigator in an inquiry conducted along these lines now functions as a kind of book-keeper, collecting and tabulating information voluntarily given to him by his subjects and acting on his knowledge in such a way as to create the kind of grouping they desire. The sociometrist is in this way developing the spontaneity of each individual by placing him in groups where his personality will most easily develop and flourish.

Since he is inspired by the twin principle of spontaneity and creativity, the sociometrist differs to some extent from the gestaltist: for him the whole is not 'holier' than the parts which compose it, since it is brought into being by those parts. The gestalt, in fact, is the creation of the 'gestalter' and does not exist beforehand.[35] In this respect the philosophy of Moreno departs from that of George Herbert Mead, which in many essentials it so closely resembles. Whereas Mead would explain the individual only in terms of the group, Moreno also explains the group in terms of the individual. Thus the group is influenced as much by the individual as the individual by the group. Mead's division of the self into the 'me' and the 'I' corresponds fairly closely to Moreno's distinction between the 'cultural conserve' of acquired attitudes in man and the spontaneity factor which enables him to create or reconstruct his environment. The difference is in emphasis. In Mead's view society exists first and

21

mind arises through gesture and language within that society: the self develops as a result of the individual's taking over the attitudes and habits of society, but there remains in that self a distinction between the 'I', which is individual and constantly changing in unpredictable ways, and the 'me', which is passive and receptive to social influences.[36] For Moreno the communication between individuals is not accounted for only by gesture and language, but can best be described as a tele or psychological current—'a feeling which is projected into distance: . . . transmitted from one individual to another'. It is through the operation of such communications that groups or societies arise, and it is because of the spontaneity factor in man that such groups and societies are constantly undergoing change and reconstruction. Moreno claims that whereas in Mead's philosophy the 'present' is always static and detached from the future, in his philosophy the 'moment' is always dynamic and creative.[37]

This forward-looking character likewise distinguishes Moreno from the psychoanalysts. Instead of probing back into the past to discover the cause of neurosis, Moreno induces his patient to face new situations or to force his past experiences into the present by acting out his problems on the psychodramatic stage, studying him always in a human group and never in isolation. The emphasis both in psychodrama and in sociometry is always on two-way relations— the processes of interaction between one individual and another, between an individual and a group, between a small group and a large group, between groups and total communities. By these methods it is possible not only to observe an individual's status in his family, neighbourhood or work-group, but also to view those family, neighbourhood or work-group units in relation to the town or district in which they function. The sociometrist working on a small scale to solve disciplinary problems in a school, college or factory is using the same methods, essentially, as the group of sociometrists who investigate the causes of delinquency in a large industrial town.

It has been suggested that the graphic presentation of sociometric data is misleading and futile, since any one sociogram can at best depict only the momentary feelings of a group of individuals towards one another. Even half an hour after the choices have been written down they may cease to be true owing to the appearance of interrelationships arising out of new situations. To some extent this is true, as Moreno himself admits, but it is important to note the conditions laid down by Moreno and Jennings for the collecting of sociometric data. Every sociometric choice expressed by a subject must be in relation to one particular criterion: that is to say, he must choose his associates for a particular task, occupation or amusement. A test which merely asks the subject to name his friends is not in Moreno's sense a sociometric test at all, though it may afford interesting supplementary information. The use of different criteria with the same group may reveal different groupings. In 1947 [38] Jennings distinguished carefully between two kinds of group which such concurrent testing could reveal—the psyche-group, which she defined as 'an interpersonal structure where the uniqueness of the individual as a personality is appreciated and "allowed for" with varying degrees of spontaneous indulgence and affection', and the socio-group which 'has psychological structure in relation to a socio-criterion important enough to cause interpersonal choice to arise distinctly in relation to it'. She emphasises the importance of creating opportunities for the existence of both kinds of group. In any healthy community the members of psyche-groups will be drawn from a cross-section of the socio-groups: even children learn to distinguish between one kind of social occupation and another in distributing their choices. A group which divides into the same cliques for every kind of activity shows poor social integration compared with one which varies its grouping according to different situations. Jennings notes that such cliques tend to form if the atmosphere of the socio-group is regimented. Where the organisation is democratic, on the other hand, there is a far lower correlation between socio-group structure and psyche-group structure, and better relationships therefore exist in the community as a whole.

A second criterion too often ignored by investigators using sociometric techniques is that the criterion must have meaning for the subject. If he is asked to name those with whom he would like to sit at meal-times he should know that his expressed choices will be considered when seating arrangements are made.[39] This explains why sociometric testing lends itself simultaneously to research and to therapy and why the fear of mixing the two is unfounded.[40] Jennings gives as a further condition that the criterion should be repeatable at intervals without any lessening of the value of choosing. Here again, research and therapy are both brought into play, for by repeating the test the investigator can measure the effects of his earlier placement and at the same time plan further replacements if necessary.

Clearly no studies such as those undertaken at Hudson could proceed far without discoveries being made about the nature of leadership. It was found that leaders emerged in many different ways. Some established their positions slowly and then maintained them. Some shone suddenly for brief periods and were as suddenly eclipsed. Some were accepted only in certain situations. Some were consistently recognised as leaders from the week they entered the group. Jennings noted from her study of one particular cottage group that leadership appeared to be a process of choosing as well as being chosen. A girl might be the centre of many attractions, but if she herself sought the companionship of others who were indifferent to her she was hardly in a position of leadership. This seems to be the distinction between leadership and mere popularity. An individual is an accepted leader only if she is in a position to influence the majority of the group. If she receives choices merely from her own particular clique or from scattered individuals in whom she feels no interest she is not in a key position. Social status therefore depends not only on the number of incoming choices but also on the degree of reciprocation. When the grouping of girls in a dining-room was modified at eight-weekly intervals on the basis of successive tests it was found that a steady increase in the number of mutual choices and a steady decrease in the number of unreciprocated outgoing choices took place. Similar evidence was produced when sixteen girls who, on their arrival at Hudson, had been placed in cottages without sociometric testing were compared with a number of others who had been assigned to cottages on the basis of expressed affinities with housemothers and with girls in key positions in cottage groups. This study showed that sociometric assignment helped newcomers to adjust themselves more easily to their surroundings and protected them against 'social blocking' at an early stage.[41]

The use of these methods has extended rapidly and many educationists are adopting them in schools and training colleges.[42] Zeleny, Bonney, Partridge and others have welcomed sociometry as an instrument for discovering and where necessary redirecting psychological currents in the classroom. All testify to its value as an aid to the teacher in his task of creating the best kind of learning situation. The work of the Toronto group (Northway, Frankel and Potashin) shows that isolated children tend to remain isolated if no

24

measures are taken on their behalf, but that many of them can be helped towards more secure positions in their group. Shoobs demonstrated that the use of sociometric procedures in the grouping of children and the appointment of leaders enabled the teacher to organise the class so that isolates, rebels and conformists could work together more adequately. Kuhlen and Bretsch found that physical and emotional problems were most frequent among the unaccepted members of a group of adolescent boys and girls. McClelland and Ratcliff reported that they were able to improve the cohesion of a class of junior high-school children by devising opportunities for group activity and giving isolates specific jobs and responsibilities which brought them into greater prominence.

Various attempts have been made since 1940 to improve the statistical accuracy of sociometric measurements. Zeleny has devised a method of measuring social status by the use of a five-point scale: each subject is asked to express his attitude to each other subject as one of five degrees of intensity, ranging from complete acceptance (a first choice) to complete rejection (a last choice). He calculates a social status index by the use of a formula based on the average intensity of attitudes expressed towards the individual plus or minus the average deviation of individual attitudes from the average attitude. Howell has attempted to measure leadership by the use of a list of statements ranging from absolute acceptance to absolute rejection and corresponding to the Thurstone attitude scale, and has found that these scores correlate highly with Zeleny's social status scores. In Northway's Social Acceptability test four different criteria are used and scores are calculated by the summation of weighted choice values; charts are drawn by a target method, those in the highest quartile being plotted in the centre of the diagram and those in the lowest on the outside. Bronfenbrenner claims to have invented a constant frame of reference for all sociometric research, which will enable investigators to follow up sociometric growth studies and to examine sociometric data in relation to other data. He attributes the lack of this kind of research to the as yet unsatisfied need for methods for identifying statistically significant data and for comparing relationships in diverse sociometric situations. He uses a combination of Moreno's 'deviation from chance expectancy' principle and Northway's target method to devise an index which he claims to be significant regardless of the size of the group or the number of choices used.[43]

Moreno himself has remained well aware that methods of measurement will have to be refined and the instruments of exploration sharpened. As a result of experiments carried out at Hudson over several years he has proposed a new way of measuring social status so as to take into account not only the order of preferences but also their relative intensities.[44] The investigator asks the subject to distribute a given period of time among his friends or acquaintances and calculates in time units the depth or intensity of each choice expressed. At Hudson the method was applied (among other criteria) to the day-to-day choice of table companions at three meals, each of about twenty minutes' duration. These data made it possible to record not only each girl's status on any particular day, but also to determine its rate of change by comparing it from day to day and from week to week.

In reporting this new technique Moreno reminded sociometrists of their moral responsibilities towards the subjects whom they tested, emphasising that the philosophical principles inherent in sociometry were no less important than the mathematical formulations which would in time accompany it.

SUMMARY AND CONCLUSION

The research projects surveyed in this chapter all had in common the desire to study groups—in factories, recreational clubs, clinics, hospitals and classrooms—and their accumulating evidence suggests that social integration, high morale and efficiency are interdependent and that these conditions are more likely to exist in a democratic community than in a dictatorship. Children, it appears, are very capable of organising their own affairs if given opportunities to do so, and socially backward children can be helped to establish themselves in a group if they are placed with others whom they like and in situations where their talents will not pass unnoticed.

In studying all these separate researches into the dynamics of group life one becomes increasingly aware of their interrelatedness. The evidence recorded by the industrialist is supplemented or corroborated by the findings of the educationist and the social worker; the teacher in his rôle as therapist finds himself drawing on the experiences of the psychiatrist; the social field-worker discovers points of contact with the anthropologist. Cottrell and Gallagher [45] in surveying the developments in social psychology between 1930 and

1940 complained of the failure of the social psychologists to define the limitations of their subject. Yet to-day this very absence of fixed boundaries is accounted a virtue and social scientists are seeking as never before to combine and integrate their work in the effort to discover and create the conditions for mental health.

REFERENCES

1. MURPHY, L. B., AND MURPHY, G.
   'The Influence of Social Situations upon the Behavior of Children', in Murchison, C. (ed.), *A Handbook of Social Psychology*. Worcester, Massachusetts: Clark University Press. 1935.
   See also:
   MURPHY, L. B., AND NEWCOMB, T. M.
   Experimental Social Psychology. Revised Edition. New York and London: Harper and Brothers Publishers. 1937.
   LUNDBERG, G. A.
   Social Research. A Study in Methods of Gathering Data. New York: Longmans, Green & Co. 1942.
   MANNHEIM, K.
   Diagnosis of Our Time. London: Kegan Paul, Trench, Trubner & Co., Ltd. 1943.
   FLEMING, C. M.
   The Social Psychology of Education. London: Kegan Paul, Trench, Trubner & Co., Ltd. 1944.
   YOUNG, KIMBALL
   Handbook of Social Psychology. London: Kegan Paul, Trench, Trubner & Co., Ltd. 1946.
   FLEMING, C. M.
   Adolescence: Its Social Psychology. London: Routledge and Kegan Paul Ltd. 1948.
2. MORENO, J. L.
   Who Shall Survive? Washington: Nervous and Mental Disease Publishing Co. 1934.
   LEWIN, K.
   A Dynamic Theory of Personality. New York and London: McGraw-Hill Book Co. Inc. 1935.
3. For recent reports of the work of the former, see BRIDGEWATER, J., *A Study of Psychodrama as a Classroom Technique*, and BASU, A., *A Descriptive Study of a Group of Adolescents at a Youth Club*. Unpublished M.A. Theses. University of London. 1949 and 1950.
4. HOGGARTH, N. R.
   'The Relative Values of Certain Individual and Group Methods used in Practice Periods in the Teaching of Elementary Mathematics.' Unpublished M.A. Thesis. University of London. 1938.

5. HORNE, D. H. T.
   'A Comparison in Methods of Teaching Science.' Unpublished
   M.A. Thesis. University of London. 1943.

6. SIMPSON, E. B.
   'Measurement of the Effect of Group Discussion on the Under-
   standing and Appreciation of Films.' Unpublished M.A. Thesis.
   University of London. 1947.

7. LAMBERT, C. M.
   'A Study of Interest in School Subjects among Secondary School
   Pupils at Different Ages.' Unpublished M.A. Thesis. University of
   London. 1944.

8. Summarised and discussed in:
   FREUD, S.
   Group Psychology and the Analysis of the Ego, Chapter II. Vienna:
   The International and Psycho-analytical Press. 1922.

9. ALLPORT, F. H.
   'The Influence of the Group upon Association and Thought', *The
   Journal of Experimental Psychology*, III, 1920, pp. 159–82.

10. TRAVIS, L. F.
    'The Influence of the Group upon the Stutterer's Speech in Free
    Association', *The Journal of Abnormal and Social Psychology*, III,
    1928–9, pp. 45–51.

11. SOUTH, F. B.
    Some Psychological Aspects of Committee Work', *The Journal of
    Applied Psychology*, XI, 1927, pp. 348–68, 437–64.

12. WATSON, G. B.
    'Do Groups think more Effectively than Individuals?', *The Journal
    of Abnormal and Social Psychology*, XXIII, 1928–9, pp. 328–36.

13. SHAW, M. E.
    'A Comparison of Individuals and Small Groups in the Rational
    Solution of Complex Problems', *The American Journal of Psycho-
    logy*, XLIV, 1932, pp. 491–504.

14. DASHIELL, J. F.
    'Experimental Studies of the Influence of Social Situations on the
    Behavior of Individual Human Adults', in Murchison, C. (ed.),
    Handbook of Social Psychology. Worcester, Massachusetts: Clark
    University Press. 1935.

15. WHEELER, R. D., and JORDAN, H.
    'Change of Individual Opinion to accord with Group Opinion',
    The Journal of Abnormal and Social Psychology, XXIV, 1929–30,
    pp. 203–6.

16. JENNESS, A.
    'The Role of Discussion in Changing Opinion regarding a Matter
    of Fact', *The Journal of Abnormal and Social Psychology*, XXVII,
    1932, pp. 279–96.

17. See also:
ALLPORT, F. H.
'Psychology in Relation to Social and Political Problems', in Achilles, P. S. (ed.), *Psychology at Work*. New York and London: McGraw-Hill Book Co. Inc. 1932.

For full report see:
18. ROETHLISBERGER, F. J., and DICKSON, W. J.
Management and the Worker. Cambridge, Massachusetts: Harvard University Press. 1941.

For summaries and interpretations see:
WHITEHEAD, T. N.
Leadership in a Free Society. London: Oxford University Press. 1936.

HOMANS, G. C.
Fatigue of Workers, Chapter IV. New York: Reinhold Pub. Corp. 1941. Reprinted in Hoslett, S. D. (ed.), *Human Factors in Management*. Parkville, Missouri: Park College Press. 1946. Also in Newcomb, T. M., and Hartley, E. L. (eds.), *Readings in Social Psychology*. New York: Henry Holt & Co. 1947.

For similar investigations in England see:
BARTLETT, F. C.
'The Co-operation of Social Groups', *Occupational Psychology*, XII, 1, 1938, pp. 30–42.

FRASER, J. MUNRO
'An Experiment with Group Methods in the Selection of Trainees for Senior Management Positions', *Occupational Psychology*, XX, 2, 1946, pp. 63–7.

GILLESPIE, J. T.
Dynamic Motion and Time Study. London: Paul Elek. 1947.

RAPHAEL, W.
'A Study of some Stresses and Strains within the Working Group', *Occupational Psychology*, XXI, 2, 1947, pp. 92–101.

TENNER, C.
'Some Problems of Discipline among Adolescents in Factories', *Occupational Psychology*, XXI, 2, 1947, pp. 75–81.

Other references to the social psychological approach to industrial problems are to be found in:
OAKLEY, C. A.
Men at Work. London: Hodder and Stoughton, Ltd. 1945.

MAIER, N. R. F.
Psychology in Industry. Boston, Massachusetts: Houghton Mifflin Co. 1946. London: George G. Harrap & Co., Ltd. 1947.

GILLESPIE, J. J.
Free Expression in Industry: A Social-Psychological Study of Work and Leisure. London: The Pilot Press, Ltd. 1948.

19. ALLPORT, G. W.
'The Psychology of Participation', *The Psychological Review*, LII, 1945, pp. 177–82. Reprinted in shortened form in Hoslett, S. D. (ed.), *Human Factors in Management.* Parkville, Missouri: Clark College Press. 1946.

20. KEPHART, N. C.
'A Method of Heightening Social Adjustment in an Institutional Group', *The American Journal of Orthopsychiatry*, VIII, 1938, pp. 710–18.

21. MOWRER, O. H.
'Authoritarian vs. "Self-Government" in the Management of Children's Aggressive (Anti-social) Reactions as a Preparation for Citizenship in a Democracy', *The Journal of Social Psychology*, X, 1939, pp. 121–6.

22. For reports of this research see:
LEWIN, K., LIPPITT, R., AND WHITE, R. K.
'Patterns of Aggressive Behavior in Experimentally Created "Social Climates"', *The Journal of Social Psychology*, X, 1939, pp. 271–99.

LIPPITT, R.
'Field Theory and Experiment in Social Psychology: Authoritarian and Democratic Group Atmospheres', *The American Journal of Sociology*, XLV, 1939, pp. 26–49.

LIPPITT, R.
'The Morale of Youth Groups', in Watson G. (ed.), *Civilian Morale.* Boston, Massachusetts: Houghton, Mifflin Co. 1942.

LIPPITT, R., AND WHITE, R. K.
'The "Social Climate" of Children's Groups', in Barker, R., Kounin, J., and Wright, H. F. (eds.), *Child Behavior and Development.* New York and London: McGraw-Hill Book Co. Inc. 1943.

LIPPITT, R., AND WHITE, R. K.
'An Experimental Study of Leadership and Group Life', in Newcomb, T. M., and Hartley, E. L. (eds.), *Readings in Social Psychology.* New York: Henry Holt Co. 1947.

23. BAVELAS, A.
'Morale and the Training of Leaders', in Watson, G. (ed.), *Civilian Morale.* Boston, Massachusetts: Houghton Mifflin Co. 1942.

24. LEWIN, K.
'Group Decision and Social Change', in Newcomb, T. M., and Hartley, E. L. (eds.), *Readings in Social Psychology.* New York: Henry Holt Co. 1947. See also references in Maier, N. R. F., *Psychology in Industry*, pp. 264–6. Boston, Massachusetts: Houghton Mifflin Co. 1946.

25. See *Studies of Teachers' Classroom Personalities: Applied Psychology Monographs of the American Association for Applied Psychology,* Nos. 6, 8 and 11. Stanford University Press. 1945–6.

(i) ANDERSON, H. H., AND BREWER, H. M.
Dominative and Socially Integrative Behavior of Kindergarten Teachers. No. 6. June, 1945.

(ii) ANDERSON, H. H., AND BREWER, J. E.
Effects of Teachers' Dominative and Integrative Contacts on Children's Classroom Behavior. No. 8. July, 1946.

(iii) ANDERSON, H. H., BREWER, J. E., AND REED, M. F.
Follow-up Studies of the Effects of Dominative and Integrative Contacts on Children's Behavior. No. 11. December, 1946.

26. MORENO, J. L. (ed.)
Group Psychotherapy: A Symposium. New York: Beacon House Inc. 1945.

See also:
KLAPMAN, J. W.
Group Psychotherapy: Theory and Practice. London: Heinemann Medical Books, Ltd. 1946.

27. SLAVSON, S. R.
An Introduction to Group Therapy. New York: The Commonwealth Fund. 1943.
The Practice of Group Therapy. London: The Pushkin Press. 1947.

28. DURKIN, H. E.
'Application of Dr. Levy's Relationship Therapy to a Pre-school Summer Play Group', *The American Journal of Orthopsychiatry,* IX, 1939, pp. 583–97.

29. GABRIEL, B.
'An Experiment in Group Treatment', *The American Journal of Orthopsychiatry,* IX, 1939, pp. 146–69.
'Group Treatment for Adolescent Girls', *The American Journal of Orthopsychiatry,* XIV, 1944, pp. 593–602.

30. AXELROD, P. L., CAMERON, M. S., AND SOLOMON, T. C.
'An Experiment in Group Therapy with Shy Adolescent Girls', *The American Journal of Orthopsychiatry,* XIV, 1944, pp. 616–627.

31. REDL, F.
'Diagnostic Group Work', *The American Journal of Orthopsychiatry,* XIV, 1944, pp. 53–67.

32. SLAVSON, S. R.
Creative Group Education. New York: Association Press. 1938.

33. MORENO, J. L.
Who Shall Survive? A New Approach to the Problem of Human Relations. Washington: Nervous and Mental Disease Publishing Co. 1934.

34. MORENO, J. L.
'Group Method and Group Psychotherapy', *Sociometry Monographs.* No. 5. New York: Beacon House Inc. 1941.
See also:

MORENO, J. L.
'Interpersonal Therapy and Psychotherapy of Interpersonal Relations', *Sociometry*, I, 1, 1937, pp. 9–76.
'The Foundations of Sociometry: An Introduction', *Sociometry Monographs*, No. 4. New York: Beacon House Inc. 1943. First published in *Sociometry*, IV, 1, pp. 15–35.

35. MORENO, J. L.
'Sociometry and the Cultural Order', *Sociometry Monographs*, No. 2. New York: Beacon House Inc. 1943. First published in *Sociometry*, VI, 3, 1943, pp. 299–344.
See also:
MORENO, J. L., AND JENNINGS, H. H.
'Statistics of Social Configurations', *Sociometry*, I, 3 and 4, 1938, pp. 342–74.

36. MEAD, G. H.
Mind, Self and Society. Chicago: University of Chicago Press. 1934.

37. MCKINNEY, J. C.
'A Comparison of the Social Psychology of G. H. Mead and J. L. Moreno' (with a comment by Moreno), *Sociometry*, X, 4, 1947, pp. 338–53.
See also:
MORENO, J. L.
'The Philosophy of the Moment and the Spontaneity Theatre', *Sociometry*, IV, 2, 1941, pp. 205–26.

38. JENNINGS, H. H.
'Leadership and Sociometric Choice', *Sociometry*, X, 1, 1947, pp. 32–49.
'Differentiation of the Psyche-group and the Socio-group', *Sociometry*, X, 1, 1947. pp. 71–9.

39. MORENO, J. L.
'Progress and Pitfalls in Sociometric Theory', *Sociometry*, X, 3, 1947, pp. 268–72.

40. MORENO, J. L.
'Sociometry and the Cultural Order', *Sociometry Monographs*, No. 2. New York: Beacon House Inc. 1943. First published in *Sociometry*, VI, 3, 1943, pp. 299–344.

41. JENNINGS, H. H.
'Structure of Leadership—Development and Sphere of Influence', *Sociometry*, I, 1 and 2, 1937, pp. 99–143.
MORENO, J. L., AND JENNINGS, H. H.
'Sociometric Methods of Grouping and Regrouping', *Sociometry*, VII, 4, 1944, pp. 397–414.
'Sociometric Control Studies of Grouping and Regrouping', *Sociometry Monographs*, No. 7. New York: Beacon House Inc. 1947.

42. ZELENY, L. D.
'Sociometry in the Class-room'. *Sociometry*, III, 1, 1940.
'Experimental Appraisal of a Group Learning Plan', *Journal of Educational Research*, XXXIV, 1, 1940, pp. 37–42.

BONNEY, M. E.
   'Values of Sociometric Studies in the Classroom', *Sociometry*, VI, 3, 1943, pp. 251–4.
PARTRIDGE, E. D.
   'The Sociometric Approach to Adolescent Groupings', *Sociometry*, VI, 3, 1943, pp. 258–63.
ZELENY, L. D.
   'The Value of Sociometry to Education', *Sociometry*, VI, 3, 1943, pp. 247–8.
NORTHWAY, M.
   'Outsiders: A Study of Personality Patterns of Children least Acceptable to their Age-mates', *Sociometry*, VII, 1, 1944, pp. 10–25.
FRANKEL, E. B., AND POTASHIN, R.
   'A Survey of Sociometric and Pre-Sociometric Literature on Friendship and Social Acceptance among Children', *Sociometry*, VII, 4, 1944, pp. 422–31.
NORTHWAY, M., FRANKEL, E. B., AND POTASHIN, R.
   'Personality and Sociometric Status', *Sociometry Monographs*, No. 11. New York: Beacon House Inc. 1947.
KUHLEN, R. G., AND BRETSCH, H. S.
   'Personal Problems of Adolescents', *Sociometry*, X, 2, 1947, pp. 122–32.
MCCLELLAND, F. M., AND RATCLIFF, J. A.
   'The Use of Sociometry as an Aid in Promoting Social Adjustment in a Ninth Grade Home Room', *Sociometry*, X, 2, 1947, pp. 147–153.
SHOOBS, N.
   'Sociometry in the Class-room', *Sociometry*, X, 2, 1947, pp. 154–164.
43. ZELENY, L. D.
   'Status: Its Measurement and Control in Education', *Sociometry*, V, 2, 1941, pp. 193–204.
HOWELL, C. E.
   'Measurement of Leadership', *Sociometry*, V, 2, 1942, pp. 163–8.
BRONFENBRENNER, U.
   'The Measurement of Sociometric Status'. *Sociometry Monographs*, No. 6. New York: Beacon House Inc. 1945. First published in *Sociometry*, VI, 4, and VII, 1 and 3, 1943.
   For evaluation of the progress of statistical methods in Sociometry see:
CRISSWELL, J. H.
   'Sociometric Measurement and Chance', *Sociometry*, VII, 4, 1944, pp. 415–421.
   'Foundations of Sociometric Measurement', *Sociometry*, IX, 1, 1946, pp. 7–13.
EDWARDS, D. S.
   'The Constant Frame of Reference Problem in Sociometry', *Sociometry*, XI, 4, 1948, pp. 372–9.

44. MORENO, J. L., JENNINGS, H. H., AND SARGENT, J.
    'Time as a Quantitative Index of Interpersonal Relations', *Socio-metry Monographs*, No. 13. New York: Beacon House Inc. 1947.
45. COTTRELL, L. S., AND GALLAGHER, R.
    'Developments in Social Psychology: 1930–1940', *Sociometry Monographs*, No. 1. New York: Beacon House Inc. 1941.

CHAPTER TWO

PLANNING AN EXPERIMENT IN A
LONDON SCHOOL

THIS experiment arose in the first place from a belief that group methods might be applied more specifically to the teaching of English Composition than they appear to have been in the past. Ever since the time of Caldwell Cook activity methods have been widely used in connection with dramatic work and oral expression, and in project work the writing of reports is frequently treated as a group responsibility; yet there seems to have been little scientific investigation into the possibility of training children to co-operate in the writing of stories, plays or poems, although a wealth of folk literature exists to prove that such activity is healthy and natural. Instead, this kind of co-operation is viewed in some quarters with distrust, and the experiment now to be reported may well be open to criticism on the grounds that group activity, while benefiting the dull or mediocre child, may have a thwarting effect on a child of outstanding artistic talent. It should be understood, however, that the children who participated were given frequent opportunities to write individually as well as co-operatively. It is not suggested that group writing should take the place of individual writing: on the contrary it was hoped, when the method was first put on trial, that the children would acquire new ideas and greater ease of expression as a result of close intercourse, and so would write more competently and with more enjoyment when thrown back on their own resources.

At its outset, then, the aim of the investigation was to produce better writers. But it was in the nature of such an experiment that this single aim should become merged with others and that the field should prove to be wider than it had originally seemed. It soon became apparent that the group method was not simply a matter of setting five or six children to pool ideas for a story. Mechanisms

35

were being put into action which might affect significantly the social relationships of the children as well as the quality of their work. The method, in fact, brought with it new responsibilities which could not be ignored or considered lightly: ill-considered allocation of children to groups might precipitate new psychological difficulties; wise grouping might help to solve existing ones. Thus the search for a more effective teaching method became also a search for a better psychological environment, and the study of the children's intellectual growth proceeded side by side with the study of their social development.[1]

The experiment was carried out in a girls' secondary school near London between January 1947 and October 1948. In January 1947 the pupils who were to take part in the experiment were in their first year, in two parallel forms with populations varying from thirty-three to thirty-seven during the six terms which followed. During the autumn term of 1946 both forms had been given the Fleming-Jenkins Tests in English, Arithmetic and General Ability. The results of these showed that the two groups were comparable in intelligence, the experimental group being slightly superior to the control group. The scores ranged from 222 to 315 for Group C (the control group) and from 217 to 311 for Group E (the experimental group); the mean and standard deviations were 262·5 and 23·77 for Group C and 272·3 and 24·17 for Group E.

During the spring term six further tests were given to assess the pupils' attainments in English Composition and to find out something about their attitudes to the subject. In view of the difficulty of marking compositions reliably,[2] two objective attainment tests, each consisting of fifty items, were constructed with a view to assessing range and accuracy of vocabulary, awareness of the less obvious differences between words used in similar contexts, appreciation of the structure of a sentence and ability to follow the logical sequence of sentences in a paragraph. Recognised statistical procedures were used to calculate the validities of the separate items, the validity of each test as a whole and the internal reliability of the tests.[3] In addition to these two objective tests of attainment, three composition tests were used. The choice of subjects for these tests was made with two aims in view—firstly to give the pupils opportunities for different kinds of writing and secondly to ensure that, in at least two out of the three, all the children should have a common fund of subject-matter on which to draw, so that the less inventive ones might not be unduly penalised; the first and second composition subjects were therefore based on the narrative material used in the two objective tests and the third was a description of either 'a room crowded with furniture and ornaments' or 'a general store in a country village'. The compositions were marked, according to an analytical scheme, in the three categories—Words, Sentences and Ideas. As a further guide to reliable marking, a five-point scale was constructed for each of these categories, in which the qualities expected for each grade were described. For these five tests the maximum score was 210 (65 for each attainment test, 30 for Composition I, 25 for Composition II and 25 for Composition III). A test of attitude to English Composition was then constructed by the Thurstone method and scored by the combined Thurstone-Likert method.[4] A hundred statements were originally compiled, largely from children's expressed opinions; they ranged from very favourable attitudes (e.g. 'I think play-writing is fascinating') to very unfavourable attitudes (e.g. 'I think keeping a diary is a waste of time and paper') and covered such varied forms of written and oral composition as letter-writing, story-telling, the keeping of diaries, play-writing, debating and public-speaking. From these, twenty-four statements were finally selected for inclusion in the test. The maximum score possible on this test was 87 (32 for the eight very favourable statements, 12 for the four favourable statements, 15 for the five unfavourable statements and 28 for the seven very unfavourable statements).*

THE FIRST SOCIOMETRIC TEST: APRIL 1947

On April 18th the following sociometric test was given: each girl was asked to write down, in order of preference, the names of four others with whom she would like to work in English lessons. The pupils in the experimental group (Class-Group E) were told that they would in future be writing compositions (stories, plays, descriptions, etc.) in groups as well as individually, and that the grouping would be arranged on the basis of their expressed choices, all receiving equal consideration. For them, therefore, the test fulfilled the conditions laid down by Moreno and Jennings

* For full details of the construction and scoring of all these tests see the writer's unpublished M.A. Thesis. London: University of London Library, 1949, pp. 56–78, and Appendices I–III.

that the criterion should have significance for the subjects being tested.[5]

Sociometric methods were used for two purposes—to collect data on the social configurations in the two groups and to provide a basis for breaking up the experimental group (and later, the control group) into smaller working units. The pupils in the control group (Class-Group C) were told that although they would not be doing composition work in groups for some time, it would be helpful for the teacher to know how they would like to be grouped if opportunities arose, say, in drama lessons, and they were promised that after not more than three terms they would be grouped for composition work too. It is realised that for them the test had less significance, but it seemed at the time (and later when they were retested in September) that they accepted this explanation and recorded their choices sincerely.

RECORDING METHODS

A note must here be inserted to describe the methods used for tabulating and charting the results of the sociometric tests, which were given periodically during the next sixteen months as the need for retesting arose. Table I (at end of book) shows the procedure adopted to record the choice for both groups in five successive tests. The method is that used by Moreno and Jennings: the entries along the horizontal lines show for any individual which other girls she chooses, and the entries in the columns show for any individual by how many other girls she is chosen. A first choice is indicated by the number 4, a second by 3, a third by 2 and a fourth by 1; total and scores are given for every child at the foot of the table. As there were ten children who entered or left the group for varying reasons during the period of investigation, not every child was involved in every test: the name of any child who was not in the class-group at the time of a test is therefore bracketed in the corresponding table for that test. Table II (at end of book) shows an analysis of the choices of the same group on three occasions: here, too, the method used by Moreno and Jennings in their investigations at the New York State Training School has been applied. In Table III (at end of book) the results of a test given to Class-Group E in May 1948, when they were asked to give their choices on each of four different criteria, are recorded by Northway's method,[6] except that the choices are not weighted, but are all entered as '1'.

A COMPARISON OF THE TWO SOCIOGRAMS: APRIL 1947

The first test revealed the existence of stars and isolates in both groups and a strongly skewed distribution of choices. In both groups there were a few overchosen individuals and many underchosen. In Group E* two girls were isolated and two received only fourth choices; there were two isolated pairs and three triangular structures. Of the four girls who received eight or more choices, Constance seemed to be in the most influential position, since she exchanged

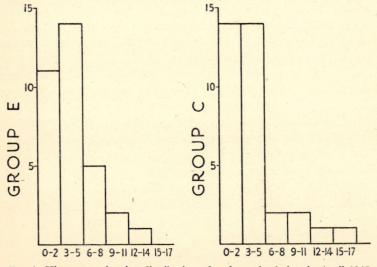

FIG. 1. Histograms showing distribution of sociometric choices in April 1947

mutual choices with two of the other three and was chosen by girls from nearly all sections of the form. No very distinct grouping was yet visible from this sociogram apart from unreciprocated choices from one pair or triangle to another, but it will be seen later that some of these structures underwent interesting developments and modifications during the following few months. In Group C† the 'stars' were more prominent than in Group E. Kathleen and Freda received seventeen and thirteen choices respectively and were linked by mutual choice. Jill attracted nine choices but reciprocated none of them. Two strong groupings were visible, one clustering round Kathleen and one round Freda. Three girls were completely unchosen and there was one isolated pair.

* See Sociogram 1, p. 41 and Table I at end of book.   † See Sociogram 2, p. 42.

In charting these results in the sociograms which follow the aim has been to show in the sociograms the pattern of social groupings in each class-group. With only one or two exceptions every name appears in the same position on the page in all sociograms. No attempt has been made to indicate status by the use of a target method, such as Northway and Bronfenbrenner have used, by which those receiving the greatest number of choices are plotted in the centre and those receiving fewest choices are plotted on the rim of a circle.[7] For the purposes of this study it seemed more important to indicate as far as possible the social groups into which each class-group divided itself and show to what extent these groupings shifted, broke up or merged with one another over a period of time. To avoid making the charts too confusing to the eye not more than three choices have been plotted, except in Sociograms 7 and 8 where up to five are shown for each child. The information given in the sociograms can be supplemented by the tables, where fourth choices are recorded. The numbers used in Sociograms 5 to 8 correspond to those used in the sociometric tables: thus, for example, 26 in Group E always refers to Sally and 32 in Group C to Nan. A key to the symbols used in the sociograms is given below.

KEY TO ALL SOCIOGRAMS

 First choice.

Second choice.

Third, fourth or fifth choice.

 Ann sends her first choice to Joan, who reciprocates only with her third choice.

 A pupil who entered the class later than the date of the test.

A pupil who was not included in the test. (See Sociograms 9 and 10.)

In Sociograms 1 and 4 the numbers 1 to 8 denote the Composition Groups to which the pupils were allocated.

In Sociograms 9 and 10 the numbers 1 to 9 denote the canteen tables to which the pupils were allocated.

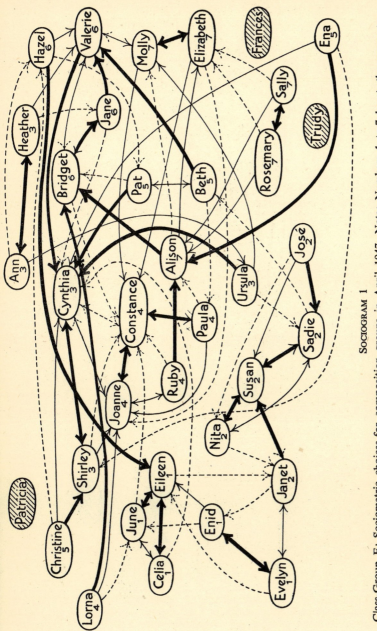
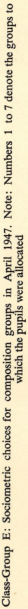

SOCIOGRAM 1

Class-Group E: Sociometric choices for composition groups in April 1947. Note: Numbers 1 to 7 denote the groups to which the pupils were allocated

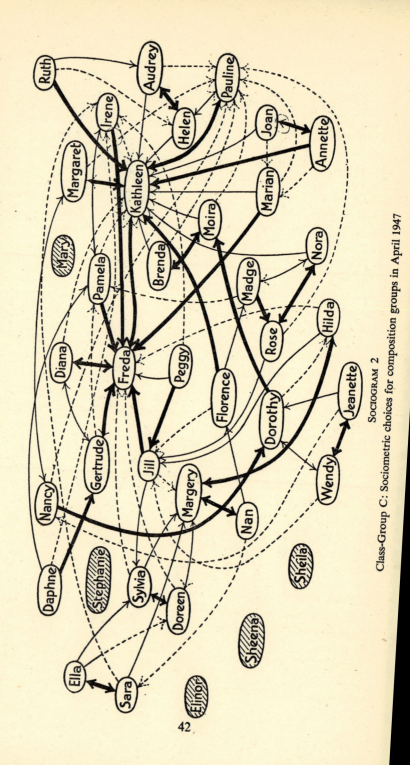

SOCIOGRAM 2

Class-Group C: Sociometric choices for composition groups in April 1947

OBSERVATIONS ON CLASSROOM BEHAVIOUR
FEBRUARY 25th TO MAY 6th, 1947

The social relationships revealed by the first sociometric test may perhaps be illuminated by some observations recorded on the experimental group between February 25th and May 6th and on the control group during the month of April. During the winter and spring terms the investigator had found Group C more lively and responsive as a form than Group E: in Group C most of the children were willing to participate in activities, whereas in Group E there was a surprisingly large number of unresponsive children who played little or no part in oral work.

On February 25th observations were recorded* during an English lesson taken with Group E by a student in training, who was in this lesson making a special effort to induce the unco-operative children to take part in the work. In the first part of the lesson, twelve girls participated continually in the discussion, five made only one suggestion each and the remaining fifteen took no part. The student tried to draw in Valerie, with whom she failed completely, and Constance, with whom she partly succeeded. During the second part of the lesson, three more children were brought into the discussion (Elizabeth, Constance and Hazel), each contributing one idea. Two others (Jane and Enid) would have made suggestions if given an opportunity, but their waving hands were not noticed and they relapsed into inactivity. Unsuccessful attempts were made to induce Valerie, Lorna and Heather to contribute to the discussion, but the question 'anything to suggest?' seemed to have a paralysing effect on them. When compared with the results of the first sociometric test of the following April, these records showed that of the ten children who participated actively in both parts of the lesson seven received five or more choices, and that of the eleven who played no part in the lesson two were completely isolated and three received only one choice each.

The prominence of these ten girls in form activities and the gradual emergence of some of the others may be further illustrated by a brief account of four consecutive dramatic periods between February 27th and March 20th. In the first lesson the class was divided roughly into three teams according to seating positions in the room. The dramatisation of 'Odysseus and the Cyclops' was

* See Fig. 2, page 44.

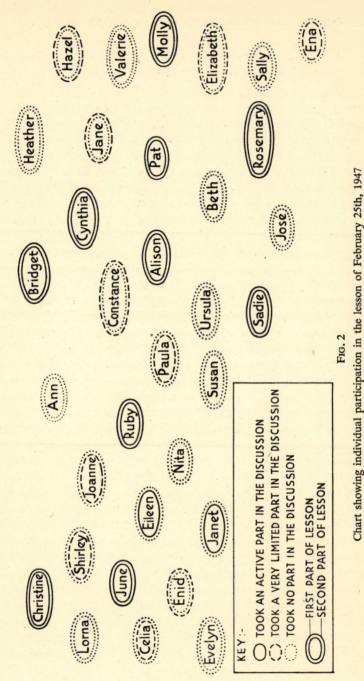

KEY :-

◯ TOOK AN ACTIVE PART IN THE DISCUSSION
⬭ TOOK A VERY LIMITED PART IN THE DISCUSSION
◯ TOOK NO PART IN THE DISCUSSION

◖─FIRST PART OF LESSON
◗─SECOND PART OF LESSON

Fig. 2

Chart showing individual participation in the lesson of February 25th, 1947

44

discussed at some length and in the second lesson, a week later, each group acted the scene to the others. On this occasion Valerie, showing initiative and taking an active interest in an English lesson for the first time, gave a surprisingly good performance which was appreciated and commented on by the girls who watched it: this seemed to be the beginning of a new rôle for her in the form and to mark the end of her timid, unresponsive phase. In the third lesson (March 13th) a ballad which the form had previously read was dramatised. The same three teams were used, but this time the acting was spontaneous and unrehearsed. In this lesson Constance came into prominence as the narrator for her group: she read fluently and confidently and her actors showed more spirit than the other teams who had less successful narrators. For the fourth lesson (March 20th) a hall with a stage was used, and the student who had taught the form on February 25th acted as observer and recorded the names of those children who contributed ideas and took part in the activity. A volunteer was asked for, to go up on the stage and start miming an action which could lead up to a scene involving several other actors. After a moment or two Ruby went up and started a 'bus queue, looking at her watch and giving signs of impatience. She was joined by seven others and eventually the 'queue' boarded an imaginary 'bus. Soon after, Valerie volunteered to play the rôle of the conductor. After a discussion the scene was acted a second time, the same children volunteering again with three additional ones. This mime was criticised on the grounds that there was 'too much falling about'. For the third mime all but three volunteered, and those who had not offered before were chosen to act the scene. This time suggestions were called out to organise the activity (for example: 'The 'bus has just skidded and the driver has pulled up with a screech of brakes'). Ruby offered to keep up a running commentary from the floor and did it extremely well. A diagram based on the student's records was constructed to show how the activity was distributed during this lesson. It was noticed that June, Bridget, Ruby, Alison and Pat participated actively in both the lessons for which this kind of record was kept, that Sadie, though diffident at first about acting, was willing to take part in discussion as on the earlier occasion and that Ursula and José were completely passive on both occasions. Valerie participated more actively than any other pupils on the second occasion, taking part in all three mimes and all three discussions.

Description of Situation.—I. A man returning home (1) finds he has come out without his door-key. He rings the bell, and receiving no answer begins to clamber up to an unlocked window. A passer-by (2) accuses him of housebreaking, and an argument follows. A policeman (3) arrives and takes control.

Group E

Girls playing the parts	Observer's comment	Girls taking part in discussion
June (1) Elizabeth (2) Constance (3)	June began the scene well, miming the business of looking for the key convincingly. Elizabeth came in fairly soon and began confidently, but petered out after a few minutes and stood on one side most of the time saying nothing. Constance was fluent and confident, and although she showed little sense of dramatic characterisation, she handled the situation competently and really investigated the affair, asking to see the man's identity card, etc. The class felt that the actors were not manly enough.	Ruby Bridget Alison Pat Ann Cynthia Evelyn Joanne Sadie

Group C

Girls playing the parts	Observer's comment	Girls taking part in discussion
Irene (1) Jeanette (2) Margery (3)	Irene spoke audibly and enjoyed herself, showing some sense of dramatic timing and taking the initiative when there was a pause in the conversation. Jeanette was diffident and ineffective, standing with her back to the audience most of the time: she made her accusation weakly, and took no action when the policeman arrived. Margery enjoyed miming the part of the policeman, but had few ideas about conversation and tended to dry up or repeat herself.	Doreen Brenda Pamela Pauline Jill

Description of Situation.—II. A librarian (1) has an argument with a talkative member (2) on the subject of the silence rule. Another member (3) joins in.

GROUP E

Girls playing the parts	Observer's comment	Girls taking part in discussion
Evelyn (1) Sadie (2) Bridget (3)	Evelyn made a poor start, merely standing about instead of miming the activities of a librarian. She attacked Sadie in an unpleasant manner, but gave no convincing reason for the silence rule, except that she would get into trouble if she let people talk. Sadie was equally rude, making uncalled for remarks about the books. Bridget came forward to join in the argument with plenty of confidence, but made little real contribution to the discussion. She elbowed Sadie out of the picture, but failed to make the scene any more convincing. The class felt that all three exaggerated and that none was really lifelike.	Alison Ruby Nita Celia June Valerie Rosemary Pat Janet Cynthia

GROUP C

Girls playing the parts	Observer's comment	Girls taking part in discussion
Pamela (1) Daphne (2) Hilda (3)	Pamela was far too domineering: she gave no reason for the rule, and merely repeated: 'If you stop talking you can stay.' Daphne was rude and truculent, reiterating that she would talk if she wanted to. Hilda took no part at all, but merely stood and watched the others. The class found the acting too exaggerated, and a discussion arose on the nature of authority and the best ways of exerting it.	Doreen Brenda Ella Helen Freda Audrey Irene Jill Pauline

47

Description of Situation.—III. A butcher (1) and two housewives (2) and (3) discuss the food problem.

	GROUP E			GROUP C	
Girls playing the parts	*Observer's comment*	*Girls taking part in discussion*	*Girls playing the parts*	*Observer's comment*	*Girls taking part in discussion*
Janet (1) Valerie (2) Shirley (3)	Janet was unreasonable, demanding the customer's ration book for half a pound of sausages and charging 3s. 6d. for them. Valerie showed confidence, initiative and co-operation in her handling of her part: she acted the rôle of an affected woman, tried to open a conversation with Shirley, argued with the butcher about the price of the sausages and invented a line to get herself off the stage. Shirley was quiet and timid at first, but warmed up after the first customer had gone.	Alison Rosemary Ena Paula Cynthia Sadie	Ella (1) Pauline (2) Brenda (3)	Ella used too much repetition and did not attempt to reason with her grumbling customer. Pauline complained that she was not getting her ration and that she could not come again the next day as she would be at work. She managed to invent a line which got her off the stage. Brenda showed no initiative, merely continuing the same argument and joining in the attack on the butcher. The class found the dialogue futile and the situation unreal.	Sylvia Daphne Wendy Margaret Hilda Pamela Jill Jeanette Irene Rose Freda

Description of Situation.—IV. A father (1) and mother (2) discuss whether their small boy should play in the street. A neighbour (3) comes in to complain about something he has done.

GROUP E			GROUP C		
Girls playing the parts	Observer's comment	Girls taking part in discussion	Girls playing the parts	Observer's comment	Girls taking part in discussion
Pat (1) Sally (2) Beth (3)	This was quite a lively scene and there was no nervousness. But neither the father nor the neighbour showed any tact or diplomacy, or even behaved with reasonably good manners. Beth barged in without ringing or knocking, and showed no willingness even to discuss the affair she had come to complain about; Pat as the father lolled in a chair when his wife and the neighbour were both standing, and made no attempt to apologise for his son's behaviour even when he saw that the complaints were justified. Sally began the scene well, initiating the conversation and inventing a friend for her son who led him astray and encouraged him to play in the street instead of going into the park. Discussion arose as to how the situation could have been handled, and what attitude the neighbour and the accused father should have adopted.	Ruby Bridget Molly Nita Alison Susan Pat Joanne Sadie Eileen	Moira (1) Jill (2) Marian (3)	The dialogue, though quite lively, quickly degenerated into a competition in abuse. Moira enjoyed acting the father and squaring up to the angry neighbour. She took the initiative when the dialogue petered out by saying: 'That reminds me'—and levelling another accusation. Marian arrived in a truculent, uncompromising mood, and merely put the family's back up. It was felt that all three might have been more diplomatic.	Annette Margaret Hilda Pamela Freda Audrey Pauline

49

Description of Situation.—V. A bus conductor (1) has an argument with a passenger (2) about the 'no standing' regulation. An inspector (3) arrives and handles the situation.

	GROUP E			GROUP C	
Girls playing the parts	*Observer's comment*	*Girls taking part in discussion*	*Girls playing the parts*	*Observer's comment*	*Girls taking part in discussion*
Molly (1) Cynthia (2) Alison (3)	In this scene, the actors evidently enjoyed themselves. The quarrel became rather violent and ended in the defeat of the conductress and the inspector. Molly gave orders without backing them up with reasons, and both she and Alison weakened their argument by repeating themselves.	Ruby Molly Constance Alison June Pat Rosemary Janet Paula Cynthia Evelyn Sadie Eileen	Joan (1) Sylvia (2) Gertrude (3)	The group made a shaky start, and the argument which developed between the conductress and her passenger was not convincing. Joan missed an opportunity to point out that shoppers should avoid using the buses during business rush hours, and Sylvia was merely rude and obstinate. Gertrude handled the situation more intelligently, giving a reason for the regulation.	Marian Diana Margaret Hilda Pamela Jeanette Audrey Irene Nan Madge Pauline

Description of Situation.—VI. A Woolworth's assistant (1) and the daughter of a village store owner (2) meet in a seaside boarding house and discuss their jobs. A cinema usherette (3) joins in.

GROUP E			GROUP C		
Girls playing the parts	Observer's comment	Girls taking part in discussion	Girls playing the parts	Observer's comment	Girls taking part in discussion
Ruby (1) Celia (2) Jane (3)	Ruby started the conversation and did most of the talking. She was natural and fluent, gave Celia leading questions to draw her out, and followed up Jane's openings; when there was a pause, she was the one who showed initiative and began a new topic. Celia was slow to start, but managed to work her way into the conversation again. Jane entered the conversation very naturally.	Not recorded	Deirdre (1) Doreen (2) Annette (3)	All three seemed rather embarrassed at first. Doreen opened the conversation and tried to keep it going but was unable to open a new topic. Annette entered the conversation unnaturally, and failed on several occasions to make use of questions put to her about her work. Deirdre volunteered no information about herself, and did not help Doreen to keep the conversation going.	Sylvia Daphne Marian Gertrude Diana Brenda Sarah Margaret Joan Jeanette Helen

51

Description of Situation.—VII. A husband (1) and wife (2) discuss gardening plans. The brother of one of them, who is on a visit (3), intervenes to give advice.

GROUP C

Girls playing the parts	Observer's comment	Girls taking part in discussion
Diana (1) Margaret (2) Kathleen (3)	Margaret opened the conversation by pointing out the expense and trouble involved in food production. She kept the conversation going and introduced new ideas—the best place for the vegetables, the flowers which were wanted for the carnival, the objection to having flowers at the front where the children could trample them down looking for lost balls, and the problem whether to spend money on fertiliser. Diana was difficult as a partner, producing no ideas of her own and being at first unable to respond to Margaret's; she eventually joined in when Margaret suggested that they should have an allotment. Kathleen contributed nothing to the conversation, merely repeating Margaret's arguments.	Not recorded

THE ORAL TESTS

When the experiment was being planned an oral test was included to supplement the test in written composition. A series of social situations was devised, each involving some kind of conversation or argument between three people. By this means it was hoped that no pupil would feel isolated and unsupported during her test. Marks were to be allotted on a five-point scale for (i) spontaneity, (ii) initiative and inventiveness, (iii) speech and general bearing. In the end, however, the attempt to assess the children in this way was abandoned, since the whole test seemed to lack validity: some of the situations proved much easier to handle than others, and even in the easier ones a child's fluency depended a great deal on the other two in her group. On the other hand the observations recorded while the tests were going on provided further evidence about the kind of human material in the two groups, and are therefore summarised

here for comparison with earlier and later observations. The order
in which the children were tested was determined by the children
themselves, as volunteers were asked for on each occasion: in Group
E these were forthcoming for the first five tests, but for the sixth
three girls had to be detailed to take the parts; in Group C volunteers came forward for all seven tests which were recorded.[8]

SUMMARY AND CONCLUSION

The tests given before the experimental method was introduced
showed that the two groups were comparable in ability and attainment. Group E did slightly better in the Fleming-Jenkins Test of

TABLE IV
SUMMARY OF SCORES FOR GROUPS C AND E:
APRIL 1947

		Group C	Group E
Fleming-Jenkins Test of Mental Ability	Mean S.D.	262·5 23·77	272·3 24·17
Fleming-Jenkins Test of Ability in English	Mean S.D.	87·22 12·21	92·3 10·79
Test of Attainment in English	Mean S.D.	63·65 13·6	63·65 11·14
Composition Test	Mean S.D.	38·7 6·32	36·9 8·68
Test of Attitude to English Composition	Mean S.D.	51·66 13·62	44·67 13·73
Sociometric Test	Mean S.D.	11·34 9·95	10·7 7·01

Ability in English and slightly worse in the Composition Test than
Group C; in the Attainment Test their mean scores were identical.
Group E showed a less favourable attitude to the subject than
Group C, and this result seemed to be borne out by the quality of
their oral work. The sociometric tests revealed that the social struc-
tures of the two groups differed considerably, the scores for Group C

having a much wider dispersion than those of Group E, and a higher mean owing to the large number of choices sent to Maureen and Rita.

Comparison of the individual scores on all these tests shows that low attainment was often accompanied by poor attitude and inferior social status, and the records of dramatic activities before the end of April show for some of these pupils a corresponding backwardness in oral work.

REFERENCES

1. For references to the teaching of English Composition see:
   HARTOG, P. J.
   The Writing of English. Oxford: At the Clarendon Press. 1907.
   HARTOG, P. J.
   Record or Message. London: Oxford University Press. 1913.
   HOLLINGWORTH, L. S.
   Special Talents and Defects: Their Significance for Education. New York: Macmillan & Co. 1923.
   LYMAN, R. L.
   Summary of Investigations relating to Grammar and Composition. Chicago: University of Chicago Press. 1929.
   MERRILL, J., AND FLEMING, M.
   Play-making and Plays. New York: Macmillan & Co. 1930.
   LAMBORN, G.
   Expression in Speech and Writing. Oxford: at the Clarendon Press. 1931.
   LYMAN, R. L.
   The Enrichment of the Curriculum. Supplementary Educational Monograph. Chicago: University of Chicago Press. 1932.
   SCRIVENS, A. G.
   'An Objective Study of the Factors Underlying Ability in Verbal Expression.' Unpublished M.A. Thesis. University of London. 1933.
   BAGLEY, D.
   'Objective Studies in the Teaching of English.' Unpublished M.A. Thesis. University of London. 1935.
   HARVARD JOINT COMMITTEE
   The Training of Secondary School Teachers, especially with reference to English. Cambridge, Massachusetts: Harvard University Press. 1942.
   SCHONELL, F. J.
   Backwardness in the Basic Subjects. Edinburgh and London: Oliver & Boyd. 1942.

LEWIS, M. M.
Language in School. London: University of London Press, Ltd. 1942.

BEACOCK, D. A.
'Playway English for To-day.' *The Methods and Influence of H. Caldwell Cook*. London and Edinburgh: Thomas Nelson & Sons, Ltd. 1943.

HAMLEY, H. R.
'The Project Method in the Secondary School', *The Schoolmaster and Woman Teacher's Chronicle*, December 1st and 21st, 1944.

LAMBERT, C. M.
'A Study of Interest in School Subjects among Secondary School Pupils at Different Ages.' Unpublished M.A. Thesis. University of London. 1944.

WATTS, A. F.
The Language and Mental Development of Children. London: George G. Harrap & Co., Ltd. 1944.

ROYSTON, P.
'An Investigation into the Relative Efficiency of Different Methods of Speech Instruction, including some Study of Factors Influencing Speech.' Unpublished M.A. Thesis. University of London. 1945.

FLEMING, C. M.
Research and the Basic Curriculum. London: University of London Press, Ltd. 1946.

GLOVER, A. H. T.
New Teaching for a New Age. London: Thomas Nelson & Sons, Ltd. 1946.

LAURENCE, M. J. P.
Citizenship through English. Edinburgh and London: Oliver and Boyd. 1946.

PINTO, V. DE SOLA (ED.)
The Teaching of English in Schools. A Symposium by the English Association. London: Macmillan & Co., Ltd. 1946.

HARTOG, P. J.
Words in Action. London: University of London Press, Ltd. 1947.

2. See:

VALENTINE, C. W.
The Reliability of Examinations: An Enquiry. London: University of London Press, Ltd. 1932.

SADLER, M., AND OTHERS
Essays on Examinations. London: Macmillan & Co., Ltd. 1936.

HARTOG, P. J., AND RHODES, E. C.
The Marks of Examiners. London: Macmillan & Co., Ltd. 1936.

CAST, B. M. D.
'An Investigation on Methods of Marking Compositions.' Unpublished M.A. Thesis. University of London. 1939.

VERNON, P. E.
The Measurement of Abilities. London: University of London Press, Ltd. 1940.

HARTOG, P. J., AND OTHERS
'The Marking of English Essays.' A Report upon an Investigation carried out by a sub-committee of the U.E.E. London: Macmillan & Co., Ltd. 1941.

MORRISON, R. L., AND VERNON, P. E.
'A New Method of Marking English Compositions', *British Journal of Educational Psychology*, II, June 1941, pp. 109–19.

3. LONG, J. A., AND SANDIFORD, P.
The Validation of Test Items. Toronto: University of Toronto Press. 1935.

VERNON, P. E.
The Measurement of Abilities. London: University of London Press, Ltd. 1940.

4. THURSTONE, L. L., AND CHAVE, E. T.
The Measurement of Attitude. Chicago: University of Chicago Press. 1929.

LIKERT, R., ROSLOW, S., AND MURPHY, G.
'A Simple and Reliable Method of Scoring the Thurstone Attitude Scales', *Journal of Social Psychology*, V, 1934, pp. 228–38.
See also:

EVANS, K. M.
'An Investigation into Teachers' Attitudes.' Unpublished M.A. Thesis. University of London. 1946.

5. JENNINGS, H. H.
'Structure of Leadership—Development and Sphere of Influence', *Sociometry*, I, 1, 1937, pp. 99–143.

6. NORTHWAY, M. L.
'Social Acceptability Test', *Sociometry*, V, 2, 1942, pp. 180-4.

7. NORTHWAY, M. L.
'A Method of depicting Social Relationships, obtained by Sociometric Testing', *Sociometry*, III, 2, 1940, pp. 144–50.

BRONFENBRENNER, U.
'The Measurement of Sociometric Status, Structure and Development', *Sociometry Monographs*, No. 6. New York: Beacon House Inc. 1945.

8. Cf. Psychodrama, described in the following:
CURRAN, F. J.
'Drama as a Therapeutic Measure in Adolescence', *American Journal of Orthopsychiatry*, IX, 1, 1939, pp. 215–31.

MORENO, J. L.
'Mental Catharsis and Psychodrama', *Sociometry*, II, 3, 1940. Republished in *Psychodrama Monographs*, No. 6. New York: Beacon House Inc.

MORENO, J. L.
'The Philosophy of the Moment and the Spontaneity Theatre',
Sociometry, IV, 2, 1941, pp. 205–26.

MORENO, J. L., AND TOEMAN, Z.
'The Group Approach in Psychodrama', *Sociometry*, V, 2, 1942,
pp. 191–6.

ZANDER, A., AND LIPPITT, R.
'Reality Practice as an Educational Method', *Sociometry*, VII, 2,
1944, pp. 129–51.

HENDRY, C. E.
'Role Practice brings the Community into the Classroom',
Sociometry, VII, 2, 1944, pp. 196–204.

MORENO, J. L.
Psychodrama. First Volume. New York: Beacon House Inc. 1946.

See also *Psychodrama Monographs*. New York: Beacon House Inc.

The following have special significance for education:

No. 3. MORENO, J. L.
The Theatre for Spontaneity.

No. 4. MORENO, J. L.
The Spontaneity Test and Spontaneity Testing.

No. 9. ZANDER, A., LIPPITT, R., AND HENDRY, C. E.
Reality Practice in Education.

No. 10. SHOOBS, N.
Psychodrama in the Schools.

CHAPTER THREE

OBSERVATIONS ON GROUPS IN THE EXPERIMENTAL CLASS APRIL 1947 TO JULY 1948

CONSTRUCTION OF GROUPS: APRIL AND SEPTEMBER 1947

WHEN the research was originally planned it had been intended that the groups should remain constant for the entire period of the investigation. It was soon realised, however, that this procedure would be psychologically unsound, since group life was by its very nature dynamic and changing. The girls were therefore assured at a very early stage in the experiment that they would be free to change their grouping whenever they wished to do so.

On the basis of the first sociometric test in April seven groups were constructed, each consisting of four or five children. Reference to Sociogram 1 (see page 41) will show that no two girls exchanging first choices were separated. Although at the time every effort was made to give each girl at least one and if possible two or three of her choices, Christine's position in Group 5 seems completely unjustifiable; to this group, apparently, were allocated the children who were difficult to fit in elsewhere, for none of the four put down any of the others as her first choice, and Ena received only her fourth choice by this placement. The other groups, it appears, were better adjusted, though Alison, Ruby, Lorna and Hazel were deprived of their first choices and nine others were deprived of their second choices. During the summer term three new girls came into the form from other schools—Frances, Patricia and Trudy. Frances was put into Group 6, Patricia into Group 5 and Trudy into Group 7.

During the summer term these groups worked together from time to time and acted plays together. For the following year (September 1947 to July 1948) the English time-table was arranged so that the form had a double period in a hall nearby which was used by the school for acting lessons. This meant that group work could be carried on in ideal conditions: the noise, inevitable in this kind of lesson, would disturb no other class, and the groups could be dispersed over a wider area than the limited form-room space would allow and so avoid distracting one another. In these conditions it was possible to observe the groups much more closely and at the same time give them more freedom.

On September 16th a double lesson was given to the writing of a character sketch. The groups were as they had been the previous term, and while they worked the following individual positions were noted: in Group 1 Enid took no part in the discussion or the writing; in Group 2 all four were actively co-operating; in Group 3 Heather took no part; in Group 4 all played some part, Ruby leading the discussion and Paula contributing a good many ideas; in Group 5 Patricia was on several occasions the object of a concerted attack by the others, who did not accept any of her suggestions; in Group 6 Bridget and Valerie monopolised the conversation, making all the decisions and apparently ignoring the other members of their group, who merely looked on and listened; Group 7 showed a co-operative spirit, Alison and Molly being the most vocal members. These observations suggested that the more united a group was the better it was likely to work, and that a discontented group might find a scapegoat. Leadership qualities were already observable in Ruby and Alison who were directing and co-ordinating the discussion in their groups.

At the beginning of the autumn term, many of the form were eager for a new grouping arrangement, and a second sociometric test was given, with exactly the same criterion as for the first. On this occasion the task of replacing the children in groups was much easier than in April, owing to the increase in the number of mutual choices (54·9 per cent of the choices being reciprocated in September as compared with 40·9 per cent in April). On the basis of this second test the form was divided into nine groups,* of which groups 1 and 2, Groups 4, 5 and 6 and Groups 8 and 9 were to combine for dramatic work, and Groups 3 and 7 were to remain as working units for both composition and drama. By this new allocation of children only two first choices were unsatisfied: June was given her second choice (Bridget) which was reciprocated, rather than her first (Eileen) which

* See Sociogram 3.

was unreciprocated, and Valerie was deliberately separated from Bridget as the alliance had already proved too strong for the other members of the group.

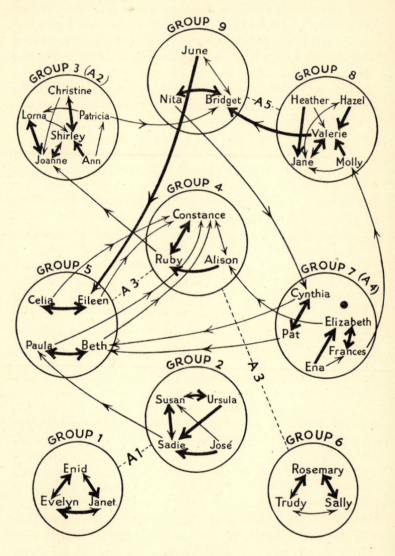

SOCIOGRAM 3

Composition Groups in Class-group E: September to November 1947

GROUP ACTIVITIES: SEPTEMBER TO NOVEMBER 1947
SEPTEMBER 22nd: MIMING OF PILGRIM'S PROGRESS

To find out whether the use of group methods had so far produced any increase in the spontaneity of the children an attempt was made to enliven the reading of Pilgrim's Progress by miming. The incidents used were Christian losing his burden, the appearance of the Three Shining Ones, the conversation with Simple, Sloth and Presumption, and the arrival of Formalist and Hypocrisy. The first paragraph was read through, and an appeal was made for volunteers to go out to

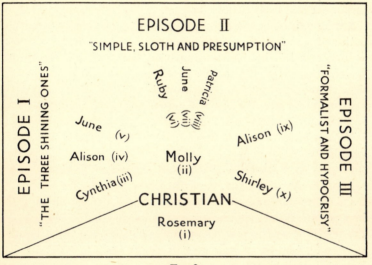

FIG. 3

the front and act the parts; when the same paragraph was read through a second time, however, the entire class sat unresponsive and no volunteer came forward to start the action. After a further request, Rosemary offered, rather self-consciously, to play Christian: she gave a weak performance, punctuated by giggles, but did start things off and was thanked for her co-operation. Next Molly took the part, entering into it wholeheartedly and without embarrassment, and this time volunteers went out quickly to take the other parts. The results are plotted above in Fig. 3.

This acting produced a temporary quickening of interest in the book. A week later the incidents of Christian's loss of his roll, his struggle to climb the Hill Difficulty and his arrival at the Arbor were acted, both actors and audience enjoying the performance. Ruby played Christian, Sally and Shirley the lions and Joanne the Porter. After this, interest flagged: the dramatisation of Christian's fight with Apollyon by Beth and Paula was entirely unsuccessful and the scene of Vanity Fair aroused little interest.

It will be noticed that ten children participated in this activity, and that four of these volunteered twice: Alison, June, Ruby and Shirley. As Shirley had been among the slowest to come forward in the mime lesson on March 20th, this showed some improvement. It could not really be said, however, that the form as a whole was any more responsive and lively than in the past.

Stories written by these new groups during a lesson on September 29th and snatches of conversation recorded while they were being written revealed that some groups were better able to co-ordinate their activities than others. The stories begun by Groups 4 and 1, of which Constance and Janet, who had been first and third in the ranking order for the April Composition Test, were members, seemed better thought out and constructed than the others, whereas in Group 6, consisting of two girls whose composition scores had been below the mean in April and one new girl, progress was so slow that very little written work had been achieved by the end of the lesson. On the other hand, the written observations on Groups 8, 9, 5 and 6 showed that discussion was not limited to the brightest members of those groups and that even children who scored low marks in the test proposed improvements and pointed out errors. Heather (Group 8), who was always excessively shy and timid in class, had been frequently absent, occasionally playing truant, and was reported to be unhappy at the school, was beginning to play a limited part in group discussion.

OCTOBER 13th: THE OBJECTIVE TEST

During this double period (and during a single period later in the week) an attempt was made to discover who were the most actively participating members of each group, and which girls were emerging as leaders. An objective test of eighteen items was compiled from material on pages 314–15 and 336–7 of Dr. A. F. Watts' book, *The Language and Mental Development of Children*.

Each group in turn worked through these eighteen test items

62

under observation. Each pupil had a copy of the test in front of her, but only one wrote in the answers: this ensured that the group came to an agreement about each item of the test. The observer tried to record all the conversation and to note which children suggested solutions (correctly or incorrectly) but failed to catch all the remarks owing to the speed with which they followed one another and the inaudibility of some of the voices.

In solving items 1 to 10 (the paired sentences) Groups 1, 4, 8 and 9 worked systematically through the sentences on the left, and (on the whole) came to an agreement about each one before going on to the next, whereas Groups 2, 3, 5 and 7 tackled the problem unmethodically, working individually or in pairs instead of co-operating, and jumping from one item to another instead of working steadily down the list. (Group 6 did not do the test; two of the three members were absent on the second day of the test, and by the time the three were all attending school again, too much time had elapsed since the other groups had worked it.)

The time taken by each group to complete the test and the number of mistakes made are given below:

Group 1: 6 minutes. 1 mistake.
Group 2: 8 minutes. No mistakes.
Group 3: 14 minutes. 2 mistakes.
Group 4: 9 minutes. No mistakes.
Group 5: 10 minutes. No mistakes.
Group 7: 10 minutes. 1 mistake.
Group 8: 10 minutes. 2 mistakes.
Group 9: 5 minutes. No mistakes.

Group 9 was therefore the quickest and most accurate, and Group 3 the slowest.* The following observations were recorded:

GROUP 1

In Fig. 4 below, unbroken lines indicate correct suggestions and broken lines incorrect suggestions.

Enid was told (by Evelyn) to write in the answers. When Janet and

---

* During the same week the test was worked individually by the girls in the Control Group. The scores for Question I (10 items) ranged from 3 to 10: eleven out of thirty gained full marks, and the mean was 7·63. For Question II (8 items) the range was 0 to 8; 3 gained full marks, and the mean was 5·57. On the whole test no girl gained full marks; the range was 3 to 17, and the mean was 13·17.

Evelyn had agreed on the solution to the first item, she was still looking down the lists of sentences. When the other two looked across at her she asked: 'What shall I put?' Evelyn told her, rather impatiently, to put down the number. The test then developed into a race between Evelyn and Janet with Evelyn usually leading, and showing an impatient spirit towards both the others. Enid seemed bewildered and did little except passively write down what the others told her to. The conversation while they were working through Question II showed this state of affairs clearly (the first had been solved correctly by Evelyn):

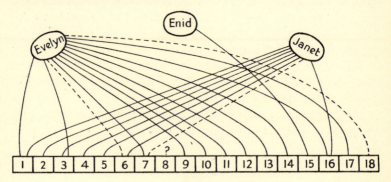

FIG. 4

Evelyn: 11 correct, 2 incorrect
Enid   : 1 correct
Janet : 7 correct, 1 incorrect

EVELYN: 'b' for number 3, don't you think?
JANET: Wait a minute.
EVELYN: Well, think quickly.

Her suggestion was accepted, and the group went on to the fifth item. Enid suggested the answer, which Evelyn accepted. Janet suggested the next two, and Evelyn agreed on the first but queried the second and provided the correct answer. In deciding number 8 there was friction again:

EVELYN: I think 'b'.
ENID: Wait a minute.
EVELYN: Well, hurry up!
ENID: You don't give me time to read it through.

But Evelyn's decision was carried without further discussion, and the only mistake on this group's paper was recorded.

GROUP 2

Sadie wrote in the answers. The conversation was disjointed and difficult to follow, as the group did not work systematically. The following attempt at recording their conversation shows that all four played some part in solving the items:

SUSAN: Number 1 goes with 3 . . . 2 with 4.

JOSÉ: I think——

SADIE: (*bursting in excitably*) 9 goes with 8!

    (*There was general agreement.*)

SADIE: (*considering the preceding item*) I don't know what number 8 means.

    (*No one took any notice, or explained the sentence to her.*)

URSULA: 5 goes with 10.

JOSÉ: No—8!

SADIE: That's wrong: number 10 goes with 8.

JOSÉ: 9 goes with 8.

SADIE: No!

SUSAN: (*irritably*) Yes it does.

JOSÉ: Number 4?

SADIE: No, I've put that for——

SUSAN: Yes! I think it is!

JOSÉ: Number 4 goes with 9. Have we done number 2?

SUSAN: 2 goes with 6. Have we done number 3?

SADIE: (*looking at a different one*) I know what this one is here!

SUSAN: Come on—let's finish this one.

While the group worked through Question II Ursula came to the fore, solving four out of the eight items. At one point Sadie said: 'I've never heard of this', but again nobody enlightened her.

GENERAL COMMENT

The group showed no effective co-operation, though no one was idle, and Susan and Sadie both showed a lively interest. Susan realised eventually that their efforts were unco-ordinated, but did nothing to improve matters. Each was working too much on her own, and although the group produced a correct solution their method lacked unity. Sadie twice expressed ignorance of the meaning of a sentence, but on neither occasion was she helped by any of the others.

GROUP 3

This group (a large one) worked through the first questions in the same disorganised fashion as Group 2. Shirley, Lorna and Patricia all tackled different items and threw out suggestions with which Joanne, the writer, could not keep pace. The search for pairs of sentences continued without system or leadership, and after nine minutes apathy set in. At this point Joanne tried to take the lead.

JOANNE: 1 and 3 together?
   (*Lorna had suggested this during the first two minutes, but no one had heard her.*)
SHIRLEY: 1 goes with 6, not with 3.
   (*Joanne looked doubtful but did not argue.*)
   It doesn't make sense with number 3.
JOANNE: (*uncertainly*) It does——

Christine muttered 'organising ability' to herself, trying to decide what it meant. Joanne and Shirley did not consult the rest of the group. In the end Joanne wrote down 3 as the answer. Question I was then finished, with a struggle, but nobody seemed satisfied. When Question II was tackled Christine came into prominence, solving four of the eight items correctly and one incorrectly. Joanne once protested: 'Wait a minute', and Lorna grumbled: 'I don't get a chance to read them.'

GENERAL COMMENT

Joanne was the only one who seemed aware that co-operation was wanting, but lacked the initiative to organise the thinking. Ann took no part at all in the work. Lorna expressed irritation at the lack of co-ordination. Christine took no part in the first ten items, but took the lead (rather aggressively) in solving the last eight. Possibly the group was too large and unwieldy.

GROUP 4

This group worked systematically down the sentences on the left, consulting each other at every stage, and explaining difficulties as they went along. Their conversation can therefore be reported more accurately, since it really was a conversation, and not merely a series of disjointed comments and suggestions. The numbers on the left indicate which item was being discussed at any given moment.

When the papers were given out Constance and Ruby consulted each other about the first item and then asked Alison what she thought. 1 and 3 were matched at once.

    2. RUBY: Isn't this like the first?
           (*Pause while all three considered it.*)
       RUBY: 6? (*Agreement.*)
    3. CONSTANCE: 2. (*Agreement.*)
    4. ALISON: 9. (*She read both sentences out: the others agreed.*)
    5. RUBY: The last one. (*Agreement.*)
    6. RUBY: 7. (*Agreement.*)
    7. CONSTANCE: Number 1?
       ALISON: I should think it would be 5.
    8. CONSTANCE: Number 1 for this?
       RUBY: Yes. Think so, Alison?
       ALISON: Yes.
  9 and 10. RUBY: What haven't we got?
       ALISON: The last one is like 4.
       RUBY: Yes—so the other must be opposite 9.
       ALISON: (*reading them out*) Yes—that would be right!

In working through Question II, Ruby asked what 'Strike while the iron is hot' meant, and Alison explained. Discussion arose over the fourth item:

ALISON: 'b'.
CONSTANCE: 'c'.
RUBY: 'Appearances may be deceptive' . . . it looks as if it's gold, but it's not gold.
ALISON: Could it be 'd'?
RUBY: It's not the first. It's not the third. So it's either the second or the fourth. (*Pause.*) All sorts of things glitter like gold, don't they?
    ('b' *was agreed on as the correct answer.*)

When Constance suggested 'b' for the answer to number 6, Ruby commented, 'Like Geometry!'

GENERAL COMMENT

This group showed excellent co-operation. No one was left behind: the group never moved on to a new item till agreement had been reached on the one in hand. They did not appear to be hurrying, yet they wasted no time. When the first question (the paired sentences) was correctly solved, all three seemed conscious of a feeling of satisfaction. In fact the whole paper was tackled with a spirit of enjoyment and friendliness.

GROUP 5

The group began by carrying on an argument as to who should do the writing. When this was decided there was some more chatter from Beth, then silence while they read through the instructions for Question I. Beth presently muttered: 'Wish I'd got my dictionary!' Then she and Eileen put their heads together and decided that 10 and 14 could be paired. Paula was consulted.

BETH: 8 and 1.
PAULA: 9 and 7.
CELIA: See if any of them goes with the one opposite number 7.
PAULA: Look! 2 goes with 6 (*read both out*).
BETH: Number 2——
    (*Celia tried to say something but was ignored.*)
BETH: Let's do number 2.

This kind of thing went on until the items were all solved. The conversation was difficult to follow, and was punctuated with remarks such as 'We've done that!' 'Which haven't we done?', etc.

To the second question all four contributed suggestions, and agreement was reached on each item. Paula queried one of Celia's suggestions and Beth queried one of Eileen's, but both were accepted in the end.

GENERAL COMMENT

The group seemed rather volatile: Beth was slow to settle down; Paula dominated the others without really leading them; Eileen took comparatively little part; Celia was ineffective at the beginning, but contributed more in the second part of the test.

GROUP 7 (Frances absent)

Elizabeth made the first suggestion, which Pat and Ena considered. Cynthia took no notice, absorbed in her own study of the paper. The conversation continued in rather an unsatisfactory way:

CYNTHIA: 10 and 4?

(*Ena made a suggestion, which was inaudible.*)

CYNTHIA: Better leave that one.

ENA: 7?

CYNTHIA: Would 9 go with the last ?

Pat, Elizabeth and Ena, having come to an agreement, suggested that 2 and 6 might be paired. Pat poked Cynthia in an effort to consult her about this, but Cynthia merely repeated: 'Do you think 9 goes with 10?' The others agreed.

PAT: Couldn't we mark them off as we do them?

CYNTHIA: (*waking up to the presence of the others again but ignoring Pat's suggestion*) 6 and 9? (*Agreement.*)

PAT: What goes with 10?

CYNTHIA: Number 4.

At this point Cynthia and Elizabeth put their heads together over number 2 and Pat and Ena did the same over number 7.

PAT: 8 goes with 1. (*Others agreed.*)

CYNTHIA: How many more?

PAT: Number 5 . . . 5 and 2! Does 9 go with 8?

ENA AND ELIZABETH: Yes!

CYNTHIA: 7 with 5?

ELIZABETH: I think 1 goes with 7.

PAT: Yes, I think so. So 6 is the only one left.

Question II was solved entirely by Pat and Cynthia.

GENERAL COMMENT

The group did not tackle Question I methodically. Pat seemed aware of the necessity for some co-ordination, but did not suggest considering the items in order. Cynthia made no attempt to identify herself with the group: when the other three were trying to solve number 3, she was considering number 10, and interrupted their thoughts by blurting out her suggestion; later when Pat tried to attract her attention, instead of trying to find out what Pat wanted, she made another random suggestion. At one point the group split into two pairs, Cynthia co-operating with Elizabeth and Pat with Ena. During the second part of the test, Elizabeth and Ena seemed to have lost all interest. The lack of co-ordination may have been due to the absence of Frances who was beginning to take the lead in this group's activities.

GROUP 8

This group showed good co-operation and worked systematically through the paper. Molly and Heather each made six suggestions, and Valerie five. When Jane seemed to be losing interest it was Valerie who aroused her attention and made her express an opinion. Hazel although she made no suggestions was following closely, and once drew the attention of the group to a mistake: Molly suggested the second one for number 7 and Hazel pointed out that they had already used it for number 3. Heather, having had two suggestions accepted in the first half of the test, was the most active member of the group in the second, joining in the general agreement on the first item, and solving four items out of the remaining seven.

GROUP 9

This group worked quickly and systematically, showing the same co-operative and friendly spirit as Group 4, and expressing satisfaction on completing the test. The conversation reveals no more than the diagram showing the distribution of correct and incorrect suggestions, and so is not given here. There was agreement on each answer written down. Errors were noted three times by June and once by Bridget.

From these observations it appeared that the small groups were on the whole better able to co-ordinate their efforts than the larger ones. In Groups 4 and 9 leadership potentialities could be seen in Ruby, Alison, June and Bridget, although in the particular situation under observation it was not so much leadership as identity of effort which was noticeable. In Groups 3 and 7 leadership was obviously needed, and although Joanne in Group 3 and Pat in Group 7 made tentative efforts to organise the activity they were not really effective. Valerie showed considerable power of leadership in Group 8, where four very different personalities were assembled—the sociable, communicative Molly, Heather, who seemed too frightened to take any part in ordinary class lessons, Jane who found the work difficult, and Hazel who appeared to be thoroughly lazy; yet this group worked as systematically as any in solving the test items. José, who in lessons appeared sometimes to be almost disappearing under her desk in her efforts to escape notice, worked confidently in her group. On the other hand, Enid and Ann were just as inactive in their

70

groups as they were in class, and Elizabeth and Ena very quickly lost interest. Evelyn, Susan and Paula seemed over-aggressive, and Beth was uncontrolled.

OCTOBER 13th: DESCRIPTION: A SHOP AND ITS OWNER

During the double period which was used for this test the groups were working on a descriptive passage, the subject being a shop and its owner. Each group was free to choose its own type of shop. Groups 1 to 5 were interrupted in this work to do the test: Groups 6 to 9 worked without interruption, and did the test later in the week when the rest of the form were engaged on individual work. An attempt was made to assess the merit of these compositions by giving each a score, expressed as a mark out of 25 and arrived at by the same process as were the individual scores in the third composition test set during the preceding April. These comparisons showed that six out of the nine groups achieved a higher score by co-operative work than the average of their individual scores when writing on a similar topic a few months before. Groups 1, 3, 5 and 8 each produced a better description than any of its members had done individually; Group 9, whose average score was the second highest, produced an inferior description by co-operative effort. The greatest improvement was achieved, not by the groups where there was outstanding individual talent, but by Group 8, where, although individual attainments were low, the group efforts were co-ordinated by effective leadership and team work. Conversely, Group 7, which seemed to lack cohesion, produced a comparatively weak description, scoring only 10, although Ena had gained a higher mark in April than any member of Group 8.

In writing these compositions two of the groups failed to keep their purpose clear, wandering from description to narrative (Groups 2 and 8). Groups 2, 3, 6 and 7 used conventional material and were content with vague, generalised phrases. Groups 1, 4, 5 and 8 introduced significant details into their descriptions, showing some feeling for colour and atmosphere and some sense of characterisation. All the group compositions were surprisingly accurate. Spelling and punctuation errors for the nine groups were as follows:

Group 1: 2 punctuation errors.
Group 2: 1 spelling error.

Group 3: 2 punctuation errors.
Group 4: No errors.
Group 5: 1 spelling error.
Group 6: No errors.
Group 7: 2 spelling and 2 punctuation errors.
Group 8: 4 spelling and 4 punctuation errors.
Group 9: 1 spelling error.

Confusion of tenses occurred in two descriptions (Groups 1 and 2), and mistakes in sentence construction in three (Groups 3, 5 and 8). It seemed, therefore, that the checking of errors which had been observed in the lesson on September 29th went on even when the groups were not being closely supervised.

OCTOBER 20th: SPONTANEOUS DRAMA*

In the hope of finding out more about the relationships within the groups an everyday situation was suggested to the form for dramatic treatment, but no suggestions were made as to how it should be acted. For this activity the composition groups combined into larger units, which will be referred to as Groups A1, A2, A3, A4 and A5 (see page 60). Each of these groups played out an imaginary scene in an underground train held up in the tube. There was no preliminary discussion or planning: thus each girl had to react spontaneously to the others in her group. A few of them went up to the stage and immediately assumed a definite character; some acted in pairs; some followed up one another's leads quickly; some took practically no active part. Details of the scenes are recorded below, in the order in which they were played.

GROUP A5

The group occupied the following positions:

    Bridget Molly June Valerie Nita Heather
                            Hazel Jane

Bridget took the initiative by complaining loudly that the hold-up would make her late for her appointment. Valerie then began to offer those sitting near her some of her rheumatic lotion, drawing an imaginary bottle out of her pocket. Then, addressing the passengers in general, she asked whether anyone could tell her the time. Jane

* Cf. Oral Tests given in April: see pp. 46–52

answered. Bridget suddenly changed her rôle, and punctuated the rest of the scene with apprehensive appeals to everybody to be careful. Nita suddenly announced that she thought the train was going to start.

GENERAL COMMENT

Bridget and Valerie tried to bring about a general interaction among the passengers. Jane responded once to Valerie and Molly joined in several times. Heather and Hazel were passive the whole time.

GROUP A3

Positions on the stage:

Trudy Rosemary Sally Beth Paula Constance Celia
                                        Ruby   Eileen

Ruby took up a position as though she had been asleep for some time and was awakened by Constance, who explained loudly and emphatically that the train had stopped. Then everybody began talking at once, and the result was so confusing that the group had to be asked to start again. The second time Beth emerged as a slow, precise old gentleman offering aspirins all round and explaining how he always carried something in case of an emergency. Constance assumed the rôle of an irritable, impatient character, but weakened her performance by repetition.

GENERAL COMMENT

This group began by acting as three, noisy, independent units—a situation which was probably aggravated by the fact that they were sitting in pairs and threes (see Sociogram 3 on page 60), Trudy, Rosemary and Sally forming one group, Beth and Paula a second, Ruby and Constance a third and Celia and Eileen a fourth. These four units never seemed to come together and interact with one another. Beth and Constance both addressed remarks to the whole group, but no conversation developed.

GROUP A2

Positions on the stage:

Ann Christine Lorna Shirley Joanne
                    Patricia

Shirley took up a position sprawling in her seat as if in a drunken sleep and maintained this rôle throughout the scene. Lorna began the conversation by consulting the other occupants of the carriage about the football pools she was doing: when she asked for a light Patricia suddenly assumed the rôle of a disapproving prude by remarking that in her young days no one thought of such things as smoking and betting. This was quickly taken up by Lorna and a quarrel developed rapidly, until Patricia moved to the opposite seat, where she found herself being used as a cushion by Shirley.

GENERAL COMMENT

This scene produced quick development of character and incident, Lorna, Patricia and Shirley interacting readily with one another. Christine and Joanne made spasmodic efforts to join in the conversation; Ann (note her position isolated at the side) took no part in the scene at all.

GROUP A 1

Positions on the stage:

Susan Evelyn José Sadie Enid
Ursula Janet

Janet was the first to speak and Sadie answered quickly. Susan offered Evelyn a sandwich, but met with no response (Evelyn acting as though she was half asleep). Susan reacted to this by expressing surprise and offering the sandwich again. During a silence Evelyn attracted attention by suddenly breaking into a violent coughing fit, to which Susan reacted by hitting her on the back. Sadie found a foreign newspaper and began to comment on it. Susan made another overture of friendship by offering Evelyn her newspaper.

GENERAL COMMENT

The conversation never really became general, but there was some interplay of character, notably between Susan (as a friendly busybody) and Evelyn (the heavy and unresponsive type). Enid and José took no part at all in the action or the conversation.

GROUP A 4

Positions on the stage:

Frances Elizabeth Ena   Cynthia
Pat

The silence was broken—after some time—by snatches of conversation between Elizabeth and Ena. Cynthia asked in an exasperated tone whether the train was supposed to be moving; receiving no answer she asked the time and was told by Elizabeth. Pat then moved over to Frances and started an inaudible conversation with her.

GENERAL COMMENT

No one took the lead in developing the conversation. The only one who attempted to convey a character was Cynthia, and she neither did nor said anything provocative enough to educe a response from any of the others.

On this occasion the individuals who played the most prominent parts were Bridget, Valerie, Beth, Lorna, Patricia and Susan. For Lorna and Susan this was a new rôle, since neither of them had hitherto shown any inclination to take part in dramatic activities. Heather, Celia, Eileen and José, who were by this time taking part in group discussions, were not yet prepared to perform in front of the class. Enid, Ann and Hazel were still as inactive on the stage as they were in their groups.

NOVEMBER 10th: THE PLANNING OF A BALLAD CYCLE

A suggestion was put to the form that the groups should collaborate to produce a cycle of Robin Hood ballads or stories in dramatised form. This project, though rather unsuccessful in itself, revealed certain facts about group structure and individual behaviour which pointed to the necessity for a new grouping.

After the groups had chosen their ballads they were dispersed round the hall to plan and rehearse their plays. During this period no group was under supervision, but from general observation it became apparent that the attitude of certain individuals, notably of Beth, Paula and Trudy in Group A3, had deteriorated and that the work was not being tackled properly. This suspicion was borne out during the last ten minutes of the session, when each group was called upon to report progress to the rest of the form. With the exception of Group A4, who seemed to have developed some plan of action, none of the groups could give any clear idea of the way in which it intended to adapt its ballad for stage presentation. The form was told that on the following Monday (November 17th) each group must be prepared to act its ballad to the rest and that those who had wasted time that morning must make it up during the week by meeting in dinner hours or going to one another's homes at the week-end. No questions were asked during subsequent lessons that week, and no further reference was made to the morning's activities.

When the ballads were acted on November 17th the groups which showed the best team-work were undoubtedly A5 and A1, who succeeded in making good use of each member (except for Hazel, who merely announced the title for her group), with the result that Enid, José and Heather really acted for the first time without noticeable self-consciousness. Group A5 chose to mime the action, using Valerie as narrator: the mime was well planned, words and actions synchronised admirably and individual performances, especially those given by June and Nita, were convincing. Group A1 had actually written out the dialogue and read it from note-books as they acted: they succeeded in concentrating all the events into one scene, and all the members of the group except Susan took part in the dialogue, Evelyn excelling as the bishop. The ballad presented by Group A2 was far less successful: the dialogue was jerky and ill-prepared and there was no attempt at grouping the characters so that they could be seen by the audience; Patricia and Shirley succeeded in conveying the mood and social position of the characters they were playing, but neither Christine nor Joanne played her part at all convincingly, and Lorna and Ann as foresters did little but sit and look on. Group A4 had evidently made some effort to prepare its play, but the result was hesitant and disjointed, chiefly because too many scenes were introduced and because the group was not large enough in number to cope with this particular ballad. Group A3 made the poorest showing of all. Constance was the narrator. Robin Hood and Little John were played by Alison and Trudy, and the foresters by Rosemary, Sally, Beth, Paula, Celia and Eileen. Ruby was called out of this lesson to go to the school dentist and so played no part. This caused a good deal of consternation, as she was to have played Little John. The group were told that they must provide a substitute and that the play must be acted without Ruby. Trudy, by virtue of her tallness, was coerced into taking the part, but showed little enthusiasm for it. Indeed, it was obvious from the beginning that she did not know what she was supposed to do or say as Little John. The only girl who acted with any vigour or understanding was Alison. There was no attempt to use the foresters to watch the fight and discuss it, to encourage Robin or threaten John. Nothing was made of the burlesque christening of Little John; and the only members of the group who showed any feeling for the dramatic possibilities of the ballad were Alison and Constance.

In the course of class discussion the group was asked how this confusion had come about. It was then admitted that the group as a whole had failed to use the lesson time adequately, that Constance, Ruby and Alison had undertaken to write the play at the week-end and take the principal parts, and that Ruby's unexpected absence had thrown them out badly. As a result, the whole form saw the necessity for all the members of a group sharing in the preparation of such a project, so that any one member could take any part at a moment's notice.

THE THIRD SOCIOMETRIC TEST: 19th NOVEMBER, 1947

The day after the acting of Robin Hood ballads Celia and Eileen came and asked to be moved into another group: they did not mind what group they joined as long as they were separated from Paula and Beth. The latter, when questioned, admitted that they had wasted time and 'fooled about' occasionally in acting lessons, though they claimed to have worked fairly consistently in composition lessons. The form as a whole welcomed the idea of regrouping, and the third sociometric test was given, still using the same criterion.* The results are given in Sociogram 4.

Certain conclusions were drawn from these findings. Firstly, it seemed that the group system might lead to the formation of small exclusive cliques, if methods were not devised by which to bring about some inter-action between the groups; secondly, an isolated triangle seemed likely to remain isolated if encouraged to work apart from other children: Rosemary, Sally and Trudy were still being disregarded by the rest of the group. Thirdly, Paula's isolation suggested that the form as a whole was beginning to discover for itself the sources of disturbance.

In constructing the new groups, it was decided that Beth should be separated from Paula and Rosemary from Trudy. Alison was asked

---

* On this occasion the control group (Class-Group C) were not given the test, as frequent testing seemed unjustifiable in their case.

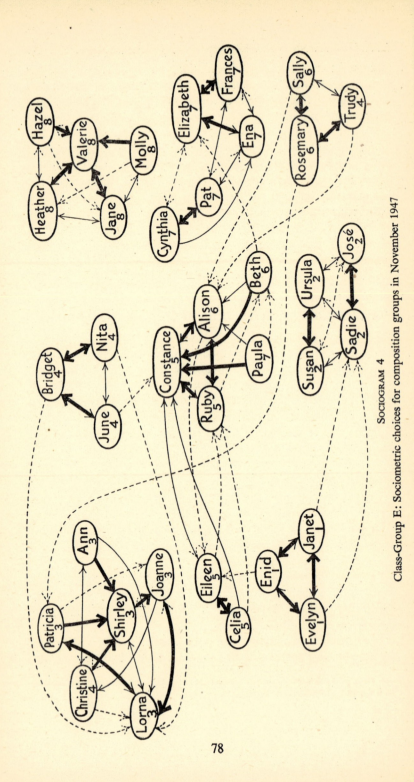

SOCIOGRAM 4

Class-Group E: Sociometric choices for composition groups in November 1947

whether, to facilitate grouping arrangements, she would work apart from Ruby and Constance. She agreed willingly to do so. She was purposely placed in a group with Rosemary and Sally who needed a stronger lead and with Beth who needed firm handling, but she was not told this.* Bridget, June and Nita were encouraged to work with girls from Joanne's group, and arranged to form a writing group with Christine and to combine with the others for dramatic work; Trudy was then absorbed into their group, where she would be likely to come under the strong influence of Bridget and June, and might be expected to work harder and with more satisfying results.

GROUP ACTIVITIES: NOVEMBER 1947 TO APRIL 1948

From time to time during this period activities were planned so as to bring about some interaction between the groups.

NOVEMBER 24th: DESCRIPTION OF THE ROYAL WEDDING

The children's experiences on the day of Princess Elizabeth's wedding had been discussed in a previous lesson, and it was agreed that each group should compose a letter to a group of Finnish children describing the various experiences and reactions of its individual members. (As the hall was not available for the lesson this group work was carried out in an ordinary overcrowded classroom.) It was found that the children had little idea of giving concrete details. On the whole they contented themselves with vague generalities, and none of the letters had much personal interest. It seemed, therefore, that a letter was too individual a form of writing to be undertaken successfully by a group.

DECEMBER 1st: ORAL PROJECT: B.B.C. INTERVIEWS

The following lesson was designed to follow up the attempt at letter-writing, and to induce some interaction between the groups. Volunteers were asked for (two from each group) to act as B.B.C.

---

* Alison's willingness to renounce her own first three choices was typical of her behaviour on many occasions: she was one of the most sociable children in the form, with a friendly attitude to both staff and girls, a lively sense of humour, and a considerable zest for work.

compères, each pair to interview one of the other groups and find out what its members had done on the day of the Royal Wedding. The following volunteered: Evelyn and Janet from Group A1, Bridget and June from Group A2, Alison and Rosemary from Group A3, Molly and Jane from Group A4 and Frances and Pat from Group A5.

Group A1, interviewed by Frances and Pat, did not warm up at all: the questioning was not skilful, and answers were for the most part restricted to 'yes' and 'no'. Frances questioned Janet but met with what appeared to be a refusal to co-operate. Exactly the same thing happened when she questioned Evelyn. Pat then questioned Sadie, who volunteered that she was going to see the film, but gave no account of how she had spent her day. Susan, when asked by Frances, admitted that she had seen the wedding on television, but gave no information about it. Ursula and José used the same blocking tactics. Frances and Pat returned to their group exhausted and defeated.

Group A2, interviewed by Evelyn and Janet, proved equally unwilling to discuss experiences. Patricia said that she had seen the King and Queen come out on the balcony of the Palace on the Wednesday night, but did not respond to further questioning about this. Ann's only comment was that she could not hear the broadcast properly because the children next door were being so noisy. Christine was a little more constructive, describing how she had gone up to town early and pushed her way to the front of the crowd (behaviour about which she seemed quite unrepentant). Joanne had listened to the service but had missed the rest of the broadcast. June (generally a communicative girl) had no comments to make, although she had listened carefully to the broadcast. Nita, who had seen the procession, could give no better account of her day than such comments as 'the procession was very nice', 'there were lots of people', and 'the cavalry were quite good', and those only in answer to specific questions. Bridget, who had also seen it, had little to report, except that she had not seen much because of the crowds, and that she had been nearer the front when the procession came back. José had seen the whole thing on television but made no comments, merely answering 'no' to a series of rather desperate questions from Evelyn.

At this point a protest was made: since both the first two groups appeared to be setting up defensive barriers to prevent the interviewers from eliciting any interesting information, the form was asked what kind of questions should have been put and what sort of responses made. The remaining groups were asked to show more co-operation with the girls acting as interviewers, and the interviewers were asked to make their questions as definite and as helpful as possible.

Group A3 showed a more friendly attitude to the interviewers, especially Ruby, Alison and Rosemary, who really tried to give some account of their activities and to describe their impressions. Rosemary was more communicative than anyone else in her group, volunteering a good deal of information about her journey up to town and responding well to questions. Bridget, as one of the interviewers, monopolised the questioning during this mock broadcast, leaving June only one of eight girls to interview and giving her little opportunity to ask any questions.

While the next group (A5) was assembling, Alison asked whether the interviewers could 'imagine things', and was told that they might handle the situation in any way they liked as long as they made it interesting and alive. After a brief colloquy with Rosemary she began by announcing that the group in the studio consisted of people from different parts of the country. Valerie, Jane and Molly all responded well to this suggestion: Jane, introduced as 'a gentleman in a grey suit and top hat', entered into the game by inventing a name for herself, saying that she had travelled down from Scotland to see the procession, giving her impressions of the London police and the beauty of the Household Cavalry, and describing the excitement felt by the people in Scotland. Molly said she had come over from Killarney a week before on her yearly visit to London, and spoke of her delight at the transformation of the palace by flood-lighting. Alison and Rosemary worked throughout this mock broadcast as a team, neither trying to monopolise the conversation at the expense of the other. Both were natural and friendly, introducing the visitors in a lively fashion, asking constructive questions and inventing some concluding remarks to round off the programme. The group, too, co-operated well and appeared to enjoy themselves.

Group A4 was interviewed by Molly and Jane: Elizabeth, introduced as a schoolgirl who had brought four of her friends along, responded rather feebly. Paula, interviewed by Jane, gave a detailed account of her day and responded well to further questions about the wedding presents, the wireless commentaries and the possibilities of television. Frances and Patricia were both quite co-operative, but Ena expressed no opinions, merely answering questions with a bare 'yes' or 'no'. The broadcast eventually petered out in confusion, no one responding to Molly's inquiry whether anyone had had any interesting experiences to tell the listeners.

As groups had obviously been handicapped by lack of first-hand knowledge, all the girls who had actually seen the procession were asked to go out and pretend to be part of the crowd lining the route, and two volunteers were asked for to act the rôle of commentators out in the B.B.C. recording van. Patricia and Sally volunteered, and in the few remaining minutes of the lesson Sally, assisted from time to time by Patricia, described the scene in the Mall just before the arrival of the procession and interviewed Bridget, Nita, Paula and Christine.

Certain interesting facts both about the groups and about individual members of the form emerge from this record. In the studio situation the first two groups appeared to block progress by giving monosyllabic answers to questions. Group A3 co-operated better, possibly because the questioning was more skilful. Group A5 was quite expertly handled by its two commentators and (apart from Hazel) responded well. Group A4 varied, two of its members showing themselves more anxious to co-operate than the others. In the imaginary situation enacted at the end of the lesson (the B.B.C. recording van in the Mall) the conversation was a good deal more spontaneous and lively, and Sally showed considerable initiative and complete self-confidence as a commentator. Jane and Rosemary were surprisingly effective both in the visitor rôle and as interviewers. The natural sociability and friendliness of Alison and Molly showed itself in their behaviour as interviewers; Bridget, if anything more competent, was dominating rather than friendly in her contacts both with the group and with her fellow interviewer. Paula spoke naturally and intelligently in both the situations in which she took part and was clearly most anxious to co-operate. At the end of the lesson the investigator was left in some doubt whether the lack of co-operation at the beginning had been due to inter-group hostility or to unsuitability of the topic for discussion.

ACTIVITIES DURING THE SPRING TERM, 1948

At the end of the autumn term the children were asked to suggest a possible composition project which could be undertaken by the groups during the coming term. After some thought Alison proposed that the form should compile a collection of stories for young children, and this idea was eagerly taken up by the others. After some discussion they agreed to find out what they could during the holidays about books written and illustrated for children under nine, and to discover by talking to such children which books were the most popular. A further discussion was held at the beginning of the spring term to pool ideas. This discussion showed that practically every girl (including those with no young brothers or sisters) had made inquiries and come back to school with ideas to contribute. One of the most noticeable features of this lesson was the enthusiasm with which Ann (an only child) participated. Throughout her first year she had seemed sulky and resentful, and as the records of group activities show, unwilling to take part in any group project; during the autumn term, however, she had begun, with some embarrassment, to take part in lessons, and went to great trouble at home to produce four or five pages of written work when most of the form were usually producing about a page and a half. When, on these occasions, she was encouraged to read out her compositions, she would blush painfully, stumble through a few lines and then thrust the paper at someone else to read for her. In spite of this shyness she obviously throve on praise, and was beginning to smile more often and look more interested during lessons.

At the end of this discussion lesson each group selected an idea, and the writing of the stories was begun on January 12th and continued until the beginning of February. To follow up this creative interest in children's stories, two parallel activities were planned for the term: the miming and acting of scenes from famous children's books, such as the *Wind in the Willows, Alice in Wonderland* and the *Rose and the Ring*; and the compilation (as a form effort) of an anthology of poems for young children, written out and illustrated by hand. Unfortunately the second project fell through, but it produced a quickened interest in the reading and learning of poetry throughout that term and led to unusually lively discussions, in which even girls who had professed to 'hate poetry' participated.

THE FOURTH SOCIOMETRIC TEST: APRIL 1948

The following changes in individual status and group structure were revealed by the fourth test. Bridget, June and Nita (an isolated triangle in November) now formed a group with Joanne, Lorna and Christine. Shirley, Ann and Patricia formed a triangle, connected by outgoing and incoming choices with every other group in the class except the group from which they had broken away. Elizabeth and Frances were seeking admission to Constance's group and received choices from Heather, Jane and Molly. Valerie and Hazel had lost status with their group but showed no inclination to join any other. Heather, Jane and Molly formed a triangle, distributing their first and second choices among themselves. Alison and Rosemary exchanged first choices; Sally's first still went to Rosemary, but her second now went to Alison. Beth gave her first three choices to Alison, Rosemary and Sally, but was not chosen by them; she and Paula had now broken apart, but neither as yet received any choices on this criterion. Paula sent her choices into three different groups— to Susan, Elizabeth, Eileen and Frances. Constance and Ruby, exchanging first choices, now sent second and third choices to Eileen and Celia and only fourth choices to Alison, who reciprocated with second and third. Cynthia and Pat were an isolated pair: they had broken away from Elizabeth, Frances and Ena, and now sent choices out to Jane, Joanne and Shirley.

After the results of this test had been studied, it was decided to find out whether the girls would differentiate in choosing companions for different activities. Each girl was accordingly asked to write down on the same paper her first three choices of companions for writing compositions, doing grammar exercises and acting in plays.* The results of this test showed that apart from a few who made the same choices for each activity, the children did discriminate. Girls who had before received choices only from a limited number of friends sprang into prominence when criteria were separated. Evelyn attracted eleven choices as a companion in dramatic activities and Bridget eight; Patricia received only two third choices on the first criterion, was isolated on the second, but received four on the third; Beth's second choice to Alison was reciprocated on the first two criteria and Paula received three on the first, five on the second and two on the third. Girls who were isolated on one criterion were, therefore, not necessarily isolated on all three. This seems to suggest that children who are less accepted socially should be given opportunities to shine in some capacity, in the hope that they might be

* A fourth criterion, eating school dinner, was also included but will be considered separately in Chapter IV.

desired as companions in at least some activity. The distribution of all the choices on these four criteria is shown in Table III (at end of book).

During the summer term the composition groups were as follows[1]:

Group 1: Evelyn, Janet, Enid, Cynthia, Pat.

Group 2: Susan, Ursula, Paula.

Group 3: Sadie, José, Trudy.

Group 4: Joanne, Lorna, Patricia, Shirley, Ann.

Group 5: Bridget, June, Nita, Christine.

Group 6: Heather, Jane, Molly, Valerie, Hazel.

Group 7: Alison, Rosemary, Beth, Sally.

Group 8: Constance, Ruby, Eileen, Celia, Elizabeth, Frances, Ena.

In arranging these groups an effort was made to keep them small, as the children themselves felt that six was too unwieldy a number and that a group of seven was quite unmanageable. It was generally felt that three or four was the ideal size for this kind of group. The girls in Group 8 were asked to divide into two sub-groups, using their own judgment, and, if they liked, changing partners from time to time. Events proved that this arrangement penalised the three who had come into the group from outside, as Constance, Ruby, Eileen and Celia were unwilling to break up. Elizabeth, Frances and Ena were on three successive occasions left to work on their own, and felt some resentment not only against the four who were excluding them, but also, it was suspected, against the investigator, who had evaded the responsibility of effecting a satisfactory grouping.

JUNE 14th: THE SECOND OBJECTIVE TEST

During this double period each of the above groups in turn worked through the following questions (taken from the first attainment test) under close observation. The children found the test difficult and no group succeeded in solving more than five of the eight items correctly. The first two items proved the easiest, the third, seventh and eighth the most difficult. The words 'lucid', 'pusillanimous' and 'equivocation' were stumbling blocks to all the groups.

CLASSIFICATION BY FRIENDSHIP

In each of the following sets of words, underline the middle one of the series:

Example: YOUTH   MAN   BABY   BOY   INFANT.

1. WOOD   FOREST   COPSE   JUNGLE   SPINNEY.
2. DELIGHTED   PLEASED   CONTENTED   EXHILARATED   SATISFIED.
3. LUCID   DARK   OBSCURE   TRANSPARENT   DIM.
4. TWIG   LIMB   BRANCH   TRUNK   SHOOT.
5. DEARTH   ABUNDANCE   MEAGRENESS   SUFFICIENCY   GLUT.
6. ESTIMABLE   PROFLIGATE   WORTHLESS   DISTINGUISHED   PRE-EMINENT.
7. CAUTIOUS   RASH   PRECIPITATE   TIMID   PUSILLANIMOUS.
8. TRUTH   EQUIVOCATION   FALSEHOOD   FACT   FICTION.

Solutions were written as follows:

	Group 1	Group 2	Group 3	Group 4
1.	Copse	Wood	Wood	Wood
2.	Pleased	Pleased	Pleased	Pleased
3.	Dim	Lucid	Lucid	Lucid
4.	Branch	Limb	Branch	Limb
5.	Sufficiency	Sufficiency	Dearth	Dearth
6.	Estimable	Estimable	Estimable	Worthless
7.	Precipitate	Pusillanimous	Precipitate	Cautious
8.	Truth	Equivocation	Fact	Equivocation

	Group 5	Group 6	Group 7	Group 8 (a)	Group 8 (b)
1.	Wood	Wood	Wood	Wood	Wood
2.	Pleased	Pleased	Pleased	Pleased	Pleased
3.	Dark	Lucid	Dim	Obscure	Lucid
4.	Limb	Branch	Branch	Branch	Limb
5.	Sufficiency	Dearth	Dearth	Sufficiency	Sufficiency
6.	Profligate	Profligate	Pre-eminent	Profligate	Estimable
7.	Cautious	Precipitate	Precipitate	Precipitate	Precipitate
8.	Equivocation	Equivocation	Equivocation	Truth	Equivocation

In Group 1 Evelyn was rather dominating and directed Cynthia what to write down on five occasions out of the eight. She explained the meanings of two words and asked two questions—one of the group in general and one of Janet in particular. Cynthia showed more willingness to co-operate than she had on the previous testing on October 13th,* and towards the end appealed to the group to think the answers out instead of putting down words at random. Evelyn responded to this, looking at Cynthia with a new respect and showing some willingness to hear her point of view. Until then she had appeared to regard her merely as the wielder of the pencil rather than as another mind to work with. In Group 2 there was very little discussion and no determined attempt to discover the meanings of unfamiliar words. In Group 3 all contributed to the discussion and three explanations of the meanings of words were offered—two by Sadie and one by Trudy—in response to questions or expressions of doubt. Group 4 was still rather indecisive, but it was better organised and worked more purposefully than on the previous testing.† All five contributed suggestions and explanations and there was no friction. (This was the first time Ann was observed to take an active part in group discussion.) In Group 5 Bridget played the most dominating part: she showed the others how to tackle the first question, corrected them when a confusion between two words arose, and did not allow them to abandon a difficulty until an answer had been agreed upon. Of the others in this group June was the most helpful. Group 6 co-operated well. Hazel, Valerie, Jane and Molly all contributed explanations of the meanings of words, and Heather, though what she said was inaudible to the investigator, was keeping up with the others and making suggestions which they could hear. In Group 7 all four were actively contributing. They showed a determination to overcome difficulties and solve the problems if possible. Although they challenged one another and did not necessarily accept one another's explanations, there was a very friendly spirit and they really worked as a team. Beth queried two statements and gave alternative explanations; Sally queried one. They arrived at the correct meaning of 'lucid' by discussion. Their conversation is reported in full below. In Group 8 trouble arose at the beginning of the lesson because Constance, Ruby, Eileen and Celia still insisted on working together: Ena complained that they had done this for

* See pp. 68, 69 (Group 7).
† See pp. 66–68 (Group 3).

three lessons and that she, Elizabeth and Frances, who wanted to work with Eileen and Celia, were being repeatedly excluded. Consequently, while Constance and her three friends were working together contentedly, Elizabeth, Frances and Ena were feeling frustrated and resentful. Among these three there was no real discussion: Elizabeth appealed to Frances for a decision three times and on four occasions wrote the word which Frances chose without question; Ena asked the meaning of 'lucid' and later put another question to the group, but on neither occasion did she receive any answer; Frances seemed rather complacent, giving Elizabeth the answers and never expecting either of the others to question her decision.

Verbatim Report: Group 7

*1. BETH: What's the first? 'Spinney?' No—'wood', 'forest' and 'jungle' are the biggest.

ALISON: 'Copse' is the smallest, then 'spinney'.

2. SALLY: 'Satisfied' first, then 'contented', then 'pleased'.

3. ALISON: 'Transparent' and 'dim'——

BETH: Why should 'dim' be the same as 'transparent'?

ROSEMARY: Sticky.

BETH: You can see through 'transparent' but not through 'dim'.

ROSEMARY: You can see through 'dim'—when it's getting dark at night.

ALISON: In the kitchen, the window is transparent at first, then it becomes dim with steam.

BETH: What about 'lucid'?

ALISON: Leave that for a minute.

4. BETH: What about 'limb'?

ROSEMARY: 'Limb' is bigger than 'branch'. That's going to be 'branch'.

5. SALLY: What's 'dearth'?

ALISON: (*laughing*) Don't look at me!

ROSEMARY: It's a long way from sufficiency to abundance.

ALISON: 'Sufficiency' is the middle one, I think.

6. ALISON: What's 'profligate'?

BETH: Something you get profit out of?

ALISON: Worthless, estimable, distinguished. . . .

* The numbers on the left indicate which question was being considered at any given moment in the working of the test.

BETH: 'Distinguished' is the opposite to 'worthless'. I should think 'profligate' goes with 'distinguished'.

ALISON: 'Pre-eminent'?

BETH: But do 'pre-eminent' and 'worthless' go together?

ALISON: 'Profligate', then.

7. ROSEMARY: 'Timid' and 'cautious' are the same.

ALISON: 'Timid' first, then 'cautious'.

BETH: 'Rash' is the opposite.

ROSEMARY (*pointing to 'pusillanimous'*): I'm not trying to say that one!

BETH: What does 'rash' go with?

ALISON: Opposite 'timid'.

BETH: Put 'precipitate'.

8 BETH: 'Fiction'.

ALISON: Fiction, fact—truth. What's 'equivocation'?

BETH: 'Fact' goes with 'truth'.

SALLY: Truth and fact: 'truth' and 'falsehood' are opposites.

ALISON: It should be 'fiction', and then 'equivocation', then 'truth', then 'falsehood' then 'fact'.

BETH: Middle one would be 'truth'.

SALLY: How?

(Alison repeated her explanation. Sally looked doubtful.)

SALLY: Oh—you're doing it in pairs. No—look!

BETH: We've got it wrong——

SALLY: Those two are opposites: truth and falsehood; fact and fiction. So 'equivocation' goes in the middle. Which did we miss out?

BETH: Number 3.

3. ALISON: 'Lucid' comes before 'dim' really. 'Transparent' and 'obscure' are the same: 'dim' and 'lucid'.

ROSEMARY: Pitch black or——

ALISON: No, not black: dim.

SALLY: Let's go up: 'lucid' or 'dim' I think.

BETH: 'Dark' is not opposite to 'dim'—it's opposite to 'transparent'.

ROSEMARY: No—'obscure' is.

BETH: Perhaps 'lucid' means transparent. I think the middle one is 'dim'.

(Here the group went back to Number 5 to consider it. Eileen read out the words.)

89

5. SALLY: 'Abundance'.
   BETH: 'Meagreness'.
   ALISON: 'Meagreness' and 'sufficiency' . . . sufficiency is about enough. We'd better put 'dearth'.
   BETH: 'Glut' is the opposite to 'abundance'.
   (*The group decided to put ' dearth'.*)

DRAMATIC ACTIVITIES: MAY TO JULY 1948

On the basis of Table III the class was divided into three groups for dramatic work. This arrangement seemed preferable to the combining together of composition groups, for two reasons: by considering the criteria separately it allowed for differentiation of choices between one activity and another; and by making each drama group a cross-section of several composition groups it made for social cohesion in the form as a whole.

During the summer term each of the acting groups chose a play, cast it and acted it to the rest of the form. Although the plays were not actually rehearsed beforehand the actors were supposed to have read their parts and the group as a whole to have discussed the staging of the play. Only three girls in the form (Nita, Christine and June) are not recorded as having played a part in one of these plays. On the whole the performances were vigorous and the responsibility for them was left entirely in the hands of the children. One group, who had chosen to act *The Stolen Prince*, asked eagerly on the morning of the performance whether they could dress up. They arrived at the hall with flowered dressing-gowns, twin dolls and a box of properties, and although they were disappointed to find that the stage was not available for them that morning, they cheerfully acted their play in a small side-room, making the best of their restricted floor-space. The nurse was played by Constance (who had learned most of her part so that she could pay more attention to the two dolls representing the royal babies), the two children by Alison and Rosemary, the fisherman and his wife by Trudy and Eileen, the prince by Beth, the gong-bearer by Paula, the property-man (with evident enjoyment) by Enid and the Chorus (with perfect self-possession) by Sally, who was understudying at the last minute for Evelyn. One of the other groups also came provided with costumes and properties for scenes from *Alice Through the Looking-Glass*, in

90

which prominent parts were played by Sadie, Evelyn, Susan, Janet and Valerie, and non-speaking parts by Ursula, Hazel, June, Heather and José.

SUMMARY AND CONCLUSION

Any attempt to interpret these records of group behaviour must to some extent be coloured by the investigator's own attitude to the children she was teaching, and may therefore be dismissed as subjective and without validity. It is hoped, however, that the following conclusions, based, not on a few weeks' study, but upon a cumulative record of fifteen months, may be considered justifiable.

The ability of a group to co-operate in literary, oral and dramatic projects seems to depend less on the talents of its individual members than on three other factors. In the first place it is important that each group should be well integrated in its social relationships, or in other words, that its members should want to work together. This was shown by the poor co-operation in Group 5 on September 16th, and by the half-hearted work of Group 8B on June 14th, 1948.* Secondly, the size of a group must be appropriate to the task for which it is formed: three or four seems the ideal number for co-operative writing; for dramatic work twelve or fifteen can work efficiently as a unit. Thirdly, in every effective grouping leadership must play an important part. In this experiment no girl was ever appointed as a leader, though groups were sometimes arranged so as not to waste leadership potentialities. In the activities described in this chapter the best leaders were not the most dominating individuals but those who were able to bring out the best in others. Alison and Valerie fulfilled this rôle perhaps better than any other girls in their class-group. Beth, Sally and Rosemary improved rapidly, both in written and oral activities, when they began to work with Alison; the uncomfortable lesson on November 24th suddenly became enjoyable when Alison took control. Valerie showed similar qualities of leadership within a narrower circle, and must be held largely responsible for the social emergence of the two diffident children in her group, Heather and Jane. Constance was recognised by the children as a natural leader from the beginning, but did not shine in the classroom until this ability had been brought into play. Dominating children like Bridget and Evelyn were not recognised as leaders by

* See pp. 59 and 87–88.

the form: they seemed to influence only small groups of children, and acted more democratically when they came into contact with challenging individuals who questioned their authority.

To the investigator, new facts about group life were continually revealing themselves as the study went on. Perhaps the most significant lesson was that even the most backward children gradually became involved in the group activities: with some this process of socialisation took the best part of a year; with others it began almost immediately. It cannot be claimed that Heather, José and Enid were playing an active part in classroom lessons even by the end of the year, but they were looking more alert and interested and were occasionally joining in discussions; on the other hand, in their own groups they often participated actively in oral work and Enid even began, towards the end, to play a prominent part in dramatic activities. It seems, therefore, that improvement in social status may bring about an increase in work efficiency, and, conversely, that deterioration in social status may impair work efficiency. The changes in attainment and attitude which were revealed by the retest in April 1948 will be considered in detail in a later chapter. Further consideration will first be given to the nature of the children's social development as it was revealed in the sociometric tests already referred to and in those now to be described and compared.

REFERENCE

1. WATTS, A. F.
   The Language and Mental Development of Children. London: George G. Harrap & Co., Ltd. 1944.

CHAPTER FOUR

A SOCIOMETRIC STUDY OF TWO CLASS-GROUPS

INTRODUCTION

DURING the four terms of the experiment all but one of the sociometric tests given to the experimental group were given also to the control group. It was hoped that by this means it would be possible not only to study the social development of the experimental group, but also to compare it with that of the control group over a period of time. In January 1948, when the experiment was in its third term, an opportunity arose of comparing the children's choices of work companions with their choices of companions in the school canteen at lunch time. Both groups were given a sociometric test on this new criterion in January; places at canteen tables were allocated on the basis of this test and a retest was given in April. The results of these tests will be discussed and compared with the other tests in the course of this chapter. An attempt was also made to relate the children's choices (on the work criterion) to such factors as home districts, previous schools and special friendships. It was possible to gauge to some extent which of the children were most stable in their friendship and which were able to establish the most satisfactory social relations with others in their form. Certain characteristics of the groups as social units also came to light as time went on. These would not have been so clear had the sociometric tests been limited to one criterion.

DEVELOPMENT OF THE CONTROL GROUP FROM APRIL 1947 TO APRIL 1948

The changes in social structure which took place in the experimental group between April and September 1947 have already been discussed in Chapter III. The structure of Class-Group C did not change so noticeably during those four months. Daphne, Moira, Brenda, Peggy and Ella showed varying degrees of improvement in status but Ella was the only one of these five girls who had really become accepted by the girls whom she chose. Marian, Annette and Joan were still unwanted, and although Joan chose Annette and Annette Marian, the three had not yet formed a definite group. Kathleen, though less of a star than in April, was still much sought after, receiving eleven choices in all, two of them first choices and three second; her first choice, now going to Irene instead of to Freda, was not reciprocated, but her second and third (to Helen and Audrey) were. Hilda, who had in April sent out unreciprocated choices to Jill and Freda, now sent them (still unreciprocated) to Kathleen, Jeanette and Brenda, receiving a third choice from Moira to whom she sent her first. Jill was again being chosen by girls in whom she showed no interest, and again choosing girls who showed no interest in her. Triangles on a two-choice basis had been formed by Gertrude, Freda and Diana and by Dorothy, Madge and Nora.* Four new girls had come into the form: Sheena and Stephanie were being kept down in the second year and so were new to the form but not new to the school; Sheila and Elinor had both been transferred from other secondary schools. The position of these girls in the form as revealed by the sociometric test was interesting: Sheena and Sheila were isolated, apart from one fourth choice each (from Nora and Daphne respectively), and Elinor completely so; Sheena and Elinor sent their first choices and Sheila her fourth to Stephanie.

By the following April the position of the underchosen girls had hardly improved at all: Marian, Joan and Annette now formed a triangle, but were still unwanted by the others whom they chose; Brenda had transferred three of her choices to a new group who did not return them—and sent only her third to Moira, who did return it; Daphne was isolated again; Elinor still received no first, second or third choices, but did receive three fourth choices including one from Stephanie to whom she sent her second; Sheena had become completed isolated. Jill and Hilda again sent out unreciprocated choices, ignoring girls who showed interest in them. Stephanie and Dorothy, choosing each other first, differed in their other choices,

* Rose, who had been connected with Madge and Nora in April, left the school in July and so did not appear in this or later sociograms.

Stephanie forming a triangle with Sylvia and Doreen, and Dorothy forming a triangle with Jeanette and Florence.*

In comparing the two groups on this criterion over the twelve-month period, it may be noted that the proportion of reciprocated choices rose more quickly in Group E than in Group C, and that the number of isolated or nearly isolated children declined correspondingly between April and September.† The frequency distributions of reciprocated choices are given below in graphic and tabular form. They suggest that whereas in Group C the formation of groups was taking place at the expense of certain isolated or underchosen children, in Group E the improvement in the status of individuals was more uniform. In Group C there were five children on the first two occasions and seven on the third who had none of their four choices reciprocated; in Group E there were five in April 1947, but only one and two respectively in the two subsequent tests. Moreover, in Group C Peggy was one of this number on all three occasions, and Ruth, Daphne, Marian and Sheena were on two occasions; in Group E, on the other hand, no girl was left in this state of frustration,

TABLE VI

FREQUENCY DISTRIBUTION OF RECIPROCATED CHOICES FOR GROUPS C AND E

	April 1947					September 1947					April 1948				
GROUP C	0	1	2	3	4	0	1	2	3	4	0	1	2	3	4
Frequency Distributions	5	10	12	4	3	5	8	10	12	1	7	5	9	8	8
Total, per cent	42·7					47·2					53·4				
GROUP E	0	1	2	3	4	0	1	2	3	4	0	1	2	3	4
Frequency Distributions	5	12	8	4	3	1	9	14	6	6	2	6	13	4	11
Total, per cent	40·9					54·9					59·5				

* The interconnection of these two groups was one of the few integrative features of this sociogram, which was characterised on the whole by exclusive cliques and excluded individuals.

† See Table II and Table V in the folder at end of book.

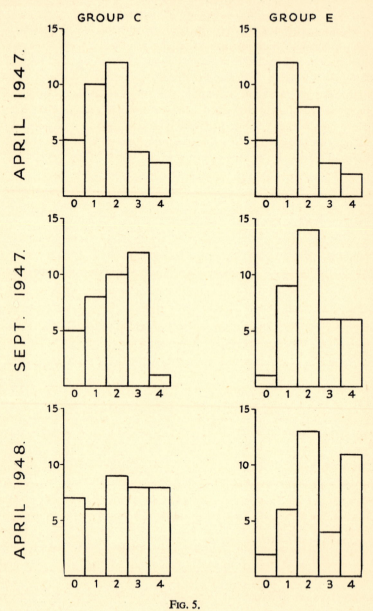

FIG. 5.
Histograms showing frequency distributions of reciprocated choices in three successive tests

for the one who failed to attract answering choices in September had not been among the five in April, and the two whose choices were unreciprocated in April 1948 were Paula and Beth, who were not yet being chosen on this criterion after their disturbing behaviour in November.

RELATION OF SOCIOMETRIC FINDINGS TO HOME LOCATIONS AND PREVIOUS SCHOOLS

An inquiry was next carried out to ascertain whether the proximity of children's homes or attendance at the same junior school had any appreciable effect on the distribution of choices. It was found that roughly two-thirds of each class-group lived within a two-mile radius of the school, and that the remaining children were scattered farther afield, over an area of approximately a hundred square miles. By the use of street reference maps of these districts, the children's homes could be fairly accurately plotted on a map of the area, using a scale of roughly three and a half inches to the mile. Sociograms showing the distribution of first and second choices in April 1947 and April 1948 were then drawn on this map, numbers corresponding to the children's homes being used as in all the tables.*

The first test showed the existence of pair and triangle formations both within small areas and at wide distances apart. In Group E the following positions were revealed by the topographical sociogram (number 5): Nita (8) and Susan (13), who came from the same junior school, exchanged first choices; Elizabeth (6) and Molly (7) exchanged first choices and sent their second to Constance (9) who lived near them and came from the same junior school; first or second choices were also exchanged by Sally (27) and Rosemary (22) who lived farther west than most of the girls, and by Ruby (1) and Joanne (36) who lived in an outlying district in the north-west and came from the same junior school. Of the unreciprocated choices sent from one district to another, eight did not reappear in September; those which did were by then mutual—June (4) and Heather (15) to Valerie (16) and Lorna (18) and Shirley (17) to Joanne (36). The previous school groups were beginning to break up: Nita and Susan (School VI) had moved apart, Nita joining Bridget and June who lived in different districts; the relationships between Molly,

* See Sociograms 5 and 6.

Elizabeth, Alison and Constance (School VII) were changing, and
Bridget (from the same school) had transferred her interests elsewhere; the group from School V was breaking up more quickly, Pat
and Cynthia, now a mutual pair, being quite unconnected with
Christine and Hazel, who no longer showed any interest in each

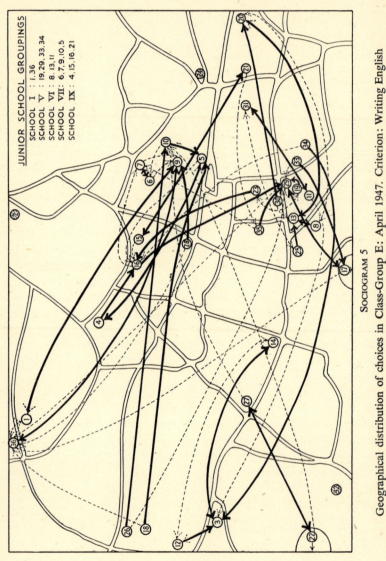

JUNIOR SCHOOL GROUPINGS

SCHOOL I : 1, 36
SCHOOL V : 19, 29, 33, 34
SCHOOL VI : 8, 13, 11
SCHOOL VII: 6, 7, 9, 10, 5
SCHOOL IX : 4, 15, 16, 21

SOCIOGRAM 5

Geographical distribution of choices in Class-Group E: April 1947. Criterion: Writing English
compositions together

other; those from School IX, on the other hand, were establishing their relationship more firmly, apart from Celia, who was cooling towards Heather and showing no interest in the other two.

In Group C the situation in April 1947 was similar to that in Group E. Sociogram 6 revealed the following relationships: mutual

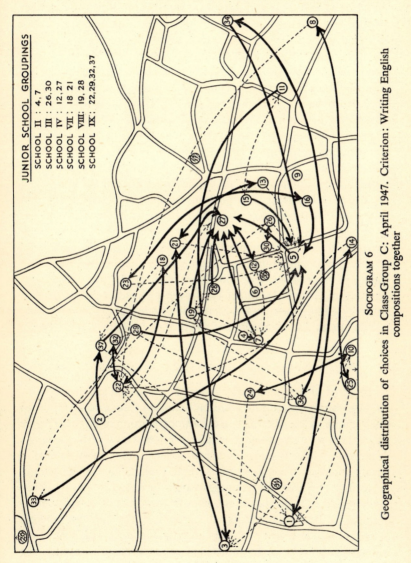

SOCIOGRAM 6

Geographical distribution of choices in Class-Group C: April 1947. Criterion: Writing English compositions together

JUNIOR SCHOOL GROUPINGS

SCHOOL II : 4, 7
SCHOOL III : 26, 30
SCHOOL IV : 12, 27
SCHOOL VII : 18, 21
SCHOOL VIII : 19, 28
SCHOOL IX : 22, 29, 32, 37

choices were exchanged both by girls living near one another and coming from the same junior school and by girls living in widely separated districts. The following unreciprocated choices sent from one district to another in April recurred in September: Jill (37) to Freda (27), Sara (14) to Margery (22), Dorothy (13) to Moira (21), Ella (25) to Sylvia (1) and Pauline (33) to Helen (26); by September Pauline had a fourth choice from Helen and Ella a second choice from Sylvia, but Jill, Sara and Dorothy were still unchosen by Freda, Margery and Moira. The relationships between Margery, Nan, Florence and Jill (all from School IX) had neither broken up nor become firmly established, except that Florence now returned Nan's choice; of the pairs from other schools, Helen and Audrey from School III and Freda and Diana from School IV had remained together, but Irene and Pamela from School VIII had broken apart, and Daphne from School II no longer chose Gertrude.

These charts seem to indicate that the friendships in both groups were to some extent influenced by the proximity of their homes and by common experiences in previous schools, especially in the first year, but that these factors became less important as time went on. It appears that the children in Group E were more able to break apart from these early influences if they proved frustrating: that is to say, groups tended either to become firmly established on a mutual choice basis or to break up altogether. Conversely, there were more children in Group C who persisted over a period of five months or more in sending their choices to others who lived near them, despite the fact that these others did not return their friendship.

INQUIRY INTO FRIENDSHIPS: DECEMBER 1947

This part of the inquiry was undertaken as a result of an exchange of views on the relation of children's choice of work companions to their choice of friends which arose among a group of Higher Degree students who were meeting regularly under Dr. C. M. Fleming's leadership to discuss sociometric problems. Some believed that if group methods were used for several subjects in the curriculum instead of only one the groupings would be different, and that children would not, on the whole, choose their friends as work companions; others believed that the groupings for different subjects would correlate highly with one another, since all would have the same friendship basis. In an attempt to investigate this matter, the children of both class-groups were asked to write down the names of those whom they considered to be their friends—with whom, for instance, they would like to go on a holiday; they were given a maximum of five choices, but were not compelled to put down as many as five if they did not want to; they were told that they need not confine themselves to the other girls in the form or even to others in the school, but were asked, in naming children unknown to the investigator, to state what school they attended or what town or county they lived in if their homes were outside the London or Home County area. These choices were plotted in the following manner: five concentric circles were drawn, the innermost one being made large enough to accommodate the numbers corresponding to the names of the children in the group; these numbers were plotted in the same relative positions as the names in the September sociograms; the schools to which choices had been sent were then listed alphabetically and numbered 1 to 70, and towns and counties beyond the school neighbourhood (that is, the area covered by the map described above) were numbered 71 to 101; every choice sent to another form in the school was indicated by an arrow going out to the first ring, choices sent to other schools in the same geographical area by arrows going out to the second ring, choices sent beyond the London and Home County area to the third ring, and choices sent overseas to the outermost ring.* This test, it is realised, cannot be called a sociometric test in the true sense of the term, since the criterion was vague and unreal and since the children had no practical motive for expressing their choices accurately and sincerely. However, the charts seem to throw light on certain group and individual characteristics and have some interest as supplements to the more genuine sociograms. At the time when the first test of this nature was given (December 1947) Group E had for two terms been working in groups for about a quarter of the total weekly school time spent on English, whereas Group C had been working either individually or (more often) as one large unit. It is perhaps significant, therefore, that whereas in Group E no child was completely isolated (neither choosing nor chosen by others in the form) and only two were unchosen, in Group C four were completely isolated and four others were unchosen. Triangles and chains in Group E were more numerous and more inclusive than those in Group C. Three girls in Group C (Hilda, Jill and Wendy) put down the names of pen-friends in South Africa

* See Sociograms 7 and 8.

or U.S.A., children they had never even met, as intimate friends, and six named cousins (Doreen, Gertrude, Pamela, Peggy, Wendy and Margery). It seemed that the choices of work companions were, at this stage, influenced more by friendship than by any other factor, but that some were beginning to differentiate between criteria in making their choices.

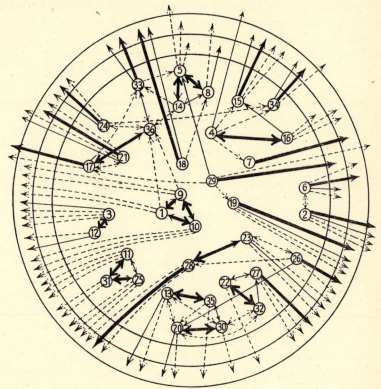

SOCIOGRAM 7

Patterns of friendship within and beyond class, school and district groupings. Class-Group E: December 1947

If the chart of friendship patterns for Group E (Sociogram 7) is compared with the choice pattern in the November test (Sociogram 4) the following facts may be noted: four triangles appear in both— Bridget, Nita and June, Enid, Janet and Evelyn, Susan, José and Ursula, Ruby, Constance and Alison; Lorna, who is well accepted in the work situation, is not named as friend by any girls in the form, and Molly is chosen only by Jane; there are two pairs of friends (Elizabeth and Frances, Eileen and Celia) who are isolated on the December criterion but accepted in groups on the work criterion in November. Ann is one of two girls chosen by Shirley as friends but receives only a fourth choice as a work companion. Cynthia, who exchanged a first choice with Shirley in April on the work criterion

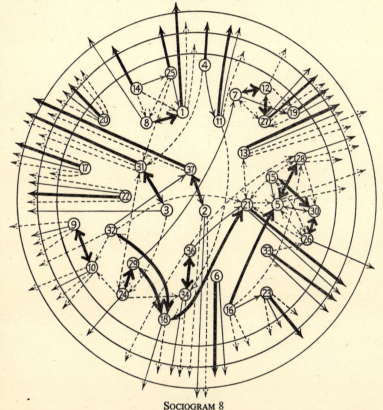

SOCIOGRAM 8

Patterns of friendship within and beyond class, school and district groupings.
Class-Group C: December 1947

but was unconnected with her in September and November, now names her as a friend but is not named by her. Beth, who does not want to work with Paula, names her first as a friend and appears second on Paula's list of friends: these two have clearly begun to differentiate between one situation and another in choosing companions and to realise that they work better apart. Heather, although she is named by two girls as a friend, does not yet regard any of the form in that light and sends all her choices out to other schools (one to her previous school). Ena chooses Beth, Paula and Sadie as friends, but not as work companions. In Group C the correspondence between friendship and work choices seems to be closer. Elinor, Sheena, Margery and Marian are completely isolated on the friendship criterion, sending all their choices outside and attracting none from the rest of the group; three of these were practically isolated in the September test on the Composition Group Criterion (Table VI). Annette chooses Marian first on both criteria. The strong friendship clusters round Kathleen and Freda are observable in both sociograms.

When the two friendship charts are examined from the point of view of mutuality of choice, it is found that eight choices sent by girls in Group C to others in the form are unreciprocated and five such choices are unreciprocated in Group E. There are three mutual first choices in Group C as compared with seven in Group E. One girl in Group C (Margaret) and two in Group E (June and Joanne) send no choices outside their own class-group; three in Group C (the isolates) and three in Group E (Molly, Heather and Pat) send all their choices to other schools; Sheena, the fourth isolate in Group C, sends three to the north of England, one to another school in the Home Counties and one to another form in her own school.

All these facts in conjunction suggest that the experimental group was becoming better integrated than the control group. The patterns of friendship seemed more inclusive in Group E than in Group C, where the existence of cliques and isolates was more apparent.

PLACEMENT AT CANTEEN TABLES: A NEW CRITERION

In January 1948 an opportunity arose of examining these friendship patterns by means of a genuine sociometric test. To facilitate arrangements in the school canteen during the lunch hour and to enable the senior girls sitting at the heads of tables to acquire more influence over the children, it was decided that the first, second, third and fourth forms should be allocated to specific tables instead of sitting at different ones each day according to chance. The girls who stayed to school dinner were accordingly asked to write down the names of those with whom they would prefer to be placed, four choices being allowed to each girl. Sociograms were constructed for eleven forms in the school and table allocations were made on the basis of these expressed preferences. The sociograms for the two class-groups involved in the present research are given here.*

The differences in structure between Groups E and C in January as revealed by Sociograms 9 and 10 were startling. Group E had no isolates: apart from Rosemary who received only one choice (from Trudy),† no one had fewer than two incoming choices. In Group C six girls were completely unchosen (Pauline, Margaret, Sheena, Elinor, Sara and Madge‡) and three others were chosen only once (Marian, Annette and Brenda). In Group E long chains of children in mutual choice relationship existed, forming networks of attraction linking one group with another: Rosemary was the only individual in the form who was not included in one or other of these structures (triangles, squares and chains). In Group C, on the other hand, there were four triangles, three squares and two groups of five involving between them only seventeen girls in the form; twelve girls (including the six isolates) were excluded from the triangles, squares and chains in this sociogram. Furthermore, a comparison of the two sociograms on the basis of mutuality of choice revealed that 55·9 per cent of the choices were reciprocated in Group C as compared with 63·6 per cent in Group E.

When the structures of the two groups were compared after three months Group C was found to have improved noticeably. The number of isolates and near-isolates was reduced from nine to two, the percentage of reciprocated choices had risen to 63·6 and distribution had become more uniform; furthermore, the triangles and chains had become more inclusive than they were in January, only two girls being now left outside them—Sheena who was still completely unwanted and Hilda who was chosen only by Nan and Florence. The distribution and percentages of reciprocated choices for the two groups in January and April are given below in Table VII and in Figure VI.

---

* See Sociograms 9 and 10.

† Sally, who would probably have chosen Rosemary, did not stay to school dinner, and so was not asked to name her choices on this criterion.

‡ Madge would probably have been chosen by Nora, who did not stay to school dinner and so was not asked to name her choices on this criterion.

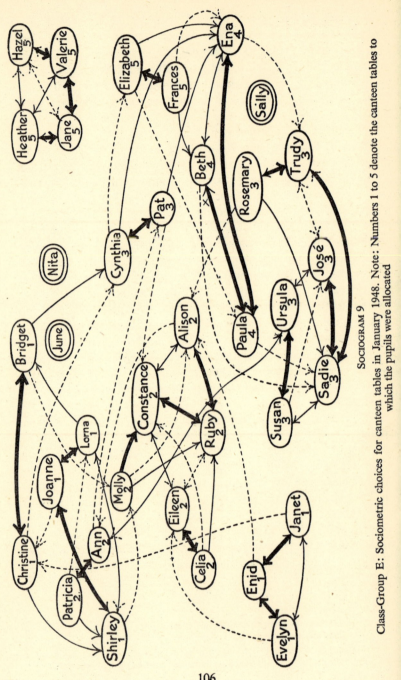

SOCIOGRAM 9

Class-Group E: Sociometric choices for canteen tables in January 1948. Note: Numbers 1 to 5 denote the canteen tables to which the pupils were allocated

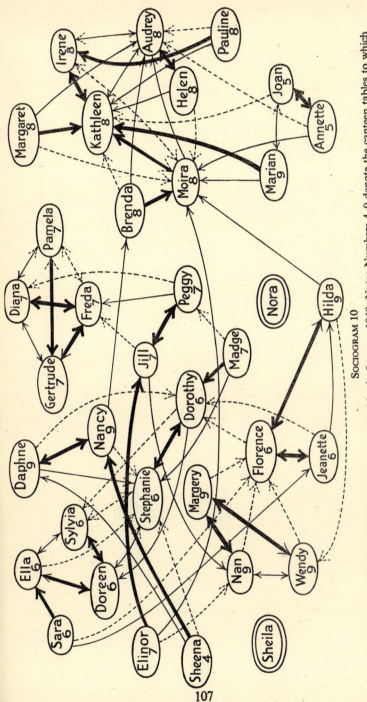

SOCIOGRAM 10

Class-Group C: Sociometric choices for canteen tables in January 1948. Note: Numbers 4–9 denote the canteen tables to which the pupils were allocated

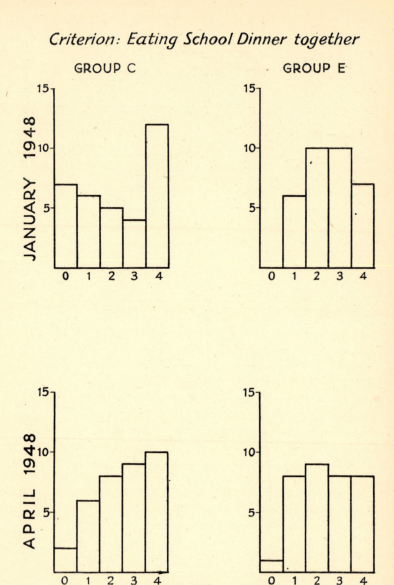

Criterion: Eating School Dinner together

FIG. 6

Histograms showing frequency distributions of reciprocated choices in two successive tests

TABLE VII

FREQUENCY DISTRIBUTIONS OF RECIPROCATED CHOICES FOR GROUPS C AND E

	January 1948					*April* 1948				
GROUP C	0	1	2	3	4	0	1	2	3	4
Frequency Distributions	7	6	5	4	12	2	6	8	9	10
Total, per cent	55·9					63·6				
GROUP E	0	1	2	3	4	0	1	2	3	4
Frequency Distributions	0	6	10	10	7	1	8	9	8	8
Total, per cent	63·6					60·3				

The changes may be partly explained by a comparison of the placements for Group C in January with the choice distribution on the same criterion in April (Sociogram 10). Certain individual changes in status took place during the intervening three months in each table group: at Table 6 Sara, who had been isolated in January, was by April exchanging a first choice with Ella; at Table 7 friendships developed between Jill and Pamela and between Madge and Peggy, and in April Madge (isolated in January) was chosen by Elinor; at Table 8 neither Margaret nor Pauline remained isolated, the one exchanging mutual choices three months later with Audrey and the other with both Audrey and Kathleen; at Table 9, Nancy and Daphne developed friendly relations with Margery and Marian, whereas Joan and Annette who were placed at Table 5 with girls from Group E remained isolated from the rest of their form.

THE PSYCHEGROUP AND SOCIOGROUP STRUCTURES AS REVEALED IN THE SOCIOGRAMS OF APRIL 1948

When the sociograms for the same group on two different criteria are compared it becomes apparent that many children were able to differentiate in choosing companions for different functions. In April 1948 Group E, after a year of group work in English, seemed more aware of this possibility of diverse choosing than were Group

C, who had not been taught by this method. Comparison of the sociograms showing the distribution of choices of co-workers in composition lessons and of companions in the school canteen revealed the following differences between the two groups:

Group C
{
16 made 3 identical choices on 2 criteria.
13 made 2 „ „ „ „
4 made 1 „ choice „ „
2 differentiated in all three choices.
}

Group E
{
8 made 3 identical choices on 2 criteria.
19 made 2 „ „ „ „
3 made 1 „ choice „ „
4 differentiated in all three choices.
}

The sixteen in Group C who chose alike on both criteria were drawn from three exclusive groups which began as clusters round Kathleen, Freda and Sylvia; of the eight in Group E who chose alike, three (Constance, Ruby and Eileen) formed a triangle on both criteria, and the other five were from different sections of the form. Of the six in Group C who chose differently, one (Sheena) was an isolate, three (Peggy, Madge and Brenda) were unchosen on all criteria and one (Margery) was at the time of these tests failing to attract work companions; the remaining one (Nancy) was, by differentiating in her choices, establishing mutual relationships on both criteria. In Group E three of the seven who chose differently (Pat, Cynthia and Valerie) were girls who had deteriorated in social status, three (Ena, Beth and Paula) were accepted by others as canteen companions but not as co-workers, and one (Rosemary) was accepted in a work group but only once chosen as a canteen companion.

When charts were made showing the patterns of friendship existing within and beyond the two class-groups in April 1948 (compare Sociograms 7 and 8 showing choices on the same criterion in December 1947), it was found that a close relationship existed between choices of canteen companions and choices of 'friends'. Of the twelve children who made different choices on the 'work' and 'canteen table' criteria, ten made identical choices on the 'friendship' and 'canteen table' criteria: thus in Group E Beth chose Paula and Trudy, Paula chose Sadie and Trudy, Rosemary chose Alison, Valerie chose Hazel, Ena chose Constance, Pat chose Cynthia and Cynthia chose Ena, and in Group C Margery chose Nancy, Peggy chose Jill and Brenda chose Moira, both as 'friends' and as table companions.

In Group E it was possible by April 1948 to distinguish to some extent between sociogroups and psychegroups, as described by Helen Jennings in 1947.[1] The social development of this group seems to support her contention that sociometric testing should not be limited to a single criterion, and that children should be given opportunities to form different groups for different purposes. The fact that a greater proportion of children in Group C made no distinction in the two kinds of choice also supports her view that these distinctions are more likely to be made by a group which is led democratically. The group method of teaching, since it throws more responsibility on the children and does not impose the same formal discipline as the classroom method, may perhaps be described as more democratic and therefore more likely to encourage the existence of different groupings in the same class.

At the end of April Group E was given an additional test, in order that this possibility might be a little further investigated. The girls were on this occasion asked to record on the same piece of paper three choices for each of four criteria: writing compositions together, doing grammar exercises together, acting in plays together and sitting at canteen tables together. It was found that on the fourth criterion only one girl (Ena) changed her previous choice, and the sociogram corresponding to that criterion was revised accordingly. On the first criterion various changes took place as a result of separating the three activities connected with English lessons. The results for all four criteria are recorded in Table III in the folder. Sociograms constructed from this table showed how certain individuals won recognition when criteria were separated and have already been discussed in Chapter III. Table III brings other interesting facts to light. By reading horizontally it is possible to find out the number of other girls with whom each individual wished to associate. Although each girl's three choices could have been bestowed on the same friends for all four activities, only one in fact so limited herself (Nita) and she could not choose table companions as she did not stay at school for lunch. Of the rest, seven named four girls, twelve named five, eleven named six, four named seven and one named eight in covering the four criteria. The scores (calculated by the summation of all incoming choices) ranged from 2 (Pat and Beth) to 36 (Alison), the mean being 10·23, and the standard deviation 7·9. Apart from Valerie, whose loss of status was difficult to account for, the girls who had low scores (5 or less) were those who had been the least effective in their groups during English lessons, and most of those with high scores (20 or more) were those who had been effective in their groups. A further sociometric test in July might have yielded interesting results, as changes in grouping were taking place at the time of the April tests and some of the less accepted children were beginning to develop socially during the summer term which followed. The investigator, however, knowing she would not be teaching the form in the autumn term, did not feel that such a course of action would have been justifiable.

STABILITY OF FRIENDSHIPS AS REVEALED BY THE SOCIOMETRIC TESTS

There is a commonly accepted belief that the friendships of adolescents are unstable. The evidence from these sociometric tests, spread over a twelve-month period, neither wholly supports nor wholly repudiates this view. It seems, in fact, unwise to attempt such a generalisation. Children's friendships, it appears, may be remarkably stable or may shift and vary from month to month or even from week to week. Certain children in both groups were noticeable for their unwavering attachment to certain others. In Group E Sally persistently chose Rosemary before anyone else, even though Rosemary transferred her first choice first to Trudy, soon after her arrival in the form, and later to Alison after she had worked with her for some weeks in the same composition group; moreover, Sally's second and third choices invariably coincided with Rosemary's first and third on those occasions when Rosemary put her name only second. Similarly, Enid persistently chose Evelyn and Pat Cynthia. Enduring friendships in this group occurred between Elizabeth and Frances, Eileen and Celia, Constance and Ruby and, after the first regrouping, between Susan and Ursula and between Sadie and José.

Ann, who had shown some tenacity in choosing her companions in school and had gradually worked her way into a mutual relationship with Shirley and Patricia, named Shirley as a friend both in December and in April and was named by her. Her out-of-school friendships, apart from one at her previous school, seemed more transitory, for the names of girls in East Anglia, the Midlands and London included in her first list did not reappear in her second. Heather named no friends in school in December, but by April her list consisted of two girls in her own form, who both named her, and two others in other forms in the school. In Group C, Madge and Nora, Sylvia and Doreen, Sheila and Wendy had lasting friendships, while Brenda, Helen, Jill and Peggy were noticeable for their unchanging feelings towards Moira, Audrey, Freda and Jill respectively. It is interesting to note that of the children in Group C who were repeatedly isolated, three (Daphne, Sheena and Brenda) considerably changed their lists of friends from December to April, and that the other two (Marian and Elinor) repeated on the second occasion choices they had made on the first. Marian and Elinor were both acquiring friends in the form by April. The other three were not. Peggy, Jill and Hilda showed rather more stability in their choice of 'friends' than in their choice of work companions.

The growth of these friendships did not appear to be unrelated to the classroom and lunch-hour activities in which the children were participating. Indeed it almost seemed at times that the teacher who organised group activities had power to bring about new tele-relationships among the children, and might unwittingly promote the growth of new friendships or break up old ones. It would seem, therefore, that the allocation of children to groups should be under-taken only with a full knowledge of the responsibilities involved.

SUMMARY AND CONCLUSION

By May 1948 seven sociometric tests had been given to both the experimental and the control groups. Between January and April Group C as well as Group E had been arranged at canteen tables on the basis of expressed preferences, but had not yet worked in groups during English lessons, as Group E had done for three terms. The findings of all these tests seemed to indicate that the children in the experimental group became better adjusted to one another during this twelve-months' period than those in the control group. Shy, undemonstrative children had won acceptance in both work and leisure situations, and others had begun by January to choose different companions for different activities and so were widening their circles of acquaintance. The assumption that the group activities in the English lessons had assisted in this development was supported in January and April by a comparison of the responses of Group C to the first and second tests on the canteen table criterion. The retest showed that the table grouping had promoted new friend-ships and enabled hitherto isolated children to acquire notice. The geographical groupings and friendship patterns studied between November 1947 and April 1948 were not, therefore, irrelevant issues. Anything which could contribute to a better understanding of these social configurations was of service to the investigator in interpreting individual and group behaviour and in assessing the effects of the experimental method: the wider the context studied, the more valid were such interpretations likely to be. The observations on the experimental group recorded in Chapter III cannot be adequately interpreted without reference to the sociometric data discussed in this chapter, and even after this combined study much of the total picture remains hidden. Conversely, the sociograms showing the tele-relationships in the control group need to be interpreted by a closer study of the smaller groupings within the class unit—a study which became possible only when these smaller groups were working less formally and more spontaneously than they could do in the classroom setting.

In May, the experimental method was introduced with Group C, groups being constructed for oral and written composition and for dramatic work. The first part of this secondary investigation, covering the period between April and September 1948, and including the findings of a further sociometric test at the beginning of the autumn term, will be reported in Chapter VI. Some consideration will first be given to the results of the retests in attainment and attitude which took place before the experimental method was introduced with the control group.

REFERENCES

1. JENNINGS, H. H.
   'Differentiation of the Psychegroup and the Sociogroup', *Sociometry*, X, 1, 1947, pp. 71–9.
   'Sociometry of Leadership: based on the Differentiation of Psychegroup and Sociogroup', *Sociometry Monographs*, No. 14. New York: Beacon House Inc. 1947.

CHAPTER FIVE

FURTHER STATISTICAL DATA: TESTS OF ATTAINMENT AND ATTITUDE

I n April 1948 the tests of attainment and attitude described in Chapter II were given to both forms for the second time, to ascertain whether the progress of either group during the period of the experiment had been significantly superior. The mean scores and standard deviations for 1947 and 1948 given below show that Group E improved more than Group C in all three tests.

TABLE VIII

SUMMARY OF TEST SCORES: 1947 AND 1948

		April 1947			April 1948		
		Attain-ment Test	Composi-tion Test	Attitude Test	Attain-ment Test	Composi-tion Test	Attitude Test
GROUP C	MEAN	63·65	38·7	51·66	76·85	44·8	52·5
	S.D.	13·6	6·32	13·62	12·29	6·99	15·57
GROUP E	MEAN	63·65	36·9	44·67	80·85	48·56	51·5
	S.D.	11·14	8·68	13·73	13·73	5·25	12·74

TESTS FOR SIGNIFICANCE

To determine whether these differences were significant, the following statistical procedures were used, the mean scores for the control and experimental groups being first considered separately and then in relation to one another.

A. *The significance of the difference between the means for the separate Groups C and E in April 1947 and April 1948: i.e. the improvement within the group itself.*

Using the procedure outlined by Peters and van Voorhis* for the determination of the significance of the difference between the means of two correlated series,[1] and also the section of Fisher's table for the distribution of it given by them in this connection, the following figures arise:

I. *Group C.*

  1. *Attainment* (objective test).

$$t = \frac{13 \cdot 2}{1 \cdot 844} = 7 \cdot 16; \; n = 29 \text{ (degrees of freedom).}$$

Referring to the table for t, this value is highly significant, being more than significant at the 1 per cent level.

  2. *Composition.*

$$t = \frac{6 \cdot 1}{0 \cdot 777} = 7 \cdot 853; \; n = 29 \text{ (degrees of freedom).}$$

Referring to the table for t, this value is highly significant, being more than significant at the 1 per cent level.

  3. *Attitude.*

$$t = \frac{0 \cdot 84}{2 \cdot 602} = 0 \cdot 3228; \; n = 29 \text{ (degrees of freedom).}$$

Referring to the table for t, this value is significant only at the 80 per cent level; therefore there is no justification for saying that there is a significant improvement in this case.

---

* Peters, C. C., and van Voorhis, W. R., *Statistical Procedures and their Mathematical Bases*, McGraw-Hill Book Co., Inc., U.S.A., 1940., pp. 160–7. Formula, p. 163; Table, p. 173.

$$t = \frac{m_1 - m_2}{6m_1 - m_2}, \text{ where } 6m_1 - m_2 = \sqrt{\frac{\bar{6}_1{}^2 + \bar{6}_2{}^2 - 2r_{12}\bar{6}_1\bar{6}_2}{N}},$$

where the suffixes 1 and 2 denote the two groups and the symbols have their usual meanings.

II. *Group E.*

  1. *Attainment* (objective test).

$$t = \frac{17\cdot2}{1\cdot701} = 10\cdot12; \; n=29.$$

This value is highly significant, being more than significant at the 1 per cent level.

  2. *Composition.*

$$t = \frac{11\cdot61}{1\cdot086} = 10\cdot69; \; n=29.$$

This value is highly significant, being more than significant at the 1 per cent level.

  3. *Attitude.*

$$t = \frac{7\cdot3}{1\cdot587} = 4\cdot599; \; n=29.$$

This value is highly significant, being more than significant at the 1 per cent level.

B. *Significance of the difference between the mean gains shown by the two groups C and E from April 1947 to April 1948: i.e. a mark of the improvement of Group C compared with the corresponding improvement in Group E.*

Using the procedure outlined by Peters and Van Voorhis* for the determination of the significance of the difference between the mean gains of two independent series over a given period of time,

* Peters, C. C., and Van Voorhis, W. R., *Statistical Procedures and their Mathematical Bases*, McGraw-Hill Book Co., Inc., U.S.A., 1940, pp. 167–76. Formula, p. 167; Table, p. 173.

$$t = \frac{(m_1 - m_1') - (m_2 - m_2')}{6(m_1 - m_1') - (m_2 - m_2')}, \text{ where } 6(m_1 - m_1') - (m_2 - m_2') \text{ is given by}$$

$$\frac{1}{\sqrt{N}} \left[\bar{6}_1^2 + \bar{6}_1'^2 + \bar{6}_2^2 + \bar{6}_2'^2 - 2r_{11}'\bar{6}_1'\bar{6}_1' - 2r_{22}'\bar{6}_2'\bar{6}_2' \right]^{\frac{1}{2}}$$

where the suffixes 1 and 2 denote the two groups E and C respectively and the dashes the use of the first set of results, i.e. those at the beginning of the given period.

and also the section of Fisher's table for the distribution of *t* given by them in this connection, the following figures arise:

1. *Attainment* (objective test).

$$t = \frac{4}{2 \cdot 51} = 1 \cdot 594, \text{ significant only for 20 per cent}$$

(by interpolation 12·5 per cent) when $n = 29$.

Therefore the improvement shown by Group E, though better than that in Group C, cannot be said to be significantly different.

2. *Composition.*

$$t = \frac{5 \cdot 51}{1 \cdot 348} = 4 \cdot 087, \text{ significant for } n = 29 \text{ at the 1 per cent level.}$$

Hence the improvement in Group E is very significantly superior to that shown in Group C over the same period.

3. *Attitude.*

$$t = \frac{6 \cdot 46}{3 \cdot 049} = 2 \cdot 119, \text{ significant for } n = 29 \text{ at the 5 per cent level.}$$

Hence the change in attitude in Group E is greater than that in Group C, and the increase is moderately significant.

The above figures reveal that both the control group and the experimental group showed highly significant improvements in attainment (both in the objective test and in the composition test); in attitude, on the other hand, there was no significant improvement for the control group, but there was a highly significant improvement for the experimental group. When the mean gains of the two groups are considered in relation to one another (Calculation B) no significant difference is found between the gains on the objective attainment test: the improvement in Group E, that is, though greater on the face of it than the improvement in Group C, is not significantly greater; but the results of the composition test show an improvement for Group E which is very significantly superior to the improvement shown for Group C, while Group E's improvement in attitude is moderately superior to that of Group C.*

INTER-CORRELATIONS

Inter-correlations were calculated by the product-moment

* For the foregoing calculations, the investigator is indebted to Dr. D. M. Lee of the Institute of Education, University of London.

formula[2] to determine whether there was any close correspondence between the different sets of results for each group. The correlation coefficients between the first and second sets of results on the three tests were fairly high for both groups, suggesting that the ranking orders at the beginning and end of the experiment were similar. The correlation coefficients between the three tests were surprisingly different in character for the two groups: there seemed to be only a low correspondence between skill in composition and attitude to composition for the control group (0·20 in 1947 and 0·01 in 1948), but a high correspondence, especially before the experiment began, for the experimental group (0·79 in 1947 and 0·55 in 1948). The scores on the objective attainment test and the composition test showed in 1947 higher correlation coefficients for the experimental group (0·66 compared with 0·27), whereas in 1948 the correlation is higher in the control group (0·49 compared with 0·41). Those between the attitude scores and the objective attainment test scores were low in all four cases (0·01 and 0·05 for Group C and 0·39 and 0·23 for Group E): this was to be expected, since the statements in the attitude test concerned the writing of letters, stories and plays, and oral activities such as discussion and public speaking, and therefore were not directly related to the material of the objective attainment test. An attempt was also made to correlate the sociometric scores with the attainment and attitude scores. The correlation coefficients seemed to indicate that sociometric status on the criterion 'writing compositions together' was quite unrelated to achievement in English composition—a conclusion which supports the more general one reached by Zeleny in 1941[3] and confirmed by Howell in 1942[4]; neither did they suggest the existence of any close correspondence between attitude to writing and sociometric status on this related criterion. On the other hand, it may be that sociometric scores, with their heavily skewed distributions, cannot be submitted to this kind of statistical treatment, and that some procedure other than the product-moment formula is needed for correlating them with more normally distributed scores.

THE COMPOSITION SCORES

When the composition scores are examined in more detail certain interesting facts emerge which help to account for the greater improvement in the experimental group, and suggest the kinds of improvements which the experimental method helped to effect. The schedule of marks for the three composition tests in 1947 and 1948 reveals the following distribution of marks for accuracy of spelling and punctuation, accuracy of paragraphing, originality of ideas (in Composition I) and quality of story (in Composition II).

TABLE IX

SUMMARY OF SOME OF THE DETAILED MARKS IN THE COMPOSITION TESTS

1. *Accuracy of Spelling and Punctuation.*

	Group C		Group E	
	1947	1948	1947	1948
Composition I				
Full marks	6	7	1	7
No marks	0	0	5	0
Composition II				
Full marks	4	7	2	7
No marks	4	1	5	1
Composition III				
Full marks	6	11	7	6
No marks	1	1	5	0

2. *Accuracy of Paragraphing in Composition III.*

	Group C		Group E	
	1947	1948	1947	1948
3 marks	2	11	5	15
2 marks	4	7	7	8
1 mark	8	6	5	0
No marks	16	6	13	7

3. *Number of Original Ideas in Composition I.*

Group C		Group E	
1947	1948	1947	1948
9	10	20	42

TABLE IX—*continued*

4. *Quality of Story in Composition II.*

	Group C		Group E	
	1947	1948	1947	1948
3 marks	0	8	1	10
2 marks	16	19	13	11
1 mark	6	3	5	4
No marks	8	0	11	5

Table IX suggests that accuracy of paragraphing was not noticeably affected by group work, but that inaccurate spelling and punctuation decreased more markedly in the experimental group; the number of original ideas used in the letter had hardly increased at all for Group C but had more than doubled for Group E in 1948; on the other hand Group C scored more highly than Group E in 1948 for the quality of story in Composition II. One other difference which does not emerge from this table may be noted here. In the 1948 test Group E wrote more prolifically on all three subjects; the following figures indicate the number of children in each group who wrote more than two pages in the retest:*

```
Composition   I: Group C —  0
                 Group E — 14

Composition  II: Group C —  1
                 Group E — 14

Composition III: Group C —  2
                 Group E —  6
```

THE ATTITUDE TEST

If the responses to the attitude questionnaire are examined in detail, it is possible to compare the children's reactions to different kinds of English composition, both oral and written. From the twenty-four statements the following groups were distinguished:

* Susan in Group E was the only one who exceeded two pages in the first test, and she is not included in these totals.

those concerned with letter-writing and the keeping of diaries, those concerned with story-telling, those concerned with play-writing, those concerned with discussion and public speaking and those concerned with composition lessons and composition home-work. The frequencies of favourable and unfavourable responses to these grouped statements are recorded below in Table X.

TABLE X

DISTRIBUTION OF FAVOURABLE AND UNFAVOURABLE RESPONSES TO SIX GROUPS OF STATEMENTS IN THE ATTITUDE TEST

Topic of Statements	Type of Response	Group C		Group E	
		1947	1948	1947	1948
Letter and Diary Writing (3, 7, 10, 20)	Favourable	73	98	54	68
	Unfavourable	38	22	58	41
Story-telling (1, 5, 18)	Favourable	40	50	42	65
	Unfavourable	39	35	44	39
Play-writing (2, 9, 23)	Favourable	46	42	39	27
	Unfavourable	41	46	50	52
Discussion and Public Speaking (8, 11, 13, 16, 21)	Favourable	63	52	57	69
	Unfavourable	68	88	79	69
Composition Lessons (12)	Favourable	21	21	11	22
	Unfavourable	6	9	17	8
Composition Homework (14, 19, 24)	Favourable	49	53	33	55
	Unfavourable	34	36	52	22

The following points emerge from this table: Group C showed in both years a highly favourable attitude towards letter and diary writing, ninety-eight favourable attitudes being expressed by them in 1948 as compared with sixty-eight by Group E; story-telling became more popular with Group E, twenty-three more favourable attitudes being expressed by them in 1948 than in 1947, compared with ten more by Group C; both groups expressed fewer favourable attitudes to play-writing in 1948 than in 1947. The statements concerned with discussion and public speaking show that Group C, who started in 1947 with a better attitude to this kind of activity than Group E, had by 1948 a worse attitude than Group E had started with; Group E, on the contrary, improved in almost the same proportion, twelve more favourable attitudes and ten fewer unfavourable attitudes being expressed by them in 1948. Group C changed very slightly for the worse in their attitude to composition lessons and composition home-work, whereas Group E changed very much for the better, nearly doubling their favourable responses and more than halving their unfavourable responses.

INDIVIDUAL GAINS OR LOSSES IN TEST SCORES

Although the test results as a whole seem to indicate that the group method proved beneficial to the children with whom it was used, it must nevertheless be admitted that many of the individual results are surprising and unaccountable. Table XI gives the numerical gains or losses on the attainment and attitude tests in April 1948, and, for comparison, the difference between the sociometric scores for April 1947 and April 1948. The table suggests that while for some children there was a fairly high correspondence between the scores for the different tests, for others there were wide discrepancies. Joan in Group C and Jane and Shirley in Group E scored lower marks in the attainment test in 1948 than in 1947; Brenda in Group C and Christine in Group E scored lower marks in composition in 1948. Of these five, the first three had improved and the last two had deteriorated in attitude by April 1948. Deterioration in attitude was not always accompanied by deterioration in attainment: Hilda's attitude score dropped from 72·5 to 20·5, but her composition score rose from 46 to 57. Janet's attitude score dropped from 38·5 to 35·5, but her composition score rose from 51 to 67. On the other hand, Jane, Valerie, Rosemary, Beth, Ena, Sally and Evelyn in Group E all showed considerable improvements in both attitude and composition scores, while for Enid and June in Group E and for Margery, Jeanette, Florence, Nan, Pauline and Nora in Group C deterioration in attitude was accompanied by insignificant progress in composition. Of those whose attitude to composition deteriorated, nine (Hilda, Margery, Helen, Nan and Pauline in Group C and Molly, Enid, June and Janet in Group E) lost sociometric status on the criterion 'writing compositions together', and two others (Brenda in Group C and Nita in Group E) made no appreciable improvement; yet there were at least twelve who improved substantially in attitude without any accompanying improvement in sociometric status. There seems, therefore, to be no simple relationship between attainment, attitude and social status even when the criterion is common to all three. The changes in social status which have been discussed in the preceding chapters and the observations on the behaviour of individuals in groups account to some extent for these conflicting features. The figure —7 in the fourth column for Constance, to cite an example, implying as it does loss of status with the group, is extremely mis-

TABLE XI

INDIVIDUAL GAINS OR LOSSES FOR CONTROL AND EXPERIMENTAL GROUPS FROM APRIL 1947 TO APRIL 1948

	CONTROL GROUP					EXPERIMENTAL GROUP			
	Attain-ment Scores	Composi-tion Scores	Atti-tude Scores	Socio-metric Status			Attain-ment Scores	Composi-tion Scores	Atti-tude Scores	Socio-metric Status
SYLVIA	7	10	6·5	−1	RUBY	12	19	11	5
PEGGY	23	13	12	6	EILEEN	15	12	14	0
DOROTHY	9	6	5	3	JANE	−2	17	14·5	9
DAPHNE	3	3	6·5	0	BRIDGET	8	9	12	2
KATHLEEN	11	3	1·5	−32	ELIZABETH	27	11	0	6
MARIAN	9	5	0·5	2	MOLLY	18	5	−8·5	−6
GERTRUDE	12	2	13	11	NITA	14	8	−4	1
DOREEN	22	4	0	4	CONSTANCE	12	1	18·5	−7
WENDY	26	14	4·5	7	ALISON	15	6	4	2
DIANA	26	7	14	−1	ENID	4	2	−5	−2
BRENDA	10	−6	−11	0	CELIA	17	21	−3	3
SARA	17	3	7·5	−2	SUSAN	20	7	16·5	3
ANNETTE	7	11	16	2	JUNE	29	6	−7	−5
HILDA	16	11	−52	−2	VALERIE	18	19	22	−16
PAMELA	11	1	8·5	11	SHIRLEY	−1	18	4·5	2
MOIRA	11	11	−14	15	PAT	27	12	3	−5
MARGERY	8	4	−17	−15	SADIE	24	11	2	7
JOAN	−14	5	12·5	5	ROSEMARY	13	19	15·5	7
JEANETTE	19	6	−14	6	BETH	21	15	14	−6
ELLA	7	6	23·5	2	JANET	4	16	−3	−4
HELEN	32	12	−8·5	−2	ENA	10	14	13	2
FREDA	14	6	3	−16	SALLY	38	15	19·5	3
IRENE	2	7	4·5	−4	PAULA	12	8	7	−5
FLORENCE	28	9	−3	4	CYNTHIA	17	18	10	−28
AUDREY	6	11	−13·5	10	JOSÉ	29	17	9	13
NAN	17	7	−3·5	−2	EVELYN	21	14	14·5	2
PAULINE	17	2	−1	−11	CHRISTINE	24	−3	−0·5	6
NORA	22	7	−2·5	5	HAZEL	9	9	11	2
MADGE	7	7	1	1	URSULA	27	15	9	8
JILL	8	8	19·5	0	JOANNE	20	11	13	−14

leading, since Constance was still well accepted and regarded as a leader by the majority of the form in April 1948. Her apparent loss of status was more probably one of the results of the rebalancing process which was continually going on in the form. If Jane, Sadie, Rosemary, José and Ursula were to improve in status, others must of necessity deteriorate, since the number of choices from each individual was limited. Some of the apparent inconsistencies in other parts of the table may be due to similar causes, which could only be discovered by statistical procedures beyond the scope of this research.

REFERENCES

1. PETERS, C. C., AND VAN VOORHIS, W. R.
   Statistical Procedures and their Mathematical Bases. New York and London: McGraw-Hill Book Co., Inc. 1940.
2. CHAMBERS, E. G.
   Statistical Calculations for Beginners. Cambridge: at the University Press. 1946.
3. ZELENY, L. D.
   'Status: Its Measurement and Control in Education', *Sociometry*, IV, 1941.
4. HOWELL, C. E.
   'Measurement of Leadership', *Sociometry*, V, 1942.

CHAPTER SIX

THE EXPERIMENT CONTINUED WITH THE CONTROL CLASS

INTRODUCTION

I N May 1948 a follow-up investigation was begun with the control group. Its aim was to discover whether the introduction of group activities would bring about improvements in individual status and group cohesion comparable to those which had been observed in the experimental group. It was realised that many factors must have contributed to the social development of Group E— factors such as the influence of the form mistress, social experiences outside the English lesson (in the laboratory, in the gymnasium, on the playing field), and the particular social configurations and personality patterns within the group itself—and that it could not be assumed that the group method was wholly responsible for these changes. Moreover, the construction of sociograms for nine forms in the school at the time when the new canteen arrangements were introduced (in January 1948) had shown that Group C was exceptional in having such a large proportion of isolates, and this discovery, it was felt, to some extent invalidated the group as a control in the experiment. If, however, this high proportion of isolates were reduced after a term of group activities, and the triangle and chain relationships became more inclusive, it might then be claimed that the experimental method had proved socially beneficial to two different classroom groups and might be expected to prove so with other children of this age-group.

GROUP ACTIVITIES: MAY TO JULY 1948

On the basis of the third sociometric test given in April 1948, seven groups, each consisting of five or six children, were constructed. The grouping is shown in Sociogram 11.

126

During the summer term two of the five weekly English lessons took place in the neighbouring hall (used by the school for acting lessons) on Tuesday afternoons from 2.40 to 4. Of these eighty minutes, roughly thirty-five were usually put aside for acting, though sometimes the whole double period might be used for group work or for acting.

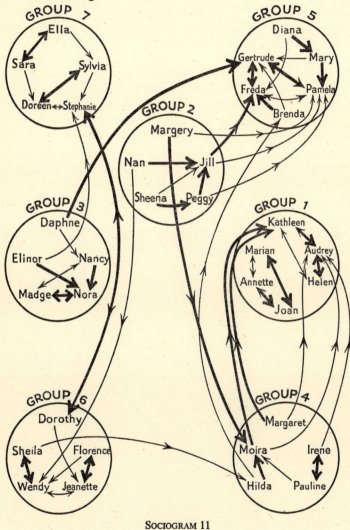

SOCIOGRAM 11

Composition groups in Class-Group C from April to July 1948

127

On May 4th the first piece of group work was planned. During the previous term the form had been reading short stories by Kipling and animal stories by Roberts. It was suggested that a study should be made of the wild animals, reptiles, birds and fishes mentioned in these (and other) stories, each group compiling information on one section of the subject, using any books of reference, pamphlets, etc., to which they had access. The material was to be arranged for a mock broadcast, each group contributing a paper. After some discussion the groups chose their topics as follows: Group 1 were to study fur-covered animals, Group 2 birds, Group 3 fishes and reptiles, Group 4 hide-coated animals, Group 5 beasts of prey, Group 6 animals living underground and Group 7 rodents. It was realised that these categories might overlap here and there, but this was not considered important. The preparation of these papers was spread over about six weeks; on two consecutive Tuesdays (May 4th and May 11th) the groups were given from 2.45 to 3.25 approximately to work on their material; on May 18th there was no lesson owing to the Whitsun holiday; on May 25th the work was completed; and on June 1st the mock broadcast was presented. The following week, as a result of discussion, the groups set to work to recast their material into more attractive forms, and on June 16th the improved versions were presented.

OBSERVATIONS RECORDED BETWEEN MAY 4TH AND JUNE 16TH

On May 4th and May 11th the groups were, as far as possible, left to develop their own methods of work, and the investigator, in going from one to another to make observations, withheld advice unless it was urgently needed. The following impressions were recorded of the way in which each group settled down to its chosen piece of work. Groups 1, 5 and 7 showed good cohesion on both occasions, and although Diana in 5 and Sara in 7 seemed to contribute little to the discussion, they were both attentive and interested. Group 6 co-operated well during the first session, Sheila and Florence both showing organising ability, but in the second they tended to work in pairs, until something Sheila said provoked general discussion and drew the group together again. The girls in Group 2, though friendly with one another, worked independently, distributing the tasks rather than co-operating over them. Group 3 showed little cohesion: Daphne provoked ridicule, Elinor was ignored and Nora only tentatively assumed the leadership. In Group 4 progress was impeded both on May 4th and on May 11th by Hilda, Moira and Pauline: these three showed little inclination to do anything but giggle at one another's remarks and attack Brenda, who seemed anxious to work seriously but unable to establish friendly relations with the group. During the first session Margaret took over the organisation, and by acting on Brenda's suggestions succeeded in subduing the unruly members. The following week Brenda again aroused hostility by aggressively criticising the group's method of working and contradicting individual girls when they made suggestions; again it was Hilda, Moira and Pauline who attacked her, but this time it was Irene (who had been absent on May 4th) who assumed the leadership and tried to make the group work as a unit. At the end of the lesson on May 11th, Brenda asked the investigator if she might change her group. The following week she was allowed to join Group 5, to which she had sent her first two choices in the sociometric test.

During the lesson on May 25th the investigator discussed the work with each group and gave advice or suggestions where necessary. Groups 1, 5, 6 and 7 all showed good cohesion, and Brenda, in her new group, was less critical and aggressive and seemed fairly well accepted by the others. In Group 3 Elinor was still isolated: Daphne and Nancy exchanged ideas on one side of the desk, and Nora and Madge on the other, but all seemed vague about the purpose of their work and quite incapable of organising it. They were given some advice and left to carry it out. In Group 2 no one seemed aware of the necessity for producing a group script: all four (Sheena was absent) were working independently, making no attempt to co-ordinate their efforts. When this was pointed out to them they seemed surprised and readily agreed to co-operate over the production of one script. The five members of Group 7, too, tended to work as independent units, but had a scheme for co-ordinating the individual contributions later. In Group 4 Irene had again assumed the rôle of leader. Margaret was very co-operative and interested in the work; Moira was still of little use to the group, but Pauline was asking questions and showing interest and Hilda was beginning to contribute suggestions.

On June 1st, when the mock broadcast was held, the following speakers were chosen by lot: Kathleen for Group 1; Peggy for

Group 2, Nora for Group 3, Margaret for Group 4, Gertrude for Group 5, Jeanette for Group 6 and Sara for Group 7. Irene volunteered to act as chairman. Of the seven readers, Peggy was the best; Kathleen, Gertrude and Nora read clearly but monotonously; Margaret's reading was disjointed and Jeanette's barely audible; Sara was nervous and inaudible at first but improved as she went on. The material compiled by Groups 4, 5 and 7 was too encyclopædic, consisting of little more than formless lists, and presented unimaginatively. Groups 1 and 3 had found more interesting material, but their handling of it was equally crude and unimaginative. Group 2, in an effort to make their material interesting, had used the story form which, the class realised, was the wrong medium for that kind of broadcast. After each paper the class was invited to put questions to the group of speakers on the platform. The discussions which arose revealed to a surprising degree psychological tensions and inter-group hostilities in the form. There seemed to be antagonism between Sylvia and Helen which showed itself in facial expression, tone of voice and verbal retaliations. Comments made by Margery and Jill called forth sharp retorts from Moira and others. Brenda seemed to be desperately trying to establish herself in the form: all the time the speakers on the platform were reading their scripts she was checking their descriptions by comparing their verbal accounts with coloured plates in a book on natural history which she had on the desk in front of her. When Irene, trying (as chairman) to direct the discussion, asked a question about the difference between a camel and a dromedary, Brenda was able to describe, very accurately, the picture in her book, and for the first time really held the attention of the class. During the last ten minutes of the lesson a general discussion was conducted on the way in which the papers had been presented and possibilities of using the interview method and dramatising some of the material were weighed up. It was decided that one more lesson should be put aside for the redrafting of the same material into more attractive forms, and that the mock broadcast should be repeated after about a week.

During the lesson on June 8th, when the groups were recasting their material, further observations on the groups were recorded. Again Groups 1, 5 and 6 worked wholeheartedly and efficiently. The five members of Group 2 were now co-operating, but in Group 7 each girl was working independently. When it was discovered that, although all were working on a common theme, each was handling it in her own way, the investigator suggested that the work should be tackled by the group as a whole to ensure that no inconsistencies were left in the final version. Group 3 seemed completely apathetic: when inquiries were made Nora and Daphne replied, somewhat complacently, that the contributions had been handed over to Elinor, who was to put them together. No attempt was being made to discuss how this should be done. The responsibility for the task was being handed on to the one member who had been absent during the previous fortnight, and nobody seemed prepared to help her with it or even to talk it over with her. The necessity of either distributing the work fairly or co-operating to complete it was pointed out to the group, and they rather sheepishly returned to the task. The work of Group 4 was again hampered by Pauline and Moira, but, stimulated by Irene's leadership and by Margaret's criticisms and enthusiasms, they both adopted a more serious attitude to the work as the lesson went on, and towards the end were beginning to offer constructive suggestions and take part intelligently in the discussion. When the revised 'broadcasts' were given on June 16th, the most successful were those prepared by Groups 2, 6 and 7 and the least successful those by Groups 1, 3 and 4.

In the course of these six weeks psychological trends which had never revealed themselves in the more formal classroom lessons became apparent. Reasons for the social isolation of certain individuals came to light when the groups were observed in a more informal work situation: Brenda aroused hostility, Daphne provoked ridicule and Elinor was merely unnoticed; isolation might, then, be caused by dislike or merely be the result of neglect. Brenda's critical, aggressive attitude in Group 4 seemed to spring from lack of respect, and when she joined a more stable group where no time was being wasted she gradually relaxed and became more friendly. Daphne appeared over-anxious to please and adopted a dominating attitude towards others without showing any ability to lead them. Elinor was obviously too shy and diffident to make any impression on a group in which she had no friends. Irene and Margaret in Group 4, Freda and Gertrude in Group 5, Sheila in Group 6, and Sylvia and Doreen in Group 7 all showed leadership potentialities during these first few weeks. Florence, who was exceptionally timid and retiring in class and had been mentioned in staff meetings as a nervous child who needed gentle handling, seemed perfectly confident in her group, and took an active and intelligent part in all its discussions. Pauline and Moira, whose efforts in class were apt to be spasmodic, showed little power of concentration when the group work began, but acquired a more serious attitude as it went on; Hilda, in the same group, improved similarly, especially after Brenda, whom she had baited a good deal, had left the group. Sheena, Elinor, Diana, Wendy and Sara appeared to be taking little or no part in the group discussions.

JUNE 15TH: OBSERVATIONS ON GROUPS WORKING AT A VOCABULARY TEST

During a double period on June 15th each group worked through the following question (from the first attainment test) under observation.*

MATERIAL USED FOR VOCABULARY TEST

In each of the following sets of words, underline the middle one of the series.

Example: YOUTH   MAN   BABY   BOY   INFANT.

1. WOOD   FOREST   COPSE   JUNGLE   SPINNEY.
2. DELIGHTED   PLEASED   CONTENTED   EXHILARATED   SATISFIED.
3. LUCID   DARK   OBSCURE   TRANSPARENT   DIM.
4. TWIG   LIMB   BRANCH   TRUNK   SHOOT.
5. DEARTH   ABUNDANCE   MEAGRENESS   SUFFICIENCY   GLUT.
6. ESTIMABLE   PROFLIGATE   WORTHLESS   DISTINGUISHED   PRE-EMINENT.
7. CAUTIOUS   RASH   PRECIPITATE   TIMID   PUSILLANIMOUS.
8. TRUTH   EQUIVOCATION   FALSEHOOD   FACT   FICTION.

Solutions were written as follows:

	Group 1	Group 2	Group 3	Group 4
1.	Wood	Wood	Wood	Wood
2.	Pleased	Contented	Pleased	Pleased
3.	Lucid	Dark	Lucid	Obscure
4.	Limb	Branch	Limb	Limb
5.	Sufficiency	Sufficiency	Sufficiency	Sufficiency
6.	Pre-eminent	Estimable	Pre-eminent	Estimable
7.	Precipitate	Pusillanimous	Precipitate	Pusillanimous
8.	Truth	Equivocation	Fact	Equivocation

* Cf. Chapter III, p. 86

	Group 5	Group 6	Group 7
1.	Wood	Wood	Wood
2.	Pleased	Pleased	Pleased
3.	Lucid	Dim	Lucid
4.	Branch	Limb	Branch
5.	Dearth	Abundance	Dearth
6.	Profligate	Estimable	Estimable
7.	Pusillanimous	Precipitate	Precipitate
8.	Equivocation	Fiction	Equivocation

As on previous occasions the groups which worked most efficiently were those in which friendly relationships existed and in which there was effective leadership. Groups 6 and 7 were the most co-operative; Groups 2, 4 and 5 tackled difficulties resolutely on the whole; Groups 1 and 3 showed poor social integration and little perseverance. The most effective leaders on this occasion were Peggy in Group 2, Sheila in Group 6 and Sylvia in Group 7. The four groups which were adequately led solved four or five items; the other three solved only three items. In Group 1, which lacked leadership, only three of the six members participated in the item solution: difficulties were shelved and the working of the test was quick but superficial. In Group 4, on the other hand, where Irene took the lead, all but one (Pauline) played an active part: there was a noticeable improvement in the attitudes of Moira and Hilda, with the result that the group as a whole tackled this work more resolutely than it had tackled the writing of the 'broadcast' scripts. In Group 3 Elinor remained silent on this as on former occasions, and Daphne again did a good deal of talking, took the lead in a bombastic kind of way, yet failed to reason either with herself or with the others. In Group 7 Sylvia took the lead: she gave four explanations of difficult words, encouraged general discussion and insisted on due consideration being shown to Ella who was writing the words down ('Ready, Ella?' 'Wait for Ella!'). The most interesting interplay of character occurred in Groups 2 and 6. In Group 2 Jill began by taking the lead aggressively, giving the impression that she was trying to solve each item before anyone else had time to, but her thinking did not go very deep and she did not try to see the words in relation to one another; it was Peggy who gradually emerged as the real leader of the group, who overruled or ignored frivolous suggestions, answered questions and tried to arrive at the meanings of difficult words by starting with the ones she knew. In Group 6 Sheila was the driving force: she kept the others thinking on the right lines without being over-dominating or inconsiderate, never accepted anyone's judgment without careful thought and always presented her ideas for the others to think over. The conversation in these two groups is reported in full below.

Verbatim Report: Group 2

1. JILL: 'Boy' is the middle one—oh yes, I see!
    (*Margery began reading out the words.*)
    MARGERY: What's the end one?
    JILL (*disregarding Margery's question*): Oh! 'Wood' is the middle one.
    PEGGY (*answering Margery*): Jungle.
    (*Jill began to read out the next series.*)
    MARGERY: You might wait for us, Jill.
    JILL: I told you—'wood'. I told you what to put. The next one's 'satisfied'.

2. PEGGY: No—'exhilarated'.
    (*Margery began to read the words over.*)
    PEGGY: First 'exhilarated', then 'delighted'——
    JILL: Then 'contented'. 'Pleased' comes before 'satisfied'.
    MARGERY: I should say 'pleased'.
    (*But Margery was over-ruled, and 'contented' was written down.*)

3.   (*Jill began to read the words out.*)
    PEGGY: I should start from the end one.
    JILL: What does 'lucid' mean?
    PEGGY: Very, very dark.
    JILL: Sure? 'Lucid', 'obscure'—'lucid', 'dark'.
    PEGGY: 'Transparent' is definitely the last one. We don't know what 'lucid' means yet.
    JILL (*fatuously*): Let's put it in the middle!
    PEGGY: 'No—dark'.
    (*Dark was written down.*)

4. JILL: 'Branch'.
    (*This was accepted without discussion.*)

5. JILL: 'Glut' is the end one, I think. What does 'dearth' mean?
    (*Here followed a good deal of reading out of words.*)

JILL: I should think a glut is more than 'abundance'.

PEGGY: I should say 'sufficiency' was the middle one. What do you think, Margery?

JILL: 'Dearth' comes higher up than 'meagreness'.

(*Peggy's suggestion was accepted.*)

6.   (*Jill again read out the words, this time trying out different orders.*)

MARGERY (*after some incoherent muttering*): 'Pre-eminent': I should say that's the top one. What does 'profligate' mean? Put it at the bottom! (*giggling*).

PEGGY: No—'worthless' at the bottom.

(*Discussion followed over the meaning of 'pre-eminent'*).

JILL: I've heard a saying 'Your Eminence', so it must be pretty high.

PEGGY: What about 'estimable' for the middle one? It comes before 'distinguished'.

(*This suggestion was accepted.*)

(*Jill began to giggle over 'pusillanimous' and attempted to pronounce it.*)

JILL: 'Rash' is precipitate.

PEGGY: Start from the bottom: 'timid', 'cautious'——

JILL: 'Pusi'——! Think of words it comes from. Animus, unanimous. Pusil—must be the same as uni——

MARGERY: I wish I'd brought my dictionary.

JILL: I think 'cautious' is next.

MARGERY: 'Timid', then 'cautious'.

JILL: 'Pusillanimous' in the middle.

JILL: 'Equivocation'—calling, or something.

PEGGY: Falsehood, fiction. . . . Fiction is not the same as falsehood. What does equivocation mean?

JILL: Equi——? Latin voco, I call. Action of calling. What does 'equi' mean? Better put it in the middle (*giggling*)!

PEGGY (*thinking*): Falsehood . . . fiction. 'Fact' last, then 'truth': 'equivocation' in the middle.

Verbatim Report: Group 6

SHEILA: Middle of the series?

JEANETTE: Like youth, man, boy——

SHEILA: Oh, I see: 'baby', then 'infant', then 'boy', then 'youth', then 'man'.

1. (*Pause*) 'Spinney'? Copse, spinney, wood, forest, jungle.
2. FLORENCE: 'Satisfied'?
   JEANETTE: 'Delighted'?
   SHEILA: 'Pleased' . . . 'contented'. . . . Satisfied, contented, pleased, delighted, exhilarated.
3. DOROTHY: 'Dim'?
   SHEILA: First 'transparent', then 'dim'. What does 'lucid' mean? Oh dear! 'Obscure' is the last. 'Transparent', then 'lucid, dim, dark, obscure'.
   FLORENCE: That makes it 'dim'.
      (*General agreement followed.*)
4. FLORENCE AND JEANETTE: 'Shoot' first.
   SHEILA: Oh, I know what it is—small to big! Shoot, twig, limb.
5. FLORENCE: Crumbs! What does 'dearth' mean?
   SHEILA: 'Abundance, sufficiency, glut.' . . . Glut and greediness; sufficiency—just enough. What would 'dearth' be? Abundance means heaps. 'Sufficiency' comes before 'abundance', 'meagreness' before 'sufficiency'. I should say 'dearth' means you haven't enough.
   FLORENCE: Oh, I see—yes!
6. JEANETTE: What is 'pre-eminent'?
      (*After a long pause they decided to leave this item.*)
7. SHEILA: 'Cautious, rash, pusillanimous'—does that mean impulsive?
   FLORENCE: 'Timid.' Wouldn't 'precipitate' be the first?
   WENDY: I should think 'cautious'.
   SHEILA: So would I. What does 'pusillanimous' mean?
      (*In the end 'precipitate' was written down as the middle one of the series.*)
8. FLORENCE: 'Truth, fact.'
   SHEILA: It goes from truth to a lie. 'Equivocation': not doing it really. So the order is: truth, fact, fiction, equivocation, falsehood. 'Fiction' would be the middle one.
6. (*The group redirected its attention to this series, which had been left unsolved.*)
   SHEILA (*reminding the others*): There are two words here that we don't know. Start from 'worthless'.
   FLORENCE: What does 'pre-eminent' mean?
   SHEILA: Eminent . . . I've heard it, but I can't express it!

FLORENCE: What about 'profligate'? I should say 'profligate' comes after 'worthless'.

SHEILA: Worthless, profligate, estimable, distinguished, pre-eminent: 'estimable' is the middle one.

These records, though brief and incomplete, show, as the observations on the experimental group showed, the importance to any co-operating group of friendly cohesion and adequate leadership. They may also serve to elucidate some of the changes in group structure which were revealed by the sociometric test given the following September.

THE SOCIOMETRIC TEST: SEPTEMBER 1948

The distribution of choices for Group C in September 1948 on the criterion 'writing English compositions together' is given in Sociogram 12 below. Daphne was still isolated, as in April. Brenda was now isolated, no longer being chosen by Moira and Hilda: she was again sending her first and second choices to Moira and Irene, as in September 1947, her third to Pauline (in the same group) and her fourth to Jeanette, in whom she had hitherto shown no interest; apparently she no longer wanted to work with Freda and Gertrude, but was again seeking acceptance by the group in which she had formerly encountered hostility and from which she had asked to be removed at the beginning of the summer term. Marian, Joan and Annette were still an isolated triangle: Annette and Joan again sent their third choices to the constellation round Kathleen and Audrey, but Marian now named Jeanette and Florence as her third and fourth choices. Ella and Sara were now well accepted in their group, and Elinor had her first choice to Stephanie reciprocated and was mentioned as a fourth choice by Doreen. Sheila was now chosen by Florence and Hilda (both on her list of choices) as well as by Wendy. Dorothy and Stephanie no longer chose one another, each being fairly well established in her own group. Florence had risen in status, receiving a first choice from Jeanette as before and second choices from Sheila, Wendy, Dorothy and Hilda. Jill, Peggy, Madge and Nora now chose one another mutually: Jill and Peggy were chosen by Margery, to whom they sent fourth choices, and Jill was chosen by Helen. Kathleen, Audrey and Moira exchanged first and second choices. Helen, who still put Audrey first on her list, now appeared only third on Audrey's. Pauline was third on Brenda's list but apart from a tentative choice from Moira (who put her down fifth with a query) had none of her four choices reciprocated. Freda had lost status with her group, who now sent her only fourth choices.

Perhaps the most remarkable feature of Sociogram 12 is the high proportion of reciprocated choices. Out of a possible total of 136 there are a hundred mutual choices—a percentage of 73·5, compared with only 53·4 per cent in April 1948. The structure of the sociogram, with its well-defined groups and absence of intergroup connections, resembles that of the experimental group in November 1947 (Sociogram 3), after a term and a half of organised group activities in English. It may be of interest to compare these two sociograms on the basis of mutuality of choice: the figures are given below in Table XII.

TABLE XII

DISTRIBUTION AND PERCENTAGES OF RECIPROCATED CHOICES FOR GROUP E IN NOVEMBER 1947 AND FOR GROUP C IN SEPTEMBER 1948

GROUP E November 1947					GROUP C September 1948				
0	1	2	3	4	0	1	2	3	4
1	1	8	8	18	3	1	5	11	14
		78·5%					73·5%		

To ascertain the extent to which the children in Group C were able, by September 1948, to discriminate in choosing companions for different activities, they were asked whether they would like their drama groups to be constructed independently of their composition groups. Since a reasonable number of the form appeared to welcome this proposal, each girl was asked to record four or five choices of companions for dramatic work. It was found that nine of the form made the same choices as for composition groups: of these, seven (Sylvia, Kathleen, Moira, Audrey, Diana, Nora and Madge) gave

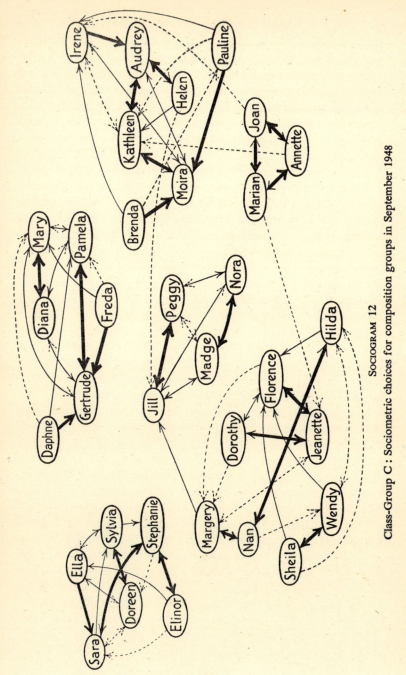

SOCIOGRAM 12

Class-Group C : Sociometric choices for composition groups in September 1948

their preferences in the same order as before, while two (Gertrude and Mary) reversed their first two and their last two choices on this criterion. Brenda, Annette, Irene, Pauline and Jill retained only one of their original choices, sending the other three to different groups for this activity: Brenda named only three girls—Irene, who had been the one member of Group 4 prepared to co-operate with her in May, and Wendy and Sheila, with whom she had had no previous socio-metric connection; Annette gave priority to Irene, Margery and Jill in her list, putting Marian and Joan only fourth and fifth; Irene named only two of her usual confederates (Moira and Pauline), putting Jill and Freda first and second, and Peggy fifth on her list; Pauline also chose Jill and Peggy, putting Moira and Helen (from her own group of friends) second and fourth, and Florence—a new sociometric choice—fifth; Jill named Peggy first on this, as on the earlier criterion, but substituted Freda, Gertrude and Mary for Madge and Nora, and put Margery fifth on her list. Other girls who showed some discrimination in choosing for different activities were Marian, Sheila, Wendy, Elinor and Helen. Daphne and Brenda, isolated on the first criterion, received a few choices on this—Daphne receiving a third choice from Pamela and a fourth from Freda, and Brenda receiving fourth choices from Sheila and Wendy; Pauline, nearly isolated on the first criterion, was mentioned as a fourth or fifth choice by Kathleen, Moira, Helen, Irene and Audrey.

In constructing groups for literary and dramatic activities, two aims were kept in mind. The composition groups were kept small and were based as far as possible on first and second choices. For dramatic activities, on the other hand, the form was divided into only three groups: The first consisted of Sylvia, Doreen, Ella, Sara, Stephanie, Elinor, Margery, Nan and Annette, the second of Irene, Mary, Diana, Gertrude, Daphne, Freda, Pamela, Marian, Joan, Pauline, Jill, Peggy, Madge and Nora, and the third of Audrey, Kathleen, Helen, Moira, Dorothy, Florence, Hilda, Jeanette, Wendy, Sheila and Brenda. This grouping gave Brenda two of her three choices and connected her both with the girls with whom she had been associating in the past and with those whom she was choosing for the first time. Annette was separated from Joan and Marian, but was given an opportunity to establish a new relationship with Margery, to whom she had given her second choice. Daphne was placed with Pamela and Freda who reciprocated her choices. It was hoped that through this grouping new links might be forged between the various sections of the form which had hitherto been so exclusive and that the class-unit as a whole might gradually become better integrated.

CONCLUSION

This second experiment, though still in its early stages, appeared by September 1948 already to have yielded interesting results. The sociometric evidence recorded after the first three months of organised group activity suggested that the experimental method might eventually effect improvements in group structure and individual status similar to those it had helped to bring about in the experimental group during the months between April 1947 and July 1948.

CHAPTER SEVEN

CONCLUSIONS AND SUGGESTIONS FOR FURTHER RESEARCH

THE experiment here reported began as a study of a method; before long it had developed into the far more interesting social study of two groups of children as they appeared in the day-to-day and week-to-week situation of the English lesson. It became evident as time went on that inter-personal relations played an important part in that situation, and that the teaching and learning processes were affected not only by the attitudes of pupils and teacher to their work, but also by the attitudes of the pupils to one another and of the class and the teacher to one another. It was possible to study the attitudes of the children to the particular kind of work under consideration (English Composition) in two ways: by the use of a scientifically constructed attitude test at the beginning and end of the experiment and by the use of observational techniques during the experimental period. These observations, combined with sociometric tests given at the beginning and end of the experiment and at intervals in the course of it, also made possible a continuous record of their changing attitudes to one another. In this way, the children were being studied not merely as learning machines register-ing (or not registering) certain impressions during formal lessons on vocabulary, sentence structure and the combination of ideas, but as personalities reacting spontaneously with one another in the effort to learn these techniques by using them co-operatively. In the informal situation of the group-work lesson, personal characteristics of individual children became more apparent to the investigator than they had ever been in the classroom. Any lesson conducted on traditional lines must by its nature be formal, even where friendly relations exist between teacher and pupils: it is necessary in the class-room situation that only one person speak at a time, and therefore that a child who wishes to ask or answer a question or to make a suggestion or comment first indicates by some conventional sign that she wishes to speak; for excessively shy, inhibited children this preliminary business of attracting attention must be an insuperable bar to participation in a discussion. There was evidence in the present experiment that in the group situation many such children, who rarely if ever took part in classroom lessons, were natural and un-intimidated when they worked in small groups with others whom they liked, and that some of them gradually came to participate actively even in the more formal lessons when the class worked as one large unit.

From the end of 1947 the canvas was deliberately enlarged to include more of the total picture: the children's reactions to one another in the English lesson were studied in terms of wider issues, such as their friendships in school and outside it, the dispersion of their homes over the hundred-square-mile area around the school and their previous experiences together in junior schools. All these inquiries yielded evidence which suggested that the children in the experimental group were becoming better adjusted to one another than those in the control group. The proportion of reciprocated choices rose more rapidly for them and children did not remain isolated from one test to another as in the control group. When the choices were plotted geographically it was found that the girls in the experimental group extended their friendships farther afield as time went on, whereas in the control group, with some exceptions, girls who lived near one another tended to band together. The attempt to find out how many had real friends in the form revealed that in the control group there were four children (three of whom lived at long distances from the school) completely isolated, neither choosing nor being chosen by others in the form, whereas in the experimental group none was so cut off. The sociometric test in January 1948, on which the allocation of children to canteen tables was based, con-firmed these findings, revealing a high proportion of isolates in the control group and a complete absence of isolates in the experimental group. Moreover, after one term of group activities, the control group began to show signs of development similar to that of the experimental group the year before: by September 1948 there were many more reciprocated choices and fewer isolates on the work criterion than in April 1948, when the secondary investigation began.

This social development did not appear to cause any diminution of intellectual progress. On the contrary, the attainment tests revealed that while both groups improved significantly in this respect, the progress made by the experimental group in English Composition greatly exceeded that of the control group. Moreover, the experimental group, who had started with a poor attitude to this kind of activity, had improved significantly by the end of a year of group activities, whereas the attitude of the control group had hardly changed at all. It is perhaps of interest to record that the Senior English mistress, who took the experimental form over in September 1948, found the children friendly and teachable, and commented particularly on their excellent attitude to the work and their willingness to tackle even dull exercises in punctuation and sentence structure with enthusiasm.

There is perhaps no subject in the curriculum which lends itself to this kind of socialising process better than English. While the present investigations were going on, the group method was being used in the third and fourth years in connection with Composition and the study of literature, and although detailed observations on these older groups were not recorded systematically, the quality of their work and the evidence of the sociometric charts supported the findings of the controlled experiment. The importance of the social incentive in education can hardly be over-emphasised. Many teachers would agree that the greatest problems in the classroom are the unresponsive, inarticulate, unapproachable individuals: naughty children can usually be provided with new interests and occupations, but socially backward children are too often either passed over and ignored or subjected to the torture of conspicuous notice. Meek,[1] discussing the problems of the adolescent, maintains that little can be done for him educationally until he has been helped to achieve 'satisfactory status with his peers', and that the teacher has a responsibility to provide him with the opportunities he needs. She points out that while experiences in which all members of the class share are valuable, a child often finds the large group 'overpowering' and retreats for fear of appearing inadequate before his fellows; yet such a pupil may be able to establish satisfying relationships in a group of three or four, and experiences in such groups may help him to feel that he is an active member of his class and so enable him to assume responsibility with greater courage and assurance.

That psychologists and teachers are becoming more aware of the relatedness of social and intellectual development has been pointed out in this country by Dr. C. M. Fleming,[2] who, in her latest book, has referred to the findings of the sociometrists and noted their implications for educationists. She emphasises again her conviction that the stresses and strains so often believed in the past to be the inevitable accompaniment of adolescence are in fact socially induced and therefore avoidable, and urges the necessity of observing the growing child from as many different points of view as possible and of studying, not isolated individuals, but individuals as members of many groups and performing many functions.

Various topics for further research have suggested themselves in the course of this investigation. Better techniques are needed for recording observations on co-operating groups; more detailed studies of children's attitudes to the various subjects in the curriculum might be carried out and devices invented for correlating these attitude scores with sociometric scores on corresponding criteria; studies of leadership and isolation in school situations, comparisons of younger with older groups on various sociometric criteria, long term studies of groups over the four, five or six years of primary or secondary school life, comparisons of similar age-groups in different types of school would all yield valuable results. No attempt has been made in this investigation to study individual 'social atoms', though such a possibility was envisaged earlier: any classroom group might yield individual case-histories of great interest to the social psychologist.

No sociometric research can ever be described as complete: therein, perhaps, lies its peculiar fascination. The field is constantly widening as the investigator becomes aware of factors related to his original topic of inquiry; and just as the original area of research extends to include or overlap with other areas of research, so the time limit advances further and further into the future. Most of the research projects suggested above could be carried out only by teams of sociometrists; yet even the fragments of sociometric research which can be undertaken by individual students of psychology may produce some evidence as to the nature of these inter-personal relations and the ways in which individuals and groups can learn to co-operate harmoniously towards common goals.

REFERENCES

1. MEEK, L. H.
   The Personal-Social Development of Boys and Girls with Implications

for Secondary Education. New York: Progressive Education Association. 1940.
2. FLEMING, C. M.
    The Social Psychology of Education: An Introduction and Guide to its Study. London: Kegan Paul, Trench, Trubner & Co., Ltd. 1944.
    Adolescence: Its Social Psychology. London: Routledge and Kegan Paul, Ltd. 1948.

PART TWO

ADOLESCENT OPINION

CHAPTER EIGHT

THE ATTITUDES OF ADOLESCENTS TOWARDS THEIR OWN DEVELOPMENT

THIS investigation into the attitudes of adolescent boys and girls towards different aspects of their own development and certain allied psychological and social concepts was carried out by means of two sets of attitude tests. The second of these was devoted mainly to a study of the attitude of the adolescents to their intellectual, social and spiritual development, while the first was a more exploratory questionnaire concerned with development as only one among five topics. The enquiry, while not conclusive in its findings, suggests that this is a field which may well repay study. As it is one hitherto hardly explored there was little guidance available for the construction of the tests, and few warnings as to the difficulties likely to be encountered in evaluation of the results. In order that the experience gained through the construction and evaluation of these tests may be available for others who may be interested in following up this study by further enquiry, the evolution of the experiment is given in some detail.

The original idea behind the investigation came from the desire to understand better the psychology that must be the basis of any effective religious education. It was the search for this understanding that led to the first set of attitude tests. 'Religion', writes Macmurray[1], 'is firmly rooted in our universal common experience. It arises from our ordinary experience of living in the world in relation with other people and to that experience it refers. . . . However tightly we shut our eyes, it makes no difference to the fact of our interdependence. Religion is simply the recognition of this fact and its importance, and true religion is its acceptance with all its implications.' It is impossible to go through the experience of living, to enter into personal relationship with other people without developing attitudes both towards these other people and ourselves—without, in short, building up some concept of human nature which will in its turn influence our relationships with people and the natural world. 'We and our attitudes of mind are part of the world', as Macmurray reminds us. Therefore, presumably, the more we can discover about people's attitudes, the more clearly shall we understand the social environment in which we live and have to bring up our children.

In the course of his life, then, man experiences both dependence and independence, both solidarity and solitariness, both his common heritage and his uniqueness. From his dependence comes his need for affection, for approval and acceptance, for recognition, all of which, along with other similar needs, are sometimes summed up as a need for 'security'. From his independence comes his need for freedom, for creativeness, for experiment, for challenge, sometimes all included in the word 'adventure'. The first two topics, then, towards which the attitude of the adolescent is to be explored are 'security' and 'adventure'. Are boys and girls in their 'teens' conscious of a need for security? What things spell security for them? Do they want adventure? If so, what kind of adventure? That these are topics pertinent to adolescence can be illustrated from the words of one of those who helped to supply the test material. In answer to the question 'What sort of things make you happy?' a girl of seventeen replied, 'Being with friends, helping them and they helping you, feeling secure and having freedom.' Here is the deliberate choice of security and freedom, or adventure, as two of the things essential to man's well-being. The first part of her answer leads up to another two of the topics selected for investigation. 'Helping them and they helping you' suggests the reciprocity, or mutuality, of relationships which, as Macmurray says, creates community. Any mention of community or society raises the question of the relationship not only of the members to each other, but of the relationship of the individual to society. The 'rights' of man are those privileges which he claims from society by virtue of his individuality; his 'responsibilities' are his recognition to society that 'we are all members one of another'. His 'rights' are a result of his strivings for independence and power, his 'responsibilities' an acceptance of the fact of interdependence. 'Rights' and 'responsibilities' then are two of the other topics towards which the adolescent's attitude is to be studied. What do these boys and girls demand as 'rights'? What do they recognise as 'responsibilities'?

The fifth subject is 'development' or 'growth'. It is characteristic of all living things that they develop, changing in size, form and structure with the passage of time. It has been suggested, however, that of all creation man is the only aspiring creature. He alone wishes to purify, strengthen and refashion himself. He alone raises development, to borrow yet another expression from Macmurray, to the level of 'intentionality'. Development is a fact of his being. Whether aspiration may properly be described as his attitude towards it is part of our purpose to discover.

This, then, gives us the five attitudes to be explored:

Security
Adventure
Rights
Responsibilities
Development

Of these, the first two represent what are now coming to be recognised as fundamental psychological needs. The last became the main topic of the investigation, and the third and fourth represent the relationship between the individual and society—a subject of importance to the adolescent.

The usual procedure in attitude testing is to present to the subjects who are being tested statements to which they are asked to respond in certain ways. Thurstone,[2] for example, asked various people to write out for him their opinions on religion and the Church, and from their writings he took some of the statements that he used in his attitude scale on the Church. It seemed that it might prove useful to collect material for these tests in a similar way, asking adolescents themselves to provide the statements as their wording might be more real and meaningful to other children who were being tested. As a convenient opportunity occurred, therefore, about two hundred girls between the ages of eleven and eighteen were asked, without previous warning or preparation, to write short answers to questions such as the following:

1. What kinds of things make you feel secure?
2. What helps you to feel independent?
3. In what ways do you feel you would most like to grow?
4. What to you are the 'rights' of human beings?
5. What is your idea of God?

and so forth.

The answers to these were delightful for their freshness, frankness and simplicity, and a most revealing source of information both about their outlook and their power of expression. The reduction of these statements to a form compatible with the purpose of a test inevitably destroyed much that was valuable as providing insight into the patterns of those things felt necessary for security, desired for development or accepted as responsibilities by different individuals. A few quotations from the answers will give some idea of what was produced. In answer to the question about security a sixteen-year-old girl replied 'A home to go to at the end of the day. Parents to go to if you are miserable. A family to support you if you are in trouble. To know that God is guiding you.' Another wrote 'a good and secure home life, a good job or happiness at school, certainty of enough to eat and enough clothes, etc., and to be with people I love and who love me.' Others wanted 'confidence in myself', 'the knowledge that I have done right', 'to be getting fairly good marks in school'. When they were asked what helped them to feel independent, one girl, about fourteen, wrote 'Being trusted and having what I say believed makes me feel independent, also being able to fathom out things by myself and being able to do things without being helped or told how.' Another wrote 'The feeling that there is no one whom you ask about small matters; that you must make up your own mind yourself.' Some of these replies formed the basis of the test on 'adventure'. There was considerable variety in the replies to the question on the ways in which they most wanted to grow, some of the older girls expressing themselves very freely. Their answers contained such ideas as 'to feel and grow in good health and be strong', 'to have a decent character, unselfish, honest, kind and generous', 'to be able to see other people's point of view', 'to be able to stand up for myself', 'spiritually to be able to understand more', 'to grow intellectually in all directions', and as an example of a complete answer, 'I would like to have plenty of self-confidence and have a good vocabulary and memory so that I never got tongue-tied or muddled. I'd like never to blush and show my emotions outwardly, especially in temper. I would like to have the personality that everyone respects, and also to have a way with children and men. I would like to have the powers of organisation. I would like to be unselfish and wise.'

This vivid little self-portrait with its mute appeal for help suggested the question as to whether an attitude test could be so framed that it would be possible to reconstruct from the responses a word picture of the individual answering it. This was not possible with the first set of tests, but from the second set it proved possible to do so with a fair measure of success, as will later be explained.

After the material had been collected the next step was to decide upon the most effective way of using it. In some way a selection of these statements was to be presented to other adolescents, both boys and girls, and their reactions to them ascertained. Before this could be done, some kind of arrangement or grading of statements would be necessary. Thurstone submitted his statements to a panel of judges for grading in order of positiveness, and then asked his subjects to indicate those statements with which they agreed. Likert[3] asked his subjects to respond to every statement but to grade their responses from the strongest agreement to the most emphatic disagreement.

As a result of a small experimental test it became apparent that it would be necessary to make a further analysis of the topics before suitable tests could be constructed. Brueckner[4] has pointed out that a certain attitude may be a generalisation arising out of a number of specific experiences. If this is a true description of the formation of an attitude it is equally true to say that many an attitude is expressed, not as a generalisation, but in terms of specific experiences, not as 'I like adventure', but as 'I like finding out things for myself', 'I like meeting new people', and so on. It is a matter of very common experience that a person may well enjoy discovering things for himself but be acutely uncomfortable at the thought of going into the company of people he has never met before. If an attitude towards 'adventure' were to be considered as an attitude to a single variable then such a difference would appear as an inconsistency. It is only when it is realised that there can be no such thing as an 'attitude toward adventure' but only various attitudes towards experiences which have in common that their outcome is unpredictable, that such a charge of inconsistency is seen to be unfounded. The same thing is true for the other topics of the investigation.

The statements on all the topics were, therefore, sorted into various groups, not at first under any special headings, but just as they seemed to belong together. After much sorting and re-arrangement of the items six divisions were decided upon: (1) Physical or General, (2) Mental, (3) Moral, (4) Social, (5) Spiritual or Religious, (6) Work. The final plan, then, for this set of tests is shown on page 154.

	Security	Adventure	Development	Rights	Responsibilities
Physical or General					
Mental					
Moral					
Social					
Spiritual or Religious					
Work					

This gave a total of thirty sections. It was then decided to have five statements in each section graded, for example, as follows:

(Physical Adventure)

A. Very positive.   I never feel happier than when I am taking risks.

B. Moderately positive.   I rather enjoy taking risks now and then.

C. Neutral.   No one should mind taking risks occasionally, but only if it seems necessary.

D. Moderately negative.   I try to avoid taking risks.

E. Very negative.   I think it is very wrong to take risks.

To each of these statements the adolescents were to be asked to make a response giving marks as follows:

4. I agree most decidedly.
3. I agree, but not very strongly.
2. I am doubtful.
1. I disagree, but not very strongly.
0. I entirely disagree.

This then was to be a test which combined features of both the Thurstone and Likert techniques.

Grading the statements so that they form a reasonably accurate measuring scale is, almost without doubt, the most difficult part of constructing an attitude test. Murphy and Newcomb[5] suggest that in all probability none of the more complex social attitudes will ever conform to such rigorous measurement. They point out that it is the experience of everyone who has ever scored attitude tests that apparently glaring inconsistencies appear in the replies of even the most sincere and conscientious subjects. This, they suggest, may be explained by the fact that consistency in such social attitudes carries with it, inevitably, some particular standard of consistency. Moreover, there are very few individuals whose attitudes concerning more than a few issues are so precise and clearly crystallised that they lend themselves to an accurate scale measurement.

These inconsistencies appear where a subject agrees both with statements graded as favourable to a topic and with those graded as unfavourable, with, for example, both A and D statements. This is a type of response theoretically impossible in an honest testee with a perfect scale; but as Murphy and Newcomb point out it frequently happens. From the point of view of the testee's score the difficulty is that the result, under these circumstances, suggests an approximately neutral attitude. A testee with a genuinely neutral attitude will have the same score. Even if we admit that the ambivalent attitude is a genuine one—and we must if we are to be true to life—how are we to devise a method of measurement which will show it? Only, it would seem, by such a careful analysis and sub-division that each scale will measure one variable and one only. The experience of scoring this set of attitude tests showed the importance of this. The second set of tests showed that it was not impossible to achieve. Some of the difficulties of grading as they appeared in this first set of tests may be briefly discussed.

Grading can be done in two ways. Either the actual ideational content of one statement may be, by common consent, more favourable to the topic in question than that of another, or the wording of one, often a matter of adverbs and adjectives, may indicate a stronger degree of support than that of another. It is where statements are graded on the basis of ideas that the charge of inconsistency can be most often levelled against the replies. Let us illustrate. The B statement in the test on Mental Adventure is 'I am glad when I have a chance of learning new things'. The D statement is 'I am a bit nervous when starting to learn something new'. Theoretically the boy or girl was expected to agree in some degree with one or other of these statements. In practice quite a number agreed with both. It takes only a moment's thought to realise that this ambivalent attitude is possible, but while a sum score on that section of the test is of little value to a teacher, a knowledge of the details of his pupil's response to the section might be extremely revealing. This difficulty could have been overcome by choosing one idea only for each section. This would have meant a very limited and impoverished survey as compared with the richness and variety of the ideas found in the spontaneous answers given by the children. The choice, moreover, of the idea could be little other than arbitrary. An attempt was therefore made to retain as many ideas as was compatible with the aim of having properly graded statements.

The other way of grading is by the use of intensifying words and phrases, 'It is my greatest wish . . .', 'I enjoy nothing better than . . .', 'I have not the slightest interest in . . .', 'There is nothing I dislike more than . . .', and so on. From this arose two difficulties. One was that some children ignored the grading and attended only to the idea, agreeing whole-heartedly with the most extreme statements. This can be illustrated by the A statement in Physical Adventure, 'I never feel happier than when I am taking risks'. A number of boys and girls seemed to agree whole-heartedly with the idea of enjoying taking risks without stopping to consider seriously whether such occasions really constituted the happiest moments of their lives. A difficulty of the opposite kind also occurred. Some children appeared to be attracted by the hyperbolic form of expression in an A or E statement as it was more colourful than a moderately expressed statement and committed themselves to an intensity of attitude which they did not really hold. A third difficulty was created by negative statements. To these it was easy to give a mark the exact opposite to that which was intended. To the D statement on Spiritual Adventure, 'It does not attract me to find out about religion', a pupil might have responded 'No, it does not', and given the statement 0, when what was meant was 'I strongly agree' and the mark 4 should have been given. These difficulties were discovered from the comments of the adolescents about the tests, and in making the second set of tests an effort was made to avoid them. It can readily be seen that such possibilities of ambiguity of interpretation can give rise to apparent inconsistencies, and that they are of the kind that could be overlooked by a panel of judges asked merely to check the grading.

This first set of tests was answered by one hundred and fifty-seven boys and one hundred and eighty-nine girls between the ages of thirteen and seventeen plus drawn for the most part from two suburban Secondary Grammar Schools. The index of reliability for each of the tests was as follows: Adventure, 0·83; Security, 0·84; Development, 0·9; Rights, 0·87; Responsibilities 0·93.

THE RESULTS

Attitude towards Adventure. The kinds of adventure towards which these adolescents show the most positive attitudes are mental adventure, the learning of new facts and the discovery of them by their own efforts, and adventure in work, that is, the finding of work in life that will give them new experience. There is very definite rejection of the routine job. The kind of adventure towards which they show the least positive attitude is adventure in social relationships. They express a certain amount of caution (more marked among the younger boys and girls) in making new friends and in meeting strangers. The boys also show an almost neutral attitude towards religion as an adventure.

Attitude towards Security. With the exception of the physical, these adolescents show a very positive attitude towards all the sources of security included in these tests: mental, the possession of knowledge; moral, the possession of a good conscience; social, happy relationships with people; and work well done. While the girls show a positive attitude towards the possession of a religious faith as a source of security, the boys on the whole, especially the older ones, do not.

Attitude towards Development. Nearly all the adolescents show a very positive attitude towards physical development, wanting to grow up strong and healthy, towards development in character and improvement in work. They also show a favourable attitude towards development in social relations. There is a less positive attitude towards development in intellectual matters but this becomes more positive as the boys and girls grow older. Girls show a more positive attitude towards spiritual development than boys, whose attitude is only very slightly positive.

Attitude towards Rights. The 'rights' towards which adolescents show the most positive attitude are the rights of all to good living conditions, the rights of all to education, to work and to religious freedom.

Attitude towards Responsibilities. Both boys and girls show a very positive attitude towards the responsibility of everyone for making the world a better place to live in, and the girls show a definite feeling of responsibility for good social relationships.

THE SECOND SERIES OF TESTS

The purpose of a second series of tests was to investigate in more detail than was possible in the first set the attitude of the adolescent to his own development. It may be said that adventure is inseparable from development, for a response to any challenge to explore inevitably results in some kind of development, and development, whether its sources are from within or whether it is a response to something from without, is itself of the nature of adventure. The conclusions of clinical psychology go to show more and more that security and development also are inseparable. It is the child who is insecure in his family relationships who finds it difficult to develop naturally in his relations with other children, and the child who has somehow failed to develop the usual skills of reading, writing and number who suffers from a feeling of insecurity towards himself and his work. While any measures therefore of the adolescents' attitude to adventure and security are natural supplements to a study of his attitude to his own development, development itself has other aspects which were not represented in the first set of tests. The test on 'Development' in the first set sought to find out only how strong in the adolescent was the desire to develop in certain ways. Any measure, however, of the attitude of an individual towards his own development should be more than a measure of desire for development. It should also be a measure of awareness of the development so far made. It is important to know not only if boys and girls want to develop, but also what they feel about the progress already made, whether they feel they are going forward, standing still or are defeated. It is important, moreover, to know whether, if they feel they are making no progress, they are the more anxious to develop or have given up hope, or whether, if they are conscious of their advance, they are complacently satisfied or the more eager to develop still further. It was with such thoughts and questions as these in mind that a second set of tests was contemplated.

It was decided that these tests should be constructed, one on the attitude towards the level of development already reached, that is, on 'Awareness of Development', another on the attitude towards future development, or 'Desire for Development'; and a third on the attitude towards certain sources of security related to the items presented in the other two tests, to be called 'Security'. These three tests were to be divided into four parts:

A. Intellectual Development.
Bi. Social Development.
Bii. Development of Independence.
C. Spiritual Development.

Neither these four aspects, nor the items which were finally selected to represent them can be considered in any way to cover all aspects of development. It was hoped, however, that an honest response to these items would give a fair picture of what any boy or girl felt about his development and of his hopes and desires for the future.

Intellectual development includes among other things growth in memory and the power of sustained concentration, development in abstract reasoning, and increased insight or understanding. These four topics were chosen for the test on awareness of intellectual development. The desire for intellectual development is represented by three topics, a desire for more information or factual knowledge, a desire for a deeper understanding, and a desire for independent mental activity, or to find out things for oneself. Security in things intellectual can come from knowledge already possessed or from the knowledge that the necessary information can be acquired. These were the two topics chosen for the test on security.

Social development has a two-fold aspect. It includes development in social contacts and also in independence. Topics must therefore cover both these aspects. Those chosen for investigating awareness of social development were increased understanding of other people, greater pleasure in meeting new people and development in co-operation. Awareness of development in independence is represented by an awareness of more frequent independent decisions, and by less concern about the opinions of both older people and contemporaries. The same three topics, of understanding, making fresh friends and greater ease in social contacts, were chosen for the enquiry into desire for development, with one general item on desire for independence. The approval of other people, both of older and more experienced people, and also of contemporaries, is one of the sources of security. This corresponds to development in social contacts and is represented in the test by two items. The security which is related to development of independence is represented by an item on the security which comes from obeying one's conscience irrespective of criticism.

Spiritual development covers a very wide field, and it was by no means easy to select representative topics. Throughout this study the emphasis has been placed on the religious rather than the æsthetic aspect of spiritual development, and the topics finally chosen refer to that. It has been suggested that people's spiritual needs are three, someone to trust, something to belong to, and something to live for. The topics chosen for the test on awareness of development were, therefore, based on these needs, a growth in the awareness of the love and care of God, a greater desire to belong to the Church, an increased interest in purpose. To these were added the general topic of a greater interest in religion. Much the same topics were chosen for the enquiry into a desire for spiritual development, desire for more knowledge and understanding of religion, the desire to know and serve God better, to improve in character and to find a purpose in life. The satisfaction of the three needs mentioned above was chosen to provide three items in the test on security.

THE FORM OF THE TESTS

To be successful a test must by its own form commend itself to the testees and enlist their co-operation. A short experiment was undertaken to discover if the adolescents preferred one form of test to another. Short attitude tests dealing with only twelve topics were drawn up in three different forms, each test containing the same topics. As an example, the three forms of one topic are given:

I. (a) I am quite sure that I shall always try to learn something new about all kinds of things.
   (b) I think, on the whole, that it is quite good to add to one's store of knowledge.
   (c) Finding out new things is all right for some people.
   (d) I do not think I shall make much effort to find out about fresh things after I leave school.
   (e) I am quite sure that when I leave school I shall leave studying behind me.

The testee was asked to say which statement best described her attitude.

II. Pamela: No more study for me when I leave school. I've no urge to know any more than I do at present.

    Daphne: I rather hope that I shall be able to go on learning.

    Bill: I'd put it more strongly. I've no intention of giving up learning just because I've left school. There are heaps of things I'm keen to know.

    Maurice: Well, I don't expect I shall make much effort to learn anything after I leave school.

    Jane: I don't feel strongly either way.

The testee here was asked to say with whom he agreed most strongly.

III. Do you want to go on learning fresh things after you leave school:

    (*a*) Very anxious to do so.

    (*b*) On the whole would like to.

    (*c*) Don't mind.

    (*d*) Am not very anxious to do so.

    (*e*) Do not want to do so at all.

The testee was again asked to say with which one response he agreed.

The adolescents, divided into three groups, answered each of these tests at two-day intervals, and were asked to say which form they found most interesting. The preferred form was Form II, the reasons given being that 'some of the boys and girls have the same kind of thoughts as my own. The enquiries were easier to understand when they were written down as conversations'; 'It seems as if real people are talking together'. The advantage of this quasi-dramatic form is its greater appeal to imagination and emotion—a point that is not without its significance if it is true that, as Brueckner says, 'Attitudes are based on emotion rather than on tested knowledge in most instances'. In Form II instead of being presented with a series of anonymous statements, as in Form I, to which his approach may be more or less academic, the adolescent is presented with a situation, in this case a discussion, and is asked to state where he stands with regard to it. This, as the girls said, is more 'real'. It is the way in which attitudes are revealed in life, for it is our attitudes which largely decide our responses.

The form next preferred was Form III. 'I like it', wrote a girl, 'because it stated quite clearly in one way or another how you felt towards different things. It is straightforward'. This straightforwardness was a feature that appealed especially to the older girls, and it is probably true that the older the child the more anxious he or she

161

is to understand clearly the point of what he or she is being asked to answer. It is interesting that the form least preferred, gaining only thirteen per cent of the votes, was Form I—the form of the first set of attitude tests.

The form finally decided upon was a combination of Forms II and III for the tests on 'Awareness of Development' and 'Desire for Development'. Form III was used for the test on 'Security', which was placed between the other two tests. This introduced a useful variety and also minimised any 'halo' effect from 'Awareness of Development' on to 'Desire for Development'.

With the combination of Forms II and III, slight modifications were made in the dramatic part of each section. The number of people taking part in each conversation was reduced from five to three by the elimination of those with the most extreme attitudes. There was no intention, however, of abandoning a five-point scale. The boys and girls were to be asked to write the name of the person with whom they most agreed. The initial letters of these names formed a simple code. In order that their responses should cover a range of five possible attitudes, they were asked to underline a name if they felt they agreed very strongly or would have expressed themselves more strongly than did the person in the test conversation. The reasons for this change were three. There was less likelihood of monotony when there were fewer remarks on each topic. With fewer remarks to read the test was shorter. Most important of all, the adolescents could no longer be drawn to a statement which was attractive rather by reason of the vividness of its superlatives than by its approximation to their own attitude. In the discussion of the first set of tests it has already been pointed out that there was reason to believe that the responses of the children had been, in some cases, unduly influenced by the attractiveness of colourful language. It was the desire to avoid this that led in this set of tests to the omission of such statements and the substitution of a method of underlining. There was some indication from the results of the first test that this might prove a useful device, for even though they were provided with a five-point scale of responses, there were some who, wishing to show how strongly they agreed or disagreed, invented methods of their own such as underlining their mark or writing larger figures. In support of this method, it is interesting to notice that the number of children who show an extreme attitude are in about the proportion that might be expected for the extreme positions in any normal distribution, that is, extreme attitudes are decidedly fewer than moderate attitudes.

Most of the children who answered the first set of tests were from two Grammar Schools in different suburbs, one for girls and the other for boys. As the boys and girls were from different schools it was difficult to decide whether certain apparent differences between them were genuine sex differences or the result of differences between the schools. It was decided therefore to have the second set answered by boys and girls attending the same school. This set was answered then by the first, third and sixth year pupils in a mixed Grammar School and by the first and third year pupils in a mixed Modern School, both in the same district. In all one hundred and fifty-eight boys and one hundred and thirty-five girls answered the tests.

The index of reliability for each of the tests was as follows: Awareness of Development, 0·88; Security, 0·79; Desire for Development, 0·96.

Scoring

The answers to each topic were scored as follows: Very positive, 2. Positive, 1. Neutral, 0. Negative, −1, Very negative, −2.

One warning about the scores must be given. An average score for a group of, say, 0·2 may have very different interpretations. It may mean that the majority of the group are indifferent with a few who have a positive attitude. On the other hand it may mean that nearly half the group are negative and only a very small majority positive. Obviously it is very important for anyone handling a group to know which of these two situations he has to face. This cannot be shown by means of an average score. A distribution of scores therefore is a much more useful way of recording the results of tests such as these.

The final form of the questionnaire is given below, and a brief summary of average scores follows in Tables I, II and III.*

ENQUIRY 1. (AWARENESS OF DEVELOPMENT)

As we grow up we change in many ways. There are things that you can do now that you could not do when you were younger. There are

* For fuller details and analytic discussion and evidence as to significance of differences see Forrester, J. F., *A Study of the Attitudes of Adolescents to their Own Intellectual, Social and Spiritual Development.* Unpublished Ph.D. Thesis. University of London. 1946.

also things that you enjoyed doing when you were younger that no longer interest you. Below you will find questions about ways in which you may feel that you have changed, and the different answers given by various boys and girls who are discussing the question. You are asked to write on your answer paper the name of the boy or girl with whom you most agree, like this:

Enquiry 1.
Section A.
1. Bob.
2. Pamela.

If you agree *very* strongly with this boy or girl or feel that you would express yourself *much* more strongly than he or she has done, underline the name you have written, like this:

1. <u>Bob.</u>

Section A

1. Do you find it easier to understand things you are trying to learn than you used to, or would you say that you find them more puzzling than when you were younger?

DICK: I don't think I notice much difference in myself.

JOAN: Lately I've been feeling that things are more difficult to understand.

BETTY: I'm sure there are things I understand now that I couldn't grasp a little while ago.

2. How about your memory? Do you think you remember things you have been told, or have learnt, better than when you were younger?

MICHAEL: I think my memory is improving as I get older.

PEGGY: I don't see much change in my memory.

RICHARD: It seems to me that I don't remember things so well as I used to.

3. Do you find it more difficult to concentrate now than when you were younger, or do you find it easier than you did?

JOYCE: I find it harder to concentrate than I used to.

BERYL: I seem to concentrate on things better than I used to.

DAVID: I don't seem to notice much change either way.

4. What about reasoning things out? Do you find it easier or more difficult?

PATRICK: On the whole, I don't notice much difference.

RUTH: I seem to find it more difficult to reason things out than I used to.

MARIAN: It seems to me that I find problems which call for reasoning easier to tackle than I did a little while ago.

Section Bi

1. Do you feel that you understand other people and their point of view better than you used to, or do you find it more difficult to understand them?

BRIAN: I find it easier to understand people and why they think and behave the way they do than when I was younger.

JIM: Lately I've been feeling that other people are more difficult to understand.

DAISY: So far as I can see there isn't much difference in the way I understand people.

2. Do you find that you enjoy meeting new people more than you did when you were younger, or less?

PHYLLIS: On the whole I don't notice much difference.

ROBERT: I think I'm more inclined to try to avoid meeting new people than I used to be.

MOLLY: I enjoy meeting new people and making fresh friends more than I used to.

3. How about the people with whom you work and play? Do you find it easier or more difficult than you used to to get on with them?

BETTY: I find it easier to co-operate with other people than I used to.

DONALD: I can't say that I notice much change in the way I get on with people.

JOAN: Lately I've been feeling that it is much more difficult to get on with other people.

Section Bii

1. Do you find that you decide more things for yourself than when you were younger, or are you more inclined to leave decisions to other people?

MAVIS: On the whole I think I decide more things for myself than I used to.

ROSEMARY: I think I am more inclined than I was to let other people make decisions for me.

PETER: I don't think I notice much change in the number of decisions I make by myself.

2. Does what older people think matter to you more than it did, or less?

BILL: I don't think that older people's opinions matter to me as much as they did.

JIM: When I'm making up my mind what to do I think more than I used to about what grown-ups will say.

DORA: What other people think affects me neither more nor less than it did.

3. What about people of your own age? Does it seem more or less important to you now than it did that you should behave in ways that they think right?

ROSE: I'm sure it seems more important to me.

MAURICE: What people of my own age think of what I do matters less to me than it did.

PHILIP: I don't notice much difference in myself.

Section C

1. What about religion? Do you think you are more interested in religion than you used to be, or less interested?

BARBARA: Religion seems more important to me than it did.

DOUGLAS: I seem to have about the same amount of interest as I always have had.

LESLIE: I've never had much interest at all.

JOAN: On the whole I would say that it appeals to me less than it did.

2. Do you feel more or less certain now than you did that God loves and cares for you?

RACHEL: I find it harder now than I did when younger to believe that God loves and cares for us.

MICHAEL: I think I am more certain about it than I was.

PETER: I don't think I've changed in what I believe.

KATHLEEN: I've never thought about it at all.

3. What about belonging to the Church? Does it seem to you more important or less important than it used to?

DENNIS: I don't see any difference in myself.

JACK: I'm not so keen as I was on belonging to the Church.

FREDA: I've never thought about it at all.

BETTY: And I'm more interested than I used to be in belonging to the Church.

4. Does it seem more or less important to you than it did that the things you do in life should be really worth while?

GWEN: I have never bothered about whether things are worth doing. I just do them.

MAURICE: I care much more than I did about whether the things I have to do are worth while or not.

ROSINA: I think, on the whole, that I think about that less than I used to.

PAUL: I don't think I've changed at all.

ENQUIRY II. (SECURITY)

We all need certain things in life to make us feel secure and happy. All people don't seem to find the same things equally important. Below you will find some questions about things that you may feel you need, or perhaps do not need. Write on your answer paper the number of the answer that is most like the one you would give, like this:

Enquiry II.
Section A.
1. *b.*
2. *d.*

Section A

1. Some people get a great feeling of satisfaction when they realise they know something well. Other people do not feel particularly disturbed when they do not know something they are asked. How do you feel?

(*a*) Very satisfied when I know.

(*b*) A little disturbed when I don't know.

(*c*) Sometimes upset when I don't know, but not always.

(*d*) Not particularly disturbed when I don't know.

(*e*) Not at all upset when I don't know.

2. Some people have this same feeling of security if they know that they can find out or learn something, even if they don't know it at

the time when they are asked. How much satisfaction do you get from knowing that you will be able to find out even if you do not know now?

   (*a*) A great deal of satisfaction.
   (*b*) A little satisfaction.
   (*c*) Am not certain.
   (*d*) Don't mind if I shall never find out.
   (*e*) Don't feel at all upset if I shall never find out.

Section Bi

   1. Some boys and girls feel secure and contented if older people approve of them. Others do not mind if they are criticised. How do you feel? Does the approval of older people help you to feel secure?

   (*a*) Helps very much.
   (*b*) Helps a little.
   (*c*) Difficult to say.
   (*d*) Doesn't make much difference to me.
   (*e*) Makes no difference at all.

   2. How about people of your own age? Does the approval of boys and girls of your own age help you to feel happy and contented?

   (*a*) Helps a great deal.
   (*b*) Helps a little.
   (*c*) Cannot be sure.
   (*d*) Makes little difference.
   (*e*) Does not make any difference to me.

Section Bii

   1. How much satisfaction do you get from doing what you think is right whatever other people may think about you for doing it?

   (*a*) A great deal of satisfaction.
   (*b*) A certain amount.
   (*c*) Cannot say.
   (*d*) Not much.
   (*e*) None at all.

Section C

   1. Some people feel happy and secure because they know that they have parents or friends whom they can trust to look after them and advise them. Other people do not need such friends and relations

so much. How much does your feeling of security depend on your having such people to help you?

(*a*) Depends a great deal.

(*b*) Depends a little.

(*c*) Cannot say.

(*d*) Does not depend much.

(*e*) Does not depend at all.

2. Some people cannot feel happy and secure unless they feel that they really belong somewhere and are really accepted as a member of that part of the community. Other people seem happy on their own. How does 'belonging' help you to feel secure?

(*a*) Helps a great deal.

(*b*) Helps a little.

(*c*) Difficult to say.

(*d*) Does not make any difference.

(*e*) Does not help at all.

3. Some people get a great sense of satisfaction when they find a real purpose in life, something worth living for and working for. Some people feel no need for this. How do you feel?

(*a*) Feel it is very important.

(*b*) Feel it is good on the whole.

(*c*) Do not mind.

(*d*) Do not think it matters much.

(*e*) Do not think it matters at all.

ENQUIRY III. (DESIRE FOR DEVELOPMENT)

Different people want different kinds of things. Girls do not always want the same things as boys, nor do young people want the same things as older folk. Below you will find questions about things you may or may not want, the various answers given by boys and girls who are talking about these questions. You are asked to write on your answer paper the name of the boy or girl in each conversation with whom you most agree, like this:

Enquiry III.

Section A.

1. Donald.

2. Maureen.

If you agree very strongly with this boy or girl, or if you feel that you would express your opinion *much* more strongly than he or she has, then underline the name you have written, like this:

1. <u>Donald.</u>

Section A

1. Do you want always to go on learning fresh things, or do you hope that when you leave school you will have done with studying?

BILL: I've no intention of giving up learning. There are heaps of things I'm keen to know.

JACK: I've no great urge to know more than I do at present.

DAISY: Sometimes I'm interested in learning new things, but sometimes it doesn't seem worth the effort.

2. Do you want to discover things for yourself or are you happiest if you are told everything you should know?

PEGGY: I haven't any particular feelings about it.

RALPH: I'm not very interested in finding out things for myself.

MALCOLM: What I enjoy is discovering things for myself without any help from anyone.

3. Are you anxious to understand things better than you do at present, or are you content with what you understand at the moment?

BRENDA: One of the things I most want is to get all the questions I'd like to ask satisfactorily answered.

JILL: Usually I accept what's told me. I'm not particularly interested in finding out why.

DICK: I'm sometimes interested in knowing reasons for things, but not always.

Section Bi

1. How do you feel about understanding other people's point of view and getting to know them better? Do you want to do so, or do you not think it necessary?

RUBY: I think I understand people well enough. There's no need to try to get to know them any better.

MONA: One of the things I think important is getting to understand other people really well.

PAUL: I suppose it's useful to know people better, but I'm not sure that I trouble about it much.

170

2. Are you interested in meeting fresh people and making new friends, or do you only feel happy when you are with people whom you know well?

JOHN: I'm not particularly keen to make new friends. The ones I have are all I need.

BASIL: I am always glad of an opportunity of meeting fresh people.

DOROTHY: I don't feel very strongly either way.

3. How do you feel about the way you get on with people, the way you work and play with them, the way you behave in company? Do you feel satisfied about it, or would you like to improve?

RUTH: I think I get on with other people fairly well on the whole. I don't feel there's much need for me to improve.

MOLLY: I wish I were better at getting along with other people and felt more at ease in company.

PHILIP: At times I think I get along pretty well, but sometimes I feel I'm not so good at it.

Section Bii

1. Do you want to be independent, to run your own life, or are you happiest when other people decide things for you?

BILL: One of the things I am looking forward to is the time when I shall be really independent and responsible for myself.

DEREK: Sometimes I like the idea of being responsible for myself, but sometimes I'm rather scared of it.

JOYCE: I don't like deciding things for myself.

Section C

1. What do you feel about religion? Do you want to know more about it or not?

ROGER: I haven't much desire to know anything about religion. It just doesn't appeal to me.

MADGE: I should like to understand better than I do what religion is all about, and what it has to do with me.

PAMELA: Some things about religion interest me, but I'm not sure if I want to know more.

2. Some people feel that what they want most in life is to 'know God more clearly, love Him more dearly and follow Him more

nearly'. Other people do not think that this matters very much. What do you think?

BARBARA: I should like to feel that I am learning to love and serve God a little better.

DAVID: I am not sure how I feel about it.

JOYCE: To be quite honest, it doesn't interest me very much.

3. Some people feel that it is very important to improve in character as they grow older. They want to find out what is right and do it. Other people don't think it matters much so long as they are happy. What do you think?

PHOEBE: Sometimes I think I'd like to be better, but often I don't bother.

ROBERT: It sounds rather priggish to me to want to improve one's character and stand up for what is right.

MICHAEL: However it sounds, I, for my part, want to find out what's right, and have the courage to do it.

4. Some people feel that it makes a great difference to them if they have a purpose in life, something to work for and live for. Other people do not want this. How do you feel?

JIM: I think this talk about a purpose in life is unnecessary. I take life as it comes.

BILL: I want to feel that I am finding out and doing the things that are most worth while in life.

DAPHNE: I'm not sure if some things really are more worth while than others.

CONCLUSIONS

AWARENESS OF DEVELOPMENT

It appears from the results of the second set of tests that the adolescents tested, on the whole, are conscious of the fact that they are developing in various ways. It is safe to say that out of the two hundred and ninety-three boys and girls who answered these tests there were none who were not conscious of some kind of development, though there is considerable variety both in the number of directions in which individuals wish to develop, and in the directions themselves, some, for example, feeling more conscious of intellectual development than social or spiritual, others more aware of progress in making social contacts than in their independence of other people.

It is interesting to notice that the results of these tests suggest that adolescents pay more attention to the opinion of adults than they are sometimes credited with doing. There is a possible explanation of this. Most of the studies on the adolescent, starting with Stanley Hall's famous two volumes, come from America, and it is possible, as Margaret Mead[6] suggests, that the psychological environment in America puts more pressure on the adolescent to revolt against the older generation in favour of deference to the opinion of his contemporaries, than it does in England. In America the boy 'is expected to go further than his father went. . . . He is furthermore expected to feel very little respect for the past. Father is to be outdistanced and outmoded . . . he did very well in his way, but he is out of date.' This position does not obtain to the same extent in England, as the results of these tests suggest. However, more investigation is needed, and a comparative study might usefully be made of the psychological environments of English children who do not set much store by the opinion of their elders and those who do.

The significance of the fact that there is no one among these two hundred and ninety-three who is not aware of some kind of development must not be overlooked, for this means that in every individual, however diffident and backward he may appear, there is some growing point for self-confidence or some last defence against regarding himself as a complete failure. Whether or not his assessment of himself is well founded or not is another matter, and a very important one, but it will be considered later.

DESIRE FOR DEVELOPMENT

If the adolescents are, on the whole, aware that they are developing, they are even more conscious of their desire to develop. Out of the six hundred and thirty-nine boys and girls who answered either the first or second of these tests there is not one who does not desire to develop in some direction. The directions in which the desire to develop seem most widespread are physical development, including the desire for health and strength, as well as for physical skills, and the desire for more knowledge, both of people and of things. They want to improve in character, and to find a purpose and meaning in life. The fact that every individual has some desire for development, some aspiration, is again of great importance to the educator, for it means that there is no child about whom a teacher need despair, no child without something in him that will respond if he is given the opportunity to fulfil his ambition. Even if there is only one way in which a child really desires to develop, that can be a growing point for desire for development in other directions, and the child who is ambitious to develop in many ways is one who will be eager to make the most of all the opportunities offered to him.

The directions in which a child desires to develop are an indication of his scale of values. If it were only the children who felt they were making progress intellectually who desired to develop still further, there would be some justification for saying that a desire to develop was a result of success; if desire to develop were confined to those who felt they were failures it might be interpreted as compensatory, but there are no grounds for explaining desire for development in such ways, for individuals vary. Where there are, however, large numbers of boys and girls who desire to improve in physical abilities, it is safe to assume that physical achievement stands high in the scale of values of most of them. Where there are a majority who desire to improve in character, it is safe to assume that character is something that is valued by youth. The desire to find significance and purpose in life which is so widespread among these boys and girls is of great importance as it gives a reason for all the other desires, the desire for more knowledge, the desire for a better understanding of people, the desire for a good character, the desire to know more about religion.

OTHER POINTS OF INTEREST

One of the striking things about the results of these tests is the small number of differences to be noticed between girls and boys, and between the younger adolescents and the older ones, and the fact that where they do occur they are seldom very great. Since children are selected for the Grammar School on the basis of intellectual rather than of social or spiritual ability, one might expect to find in those sections that deal with intellectual matters at any rate differences between Grammar School children and Modern School children. Very few of such differences, however, appear. Groups of boys and girls from both schools seem to be equally aware of the progress they have already made, and to be equally desirous of further development. This absence of differences in general obtains even when eleven-year-olds are compared with sixteen-year-olds. Such differences as there are between ages and between boys and girls are not so impressive as differences between individuals in the same group, for within any age group it is possible to find children with the most diverse views. It is a fact which tends to make an average score somewhat meaningless. It is also possible to find an eleven-year-old and a sixteen-year-old whose attitudes are more alike than two of the same age group. This suggests that the chief reasons for differences in attitudes may be, not age or sex, but personality differences which go back to constitutional or environmental differences. This immediately opens up possibilities of many fascinating studies. What kind of home life produces the most positive attitude towards the various topics? What makes a child eager to meet new people, or what makes him shrink from doing so? What kind of school organisation helps or hinders? The answers to these questions lie outside the scope of this study, but it may perhaps be suggested that by showing the differences in attitudes that exist this study has prepared the way for the more valuable study of how they are formed. It is not without significance that two children who show very negative attitudes come from unhappy home backgrounds.

INDIVIDUAL CASE-STUDIES

One of the most interesting, and possibly potentially the most useful outcome of this study has been the possibility of constructing personality sketches of the adolescents from their responses to the tests. These reconstructions can be written out very largely in the words of the test. Five of these studies were made and were sent to the school in order that the staff might express an opinion of them. They considered that on the whole they gave a great deal of valuable and accurate information about the pupils; but that there was in some cases an unreality about some of the responses to the section on religion. Some sixth-form 'portraits' discussed informally were considered remarkably accurate.

It must always be remembered that what these case studies, or character sketches, represent are not the children as they necessarily are, nor the children as their teachers see them, but as they see themselves. Where, therefore, a child's teacher agrees that the case study is accurate, he is agreeing with the child's estimate of himself. Where he happens to disagree, it does not necessarily mean that the child's self-knowledge is at fault any more than it necessarily means that the teacher's opinion is wrong. If a child declares that he wants to improve but otherwise shows little sign of such a desire, there may be two explanations. He may in reality not desire to improve. On the other hand, he may want to improve but feel incapable of doing so. This is not infrequently the case with 'shy' children who have a deceptively off-hand manner. If, therefore, a child shows by his response a desire to improve which is contrary to the teacher's estimate of him, this is to be taken as a challenge to the teacher to discover why he does not therefore improve, rather than as an opportunity for declaring that the child's opinion of himself is at fault. Should the child's knowledge of himself be inaccurate his response points all the same to his need for help and guidance. The same is true of the child's awareness of his own development, which may be either accurately or inaccurately estimated. An illustration of a study of a girl of fourteen will show what is possible.

'This girl finds it easier to understand things she is trying to learn than she used to. She feels that she can concentrate better and finds problems that call for reasoning easier to tackle than she did some time ago. She does not notice, however, much change in her memory. She has a great sense of security and satisfaction when she realises that she knows something well, but is not certain whether the fact that she will be able to acquire the necessary knowledge later on is also a source of security. She wants to go on learning and enjoys discovering things for herself with no help from anyone. There are many questions she would like to ask, and she is most anxious to have them satisfactorily answered.

'She finds it easier to understand other people than she did, and also wants to understand them better. She gets more pleasure from meeting fresh people and making new friends than she used to, and welcomes very eagerly any opportunity for doing so. She finds it easier to work and play with other people than she did and does not feel there is much need for her to improve further in that respect. The approval of both older people and contemporaries is a very real source of security to her.

'On the whole she thinks she decides more things for herself than she used to, but before she makes up her mind what to do she thinks more than she did about what grown-ups will say. She is neither more nor less anxious than she was to behave in ways that her contemporaries think right. She gets a certain amount of satisfaction from doing what she thinks right no matter what others say, but while she sometimes likes the idea of being responsible for herself she admits that she is also sometimes scared at the thought.

'She is no more interested in religion now than when younger, and admits that while some things about it interest her she is not sure if she wants to know more. On the other hand, she feels a little more certain than she did that God loves and cares for her, though she is not sure how she feels about her response, whether she wants "to know Him more clearly and follow Him more nearly" or not. She is not aware of any more interest in belonging to the Church, and although sometimes she thinks she would like to be better, she admits that often she does not bother. She realises that she cares much more than she used to that the things she has to do should be worth while, and wants both to find out and to do something in life that is worth doing. She feels that her sense of security depends a great deal on belonging somewhere and having people she can trust, and that having something to live and work for is a definite source of satisfaction.

'*Summary.* Here is a normal, happy, probably rather quiet kind of girl. Her intellectual development is satisfactory and she is interested in developing. She seems happy in her personal relationships, and is reasonably, though not strikingly, interested in being independent. She has no particular interest in religion, but has a strong interest in finding a purpose in life.'

While it is important that boys and girls should learn to know themselves as they really are, it is equally important that those who have to guide them should know what pictures these boys and girls have of themselves that they may help them to correct false pictures and to turn healthy dreams and hopes into actualities. This account of an experiment in discovering the attitudes of young people is offered in the hope that it may encourage others to seek more effective methods.

REFERENCES

1. MacMurray, John
   The Structure of Religious Experience. London: Faber & Faber, Ltd. 1936. Pp. 108–109.
2. Thurstone, L. L., and Chave, E. J.
   The Measurement of Attitude. Chicago: University of Chicago Press. 1929.
3. Lundberg, G. A.
   Social Research. New York: Longmans Green & Co. 1942. P. 229.

4. BRUECKNER, LEO. J.
'Factors Conditioning the Development of Attitudes', *Journal of Educational Research*, Feb. 1945, p. 471.

5. MURPHY, G., MURPHY, L. B., AND NEWCOMB, T. M.
Experimental Social Psychology. New York: Harper & Brothers, Publishers. 1937. Pp. 897–8.

6. MEAD, MARGARET
The American Character. London: Penguin Books, Ltd. 1944. (Published in U.S.A. in 1942 under the title *And Keep Your Powder Dry*, Ch. III.)

TABLE I

AWARENESS OF DEVELOPMENT. AVERAGE SCORES

	Grammar School			Modern School	
	1st Year	3rd Year	6th Year	1st Year	3rd Year
A 1. Boys	·74	·68	·54	·64	·71
Girls	·67	·95	·91	·67	·67
A 2. Boys	·29	·24	·37	·31	·58
Girls	·57	·64	·33	·56	·59
A 3. Boys	·03	·21	·12	·58	·42
Girls	·6	·23	·56	·23	·56
A 4. Boys	·62	·76	·96	·36	·66
Girls	·5	·86	·95	·66	·67
Bi 1. Boys	·85	·87	1·09	·53	·62
Girls	1·0	1·18	·86	·48	·74
Bi 2. Boys	·77	·61	·5	·58	·58
Girls	1·03	1·18	·24	·86	·67
Bi 3. Boys	·71	·68	·83	·42	·5
Girls	·7	·68	·43	·34	·45
Bii 1. Boys	1·09	·71	1·08	·72	·79
Girls	·97	·64	1·15	·46	·85
Bii 2. Boys	−·36	−·21	·25	−·25	−·37
Girls	−·77	−·55	−·26	−·4	−·85
Bii 3. Boys	−·15	−·37	·17	·03	·12
Girls	−·02	−·18	·00	−·34	−·22
C 1. Boys	·47	·5	·67	·39	·04
Girls	·47	·64	·47	·4	·37
C 2. Boys	·44	·29	−·08	·08	−·12
Girls	·5	·64	·29	·23	·45
C 3. Boys	·44	·16	·08	·06	−·38
Girls	·27	·18	·25	·34	−·22
C 4. Boys	·79	·68	·92	·75	·62
Girls	·87	·95	·76	·57	·67

This shows a general awareness of development in different directions at all ages, with the exception of development in becoming more independent of, or indifferent to the opinions of other people. Most of the adolescents testified to paying rather more attention to this than before. A majority, small but significant, of boys felt that they had turned away from certain aspects of spiritual development. The directions in which they are most conscious of development are in understanding and reasoning, in understanding people, and in a sense of purpose.

TABLE II

SECURITY. SCORE AVERAGES

	Grammar School			Modern School	
	1st Year	3rd Year	6th Year	1st Year	3rd Year
A 1. Boys	1·46	1·4	1·0	·82	1·04
Girls	1·33	1·23	·81	1·17	·75
A 2. Boys	1·17	1·08	1·5	1·13	1·21
Girls	1·27	1·09	1·14	·77	1·15
Bi 1. Boys	·76	·92	·92	1·03	·79
Girls	1·2	1·23	·95	·83	1·22
Bi 2. Boys	·53	·84	·92	·84	·54
Girls	·9	1·54	1·0	1·03	1·15
Bii 1. Boys	·75	1·08	1·46	·95	·75
Girls	·43	1·59	1·09	·94	·56
C 1, Boys	1·7	1·18	1·37	1·54	1·54
Girls	1·53	1·54	1·05	1·55	1·41
C 2. Boys	1·46	·79	1·17	1·03	·71
Girls	1·0	1·43	·57	·66	·96
C 3. Boys	1·35	1·5	1·71	1·38	1·29
Girls	1·6	1·82	1·34	1·26	1·59

This shows that for most of these adolescents these topics—knowledge, ability to acquire knowledge, approval of others, the approval of a good conscience, people to trust, something to belong to, a purpose—are all great sources of security. There seems to be a difference between age groups as to the strength of a good conscience, unsupported by popular approval, as a source of security (Bii 1).

TABLE III

DESIRE FOR DEVELOPMENT. SCORE AVERAGES

		Grammar School			Modern School	
		1st Year	2nd Year	6th Year	1st Year	3rd Year
A 1.	Boys	·97	1·03	1·25	·79	1·08
	Girls	·9	·86	1·0	·74	1·04
A 2.	Boys	1·12	·82	·79	·87	·96
	Girls	·97	·91	·91	·88	·71
A 3.	Boys	1·05	·95	1·0	·53	·75
	Girls	·57	1·09	·67	·51	·63
Bi 1.	Boys	·59	·5	1·0	·47	·54
	Girls	·93	·95	·91	·26	·96
Bi 2.	Boys	·5	·37	·42	·13	·71
	Girls	·73	·23	·29	·48	·26
Bi 3.	Boys	—·03	·05	·29	·08	—·12
	Girls	—·2	·23	·00	·11	·04
Bii 1.	Boys	·76	·79	·79	·76	·92
	Girls	·4	·68	·52	·17	·78
C 1.	Boys	·32	·05	·79	·32	·17
	Girls	·63	·38	·62	·63	·52
C 2.	Boys	·41	·18	·42	·58	·26
	Girls	·7	·33	·1	·8	·52
C 3.	Boys	·76	·76	1·04	·5	·78
	Girls	·83	·57	·76	·54	1·0
C 4.	Boys	·65	·63	·87	·74	·52
	Girls	·73	·67	·76	·73	·59

The desire for development appears to be strongest in a desire to go on learning, to discover things for themselves, to understanding things better, understand people better, improve in character, become more independent. The low score in Bi 3, the desire to improve in social relationship, is probably due to unfortunate wording in the positive statement, which may be interpreted to mean that the girl was not very good at getting on with people. This low score is not supported by the scores on a similar topic in the first set of tests.

CHAPTER NINE

A STUDY OF FRIENDSHIP

FRIENDSHIP as a dynamic form of personal relationship acquires special significance in the adolescent stage of human growth, when boys and girls seek among their peers in school or outside for the satisfaction of their needs for affection, sympathy and security.

By means of active participation in work and play, they develop social feeling—the feeling that they belong to a group and that they are valued and accepted by it. This experience in many ways accounts for the discipline and group solidarity of school and the study of such friendships helps adults to understand the hopes and fears, the conflicts, interests, needs and inclinations which contribute to the complex process of the social maturation of adolescent girls and boys.

Since this relation between friends is intimately personal and hence subjective, it cannot lend itself easily to objective analysis and measurement; but with the help of certain modern research techniques and by means of cautious and careful questioning supplemented by personal expression, either oral or written, it is possible to elicit some of its salient features.

The main aim of an investigation initiated in 1946 was to analyse the friendships of certain groups of pupils between the ages of twelve and fifteen, and to estimate to what extent intelligence, interest in games and sports, hobbies, general reading and success in school subjects played their part in the formation of friendly pairs. An attempt was also made to see how pupils tended to rate their friends on traits like 'politeness', 'loyalty', 'humour', 'sociability', 'physical appearance' and 'academic work'; and a subsidiary intention was to offer some observations on the problem of friendship, companionship and love, in the light of available knowledge as derived from written expression in the form of essays, and from observation of

182

boys and girls engaged in co-operative activities in the classroom and playground.

The subjects consisted of the entire group of two hundred and fifty-two pupils in a Secondary Modern School near London. Their ages extended from 11+ to 14+ (roughly twelve years to fifteen years). Their Intelligence Quotients on the Otis Quick-Scoring Beta Test (Form A) ranged from 55 to 126 and their Mental Ages from seven years nine months to fifteen years ten months. Most of them came from average middle-class families living in a small town and its neighbouring villages.

The chief method adopted was a questionnaire method more or less akin to present-day sociometric tests. The questionnaire was divided into five sections. Section A required each child to give information about himself and his interests. Section B, the main part of the questionnaire, consisted of questions relating to ten situations in which a pupil might feel the need of having friends. Each question required mention of the choice of three friends and the questions embodied in turn what could be described as companionship, identity of interests, intimacy, practical ability, intellectual ability, sympathy, adventure, security and protection, sociability and sportsmanship. Section C asked the pupil to write the names of three best friends out of all the friends mentioned in Section B, and to fill in certain information about them. In Section D each pupil was invited to rate these best friends on certain personality characteristics, and Section E was directed to form-teachers who were required to give other necessary information regarding the child concerned.

Section A

(a) Please fill in the required information about yourself:

    (i) Name ....

    (ii) $\frac{\text{Boy}}{\text{Girl}}$ .... (iii) Date of Birth...............

    (iv) Class........................... (v) School.........................

    ....

    (vi) Home Address...

    ....

(b) Read the following questions carefully and write the answers in the space provided:

    1. What is your favourite hobby? ....

    ....

2. What indoor games do you like most to play? ....

....

3. What outdoor games do you like most to play? ....

....

4. If you are in a library full of newspapers, books on travel, fairy tales, love stories, adventure, science, poetry, biography, crime—in which type of books are you particularly interested?
   (Your answer may be a type not mentioned in this list.)
....
....
....
....
....
....
....

5. What is your favourite school subject? ....

....

6. Do you regularly attend any Church or Sunday School? ....

....

7. Do you belong to any clubs or teams? ....

....

....

8. Do you go to see films? ....

9. If so, which type of films mentioned in the bracket do you like to see? (News Reel, Love-stories, Coloured-cartoons, Documentary films, Adventure, Thrillers, or any other type not mentioned in this list.)
....
....
....
....
....
....
....

Section B

Directions:
   (i) Read the following questions very carefully.
   (ii) You have to mention the names of friends in the space provided against 1, 2, 3.
   (iii) The Numbers 1, 2, 3, indicate the order of preference. Be sure to put down your first three choices. First the name

of your first choice, then your second choice, and then your third.

(iv) The questions ask you to write down the names of your friends, whether they be boys or girls.

1. If you were going to spend your day rambling or at the seaside, which friend would you like to go with you?

    1. ....
    2. ....
    3. ....

2. If you were intending to go to the pictures or a theatre and would like to have a friend with you, which friend would you select?

    1. ....
    2. ....
    3. ....

3. If you could invite a friend to your home for a weekend, or to stay with you longer, whom would you invite?

    1. ....
    2. ....
    3. ....

4. If you were asked to do some difficult work demanding practical skill, which friend would you choose to help you in your work?

    1. ....
    2. ....
    3. ....

5. If you were given some work to do requiring some real brain work, which friend would you like to help you?

    1. ....
    2. ....
    3. ....

6. If your mother or father, or someone at home were ill and you had to look after them, which friend would you like to call to assist you?

    1. ....
    2. ....
    3. ....

7. If you were to go on a rather adventurous expedition, which friend would you like to go along with you?

    1. ....
    2. ....
    3. ....

8. If you were in a position of danger and would like to have a friend by your side, whom would you choose?

    1. ....
    2. ....
    3. ....

9. If you were invited to meet a number of people whom you had never seen before and were given a choice of taking a friend with you, whom would you invite?

    1. ....
    2. ....
    3. ....

10. If you were captain of a running team to run against another school and you were asked to choose your team, mention the names of the first three whom you would like to play under your captainship. (You may have boys or girls, or both, in your team.)

    1. ....
    2. ....
    3. ....

Section C

1. Out of the friends you have mentioned in the answers above, whom would you select for a *life-long friendship*? Mention the names below in order of preference.

    1. ....
    2. ....
    3. ....

2. Fill in the required information about these three friends in the accompanying form:

1	2	3	4	5	6	7	8	9	10	11	12	13	14	15
Name of the friend.	Favourite hobby of the friend.	Out-door games the friend likes most to play	Indoor games the friend likes to play.	The type of reading in which the friend is particularly interested (Travel, Love-stories, News-papers, Adventure, Poetry, etc.).	The favourite school subject of the friend.	Does your friend regularly attend any Church or Sunday School?	Does your friend belong to any clubs or teams?	Does your friend go to see films? If so, which type of films does the friend like to see?	How long have you known this friend?	Where did you first meet your friend?	Do your parents know the parents of your friend *very well?*			
1.														
2.														
3.														

ADOLESCENT OPINION

Section D

Directions:
1. Read each question carefully.
2. The answer to each question may be any of the five types mentioned under each question as A, B, C, D, E.
3. Put down the name or names of your friends (mentioned by you in Section C (i) and (ii)) under any of the five types of the answer which you think correctly describes your friend.

1. Is your friend good at school work?

A	B	C	D	E
Very good.	Good.	Average.	Rather weak.	Very weak.

2. Is your friend polite?

A	B	C	D	E
Very polite.	Polite.	Indifferent.	Impolite.	Rude.

3. Is your friend full of fun?

A	B	C	D	E
Is very full of fun.	Is full of fun.	Neither full of fun nor dull.	Dull.	Very dull.

188

A STUDY OF FRIENDSHIP

	A	B	C	D	E
4. Is your friend adventurous?	Very adventurous.	Adventurous.	Sometimes adventurous.	Rarely adventurous.	Never adventurous.

	A	B	C	D	E
5. Does your friend work hard?	Works very hard.	Works hard.	Sometimes works hard.	Rarely works hard.	Is lazy.

	A	B	C	D	E
6. Does your friend stick by you?	Sticks by me very well.	Sticks by me well.	Usually sticks by me.	Changeable.	Very changeable.

	A	B	C	D	E
7. Does your friend get on well with other people?	Gets on very well with other people.	Gets on well with other people.	Sometimes gets on well with other people.	Rarely gets on well with other people.	Never gets on well with other people.

	A	B	C	D	E
8. Is your friend good looking?	Very good looking.	Good looking.	Neither good looking nor ugly.	Ugly.	Very ugly.

Section E

1. Name of the Pupil .... Class ....
2. Chronological Age .... 3. Height ....
4. Weight ....
5. Intelligence Quotient ....
6. How was this I.Q. found out? ....
   (The name of the Test or Tests ....
   and procedure.) ....
7. Is the pupil sociable? ....
8. Is the pupil aggressive or sub-
   missive? ....
9. What was the achievement of the
   pupil in the last examination? ....
10. Have you noticed this pupil
    having intimate friends? ....
11. If so, could you give the name or ....
    names (and the class to which ....
    they belong) of these friends? ....
12. What are the special interests of ....
    the child noticed by you? ....
13. Any other information you can ....
    give regarding the pupil's ....
    social relationship within the ....
    school or without, or any other ....
    information regarding his ....
    nature, his aptitudes, attain- ....
    ment, etc. ....
14. Socio - economic position of ....
    parents (to indicate from what ....
    sort of family the child comes). ....

190

The composite questionnaire was given in July 1947, and after about six months the investigator spent a week in the school, in December 1947, interviewing interesting cases and inquiring about the causes of changes of friends, if there were any. During the course of this week the boys and girls were asked to write an essay entitled 'My Best Friend', in which it was suggested that they might discuss (i) their conception of true friendship and companionship, and the qualities they liked most in their friends; (ii) the meaning of 'loving' a friend, whether the friend was of the same or of the opposite sex; and (iii) their feelings for friends of the opposite sex if they had any. To encourage them to express themselves freely and frankly, they were asked to write their essays anonymously. In addition to this a list of twelve geographical projects was given out to the entire school and they were asked to form into groups of two or three to carry out one of these projects as an out-of-school activity. In this fashion the results of questionnaires, interviews, essay-writing and observation of project work were pooled as an aid to the study of the problem of friendship.

All the data collected were analysed in the first instance to discover the social structure of the group and the patterns of relationships existing within the group. This was done by studying the choices distributed within the group (see Table I showing mutual choices) and by drawing sociograms on the basis of mutually reciprocated choices on each criterion (see Table II showing the composition of various constellations). Various patterns of relationships—mutual pairs, triangles, etc.—along with inter-sex choices and the implications thereof were worked out on the basis of the interviews, the opinions of the teachers and the nature of the responses on the questionnaire.

The friendly pairs formed on the basis of mutual reciprocations of 'life-long friendship' criterion were next considered with regard to the choices on the criteria, the interests, the intelligence quotient, mental age and personality characteristics. The correlations of intelligence quotients and mental ages between the friendly pairs were computed according to Fisher's[1] 'intraclass' correlation method. The simplified formula as given by Guilford[2] in connection with the correlation between interchangeable variables was used. In order to apply the test of significance, the F. values for each of the correlation coefficients was calculated and their significance was found by reference to Snedecor's Tables for F.[3] In considering the

TABLE I

MUTUAL CHOICES IN THE GROUP

Class	Number of Pupils present Receiving Mutual Choices	Per cent.	Number of Pupils present not Receiving Mutual Choices				Total	Per cent
			Complete Isolates		Unreciprocated			
			Boys	Girls	Boys	Girls		
I	77	78·6	4	2	9	6	21	21·4
II	101	91·0	1	0	5	2	8	9·0
III	33	78·6	1	0	4	4	9	21·4
IV	3	100·0	—	—	—	—	—	—
Total	214	—	6	2	18	12	38	—

TABLE II

COMPOSITION OF VARIOUS CONSTELLATIONS

Number of Pupils Forming each Constellation	Total Number of such Constellations	Number of Pupils		
		Boys	Girls	Total
2	14	12	16	28
3	3	0	9	9
4	2	0	8	8
5	1	0	5	5
6	1	6	0	6
9	2	9	9	18
11	1	11	0	11
28	1	0	28	28
42	1	30	12	42
59	1	41	18	59
—	27	109	105	214

ratings of pupils on eight of the personal characteristics the chief
interest was to find out which of these characteristics mattered most
according to these children in the choice of their friends. The ratings
were given on a five-point scale, but it was observed that the pupils
could not be relied upon to make a clear-cut distinction between A
and B, or D and E. So for convenience the five-point scale was
reduced to a three-point scale by combining the ratings of two
extremes, A and B on the one hand, and D and E on the other.
Similarly, the eight characteristics were grouped into three sub-
groups; the first group, consisting of four characteristics, 'full of fun',
'adventure', 'sticking by' and 'getting on well with other people',
was called by the general term 'character traits'. The second group,
consisting of 'good at school work' and 'working hard', was called
'work traits'; and the third group, consisting of 'politeness' and
'good looking', was called 'personal traits'.

As far as the group under investigation is concerned the evidence
obtained may be summarised as follows.

The boys and girls were not significantly different in sociability.[4]
The mean number of choices for both boys and girls was 19·85,
while the standard deviation of the scores for boys was 14·40 and
that for the girls was 13·85. Though among the boys there were more
extreme cases at both the higher and lower levels, the slight difference
(0·55) in the standard deviation for both boys and girls was not
significant, the ratio of the difference between the standard deviations
and the corresponding standard error being only 0·44.

The distribution of choices both in the group as a whole and as
revealed in inter-sex choices suggested that the selection of friends
was related to the satisfaction of psychological needs among the
children considered. Table II shows that in criterion 1 (companionship) and in criterion X (sportsmanship) there was a maximum
amount of distribution within the group, and that in the others,
except in criterion VIII (security and protection), there was a
relatively equal distribution of choices. In criterion IV (practical
ability) 30 girls chose boys, as contrasted with only 7 boys choosing
girls. The same holds true in the case of criterion V involving intellectual ability (12 boys selecting girls and 30 girls selecting boys),
criterion VII embodying adventure (15 boys selecting girls and
38 girls selecting boys) and criterion VIII embodying the need of
security and protection (14 boys selecting girls and 36 girls selecting
boys). As against this, in criterion VI, which can be described as

embodying the need of sympathy, 33 boys selected girls and 15 girls selected boys.

TABLE III

PERCENTAGE DISTRIBUTION OF CHOICES ON BASIS OF TEN CRITERIA

	Pupils Present	Outsiders	Pupils Absent	No answer
I. Companionship	69	27	4	—
II. Same Interest	66	29	4	1
III. Intimacy	65	29	4	2
IV. Practical Ability	63	29	5	3
V. Intellectual Ability	63	27	6	4
VI. Sympathy	63	29	5	3
VII. Adventure	63	30	5	2
VIII. Security and Protection	59	34	4	3
IX. Sociability	63	28	5	4
X. Sportsmanship	71	25	3	1

In the formation of groups as revealed by sociograms drawn on the basis of mutually reciprocated choices, there was a general tendency among both the boys and the girls to group themselves on a unisexual basis and where friendly relations existed between members of opposite sex, the findings revealed their unstable and insecure nature. In the essays, most of the boys and girls mentioned having friends of the opposite sex; but the girls were more outspoken and frank in their comments than the boys, and with some of the boys, mostly twelve-year-olds, instances were found not only of lack of interest but of the expression of positive dislike for girls. The dominating motive in such heterosexual friendships appeared to be associated with either physical attractiveness or popularity.

Sociograms of the group revealed the presence of complete isolates, unreciprocated choices, mutual pairs, chains and triangles of the type described by Moreno.[5] When analysed these patterns suggested that popular children tended to enlarge their groups by serving as important inter-links, whereas in exclusive pairs of two or three there might be instances of intimate friendships, whose exclusiveness tended to isolate them from the rest of the group.

Examination of friendly pairs showed that eighty-two boys out of one hundred and thirty-three mutually reciprocated choices on the 'life-long friendship' criterion and formed fifty-six pairs among themselves, whereas eighty-four girls out of one hundred and nineteen formed sixty-five pairs among themselves. The girls seemed to be more homogeneous than the boys. Only eleven pairs out of fifty-six pairs of boys were of an intimate nature, whereas in the case of girls twenty-three pairs out of sixty-five claimed intimacy.

The reciprocations among the friendly pairs on the basis of the ten criteria tended to show that all the criteria were relevant and significant during this period (see Table IV). The first three criteria seemed to be of the highest significance among both boys and girls. Among the girls, however, the sixth (sympathy) and the eighth (security and protection) were also important. On the whole, criterion V (intellectual stimulation), VI (sympathy) and VIII (security and protection) seemed to be less popular among the boys' pairs—perhaps indicating that boys during this period do not look to their friends for the satisfaction of these needs as much as girls do. In the case of criterion VII, the slight difference between boys and girls may point to the fact that adventure has no greater appeal to the friendly pairs of boys.

A study of the common interests of these friendly pairs (see Table V) revealed that belonging to the same church or Sunday school, or even club or team, played a very insignificant part in the

TABLE IV

PERCENTAGE OF FRIENDLY PAIRS ON EACH CRITERION

Criteria	Boys' Pairs (56)	Girls' Pairs (65)
I. Companionship	75	97
II. Same Interest	73	78
III. Intimacy	70	74
IV. Practical Ability	63	63
V. Intellectual Ability	59	68
VI. Sympathy	61	72
VII. Adventure	64	63
VIII. Security and Protion.	41	71
IX. Sociability	63	69
X. Sportsmanship	32	38

choice of friends. The fact that most of the friendly pairs had common interests in outdoor games, general reading and film-seeing, seemed to indicate that participating in common sports activities and having similar tastes and interests were probably the main reasons why two pupils were drawn together as friends.

TABLE V

INTERESTS OF FRIENDLY PAIRS

Interests	Percentage of Pairs having Common Interests	
	Boys	Girls
Hobby	39	35
Outdoor Games	88	78
Indoor Games	45	46
General Reading	59	71
School Subjects	41	46
Church or Sunday School	7	20
Club or Team	14	34
Film Seeing	46	68

In the selection of friends, neighbourhood also played an important part. These pupils chose their friends mostly from the same school, or on the grounds that they lived nearby, or that their parents knew the parents of their friends very well. (According to the replies received the parents of about thirty-four pairs of boys and thirty-nine pairs of girls were known to one another.)

The intelligence quotients and mental ages of forty-two pairs of boys and forty-six pairs of girls were available. An examination of the correlations between intelligence quotients and mental ages of pairs of boys and girls (see Table VI) revealed that though the correlation between the intelligence quotients of the friendly pairs of boys was +0·316, it was not high enough to be significant, and could not enable us to conclude that the intelligence quotient played any definite part in the selection of friends by boys. On the other hand, in the case of the girls' pairs, the coefficient of correlation between intelligence quotients was highly significant. (Only 59 per cent of boys' pairs gave mutual choices on this criterion, as against 67·7 per cent of girls' pairs.) The mental ages of the friendly pairs of both boys and girls also correlated significantly. It may therefore be concluded that mental maturity seems to be a significant factor in the choice of friends in this group, and similarity of intelligence also seems to be significant in the girls' choice of friends, but not in the case of boys.

TABLE VI

CORRELATIONS OF INTELLIGENCE QUOTIENTS AND OF MENTAL AGES OF FRIENDLY PAIRS

Friendly Pairs	Intelligence Quotient		Mental Age	
	r_1	F. Value	r_1	F. Value
Boys	+·316	1·61	+·374	2·25
Girls	+·543	3·45	+·451	2·70

To find out whether the ratings of their friends by the boys and girls indicated any significant trend, the value of *chi-square* (χ^2) was calculated in each case from the independence or expected values. The value in the case of boys' ratings came to 36·55, whereas in the case of girls it was 30·27. These values are highly significant.[6] It may be concluded, therefore, that:

(i) the χ^2 values indicated significant departure of the ratings from the independence values;

(ii) on the whole the 'work' traits went with the low ratings and the 'character' traits with the high ratings;

(iii) 'personal' traits seemed to have about the expected values in the case of boys, whereas in the case of girls they went with the high ratings;

(iv) both 'character' and 'personal' traits seemed to be of equal value from the point of view of girls.

Almost all the boys and girls made it clear in their essays that they believed that friendship goes deeper than mere companionship. The best friend was often described as 'somone who you are always with', 'the one liked very much', 'someone next to your own brother and sister', 'someone you can trust' and 'get on best with', 'someone you have known for a number of years', and 'you know exactly how they look upon you as a friend', 'one who shares things together', 'one who sticks by you in danger', 'one who is reliable' and 'backs you up', 'who will not let you down', 'one who likes most things that you like', 'one who is attached to you by affection and esteem', 'one who gets on without any quarrels and arguments', 'one to whom you can always turn for advice or help', 'one whom you choose', and so on.

A companion was described as a person 'that you go with in your work', 'one who sits by you at school or on the bus', 'one you know slightly', 'a person you often meet at school or at a party and enjoy yourself with in a friendly way', 'one you would find it rather difficult to trust or tell secrets', and so on.

In describing their friends boys rarely mentioned anything about the physical appearance of their friends, whereas girls described the physical appearance of their friends in addition to mentioning their other characteristics. The qualities most admired in friends were 'adventure', 'humour', 'sportsmanship', 'generosity', 'kindness to animals', 'sociability', 'respect for parents', 'keeping promises', 'politeness', 'cheerfulness', 'having the same likes and dislikes', 'good looks', 'lovely disposition', 'neatness, tidiness', and so on.

It is evident that intimacy, duration and depth of feeling were thought of as the main characteristics that distinguish true friendship from mere companionship. Friends came together not only because they played the same games or liked each other, but also because they had common likes and dislikes and possessed certain personal qualities which both boys and girls thought desirable. Thus personality traits and motives, as well as physical appearance and activities, played an important part in determining intimate friendships.

A complexity of emotional relationship was revealed when the meaning of 'I love my friend' as given by the children was analysed. The feeling of affectionate friendly love was often closely associated with other feelings of gratitude, appreciation of the friend's nature, deep concern and a desire to be always with the friend. From their statements it is perhaps hazardous to say anything definite regarding the nature of love as understood by these boys and girls. However, in talking of 'loving' a friend of the same sex, these pupils tended to imply friendly devotion and warm feelings. In talking about 'loving' a friend of the opposite sex, they seemed to be aware of a mixed feeling of attraction and affection.

It is also difficult to decide how far this idea of love was identical with a growing sexual urge. One thing that came out clearly from their statements was that they were aware of an intense desire to love and be loved. This love between two adolescent friends is a complex phenomenon which involves their whole personality—their likes and dislikes, their emotional and intellectual characteristics and the degree of attraction and affection existing between them. Beneath the obvious unisexual friendships revealed at about the age of eleven to twelve, the beginnings of heterosexual interests are clearly evident.[7]

The present writer is inclined to think, after analysis of the essays of these children, that though this feeling of love or affection may manifest itself in bodily actions or gestures in some children, nevertheless the very fact of being with the friends they love is in itself a pleasant experience. Their love is social in origin though individual in its manifestations. It seems to be an extension of the same feeling which a child has for his parents, brothers and sisters. It only later acquires a sexual significance as he becomes aware of heterosexual feelings.[8]

During early adolescence these children tended to choose their friends not only from their neighbourhood, that is from the same school and from the families with which their own family was well acquainted, but also because they were alike mentally and physically, and because they more or less resembled each other in tastes and temperament and had the same likes and dislikes. Some examples also tended to show that friendship might exist between two individuals not only on the basis of similarity of personality, but on the basis of mutual understanding and appreciation of dissimilarities as well. The important point to be borne in mind is that whatever might be the type of friendship it served to satisfy the growing needs of children. The need for friendship was indicative of the need for affection and love, the need for security and identification and the need for coping with growing self-consciousness. The type of friends selected depended upon the degree to which the friends would satisfy these needs.

The implications of the above results have obvious relevance to discussions of the problems of school organisation, mental hygiene, and group and individual activities.[9]

Further research might usefully be attempted along three lines.

The characteristics of isolates, exclusive pairs and unreciprocated choices in a group might be studied so as to help them to adjust themselves more adequately to the social life of the school and to discover ways in which they might become acceptable to other boys and girls.

Instances of change in friendships might be investigated in order to discover what influences such changes. (They may be related to pubescence or to variations in social experience and adjustment.) It would also be interesting to study the relationship between the factors that make for friendship and the duration of friendship. (It may be that friendships based on compensatory factors are liable to change.)

An analysis of the various characteristics entering into the formation of friendships at different levels would also be highly interesting. Some children form friendships with very popular children, or with children with superior achievements in academic subjects or sports, or with children having stronger physique than they. In such cases there may be an effort at what might be called 'social climbing'. In some cases this process is reversed—that is, the superior children select friends of inferior achievements. Most friendships seem to be formed among children of the same level and with similar achievements and similar interests. It may be that friendships on the same level indicate stability, whereas on the other two levels they may indicate maladjustment of personality.

REFERENCES

1. FISHER, R. A.
   Statistical Methods for Research Workers. Edinburgh and London: Oliver and Boyd. 1942. (Eighth edition.)
2. GUILFORD, J. P.
   Psychometric Methods. New York: McGraw-Hill Book Co. 1936. Pp. 371–372.
3. SNEDECOR, G. W.
   Statistical Methods. Iowa State College Press. 1940 (Third edition).
4. With this finding may be compared a similar one in:
   HENDERSON, N. K.
   'A Study of Sociability.' Unpublished Ph.D. Thesis. University of London. 1949.
5. MORENO, J. L.
   Who Shall Survive? Washington: Nervous and Mental Disease Publishing Co. 1934.
6. See GARRETT, H. E.
   Statistics in Psychology and Education. London: Longmans, Green & Co. 1947 (Third edition). Table 32, p. 242.
7. For a discussion of the mental state of friendship-love, see:
   IOVETZ-TERESCHENKO, N. M.
   Friendship-Love in Adolescence. London: George Allen & Unwin, Ltd. 1936.

SUTTIE, IAN D.
The Origins of Love and Hate. London: Kegan Paul, Trench, Trubner & Co., Ltd. 1935.

8. In this connection see the discussion of the process leading toward heterosexual adjustment in adolescence as given by:

CAMPBELL, E. H.
'The Social-Sex Development of Children.' *Genetic Psychology Monograph*, 21, 1939, pp. 461–552.

9. See MEEK, L. H.
The Personal-Social Development of Boys and Girls with Implications for Secondary Education. New York: Progressive Education Association. 1940.

PARTRIDGE, E. D.
Social Psychology in Adolescence. New York: Prentice-Hill Inc. 1939.

HOLLINGWORTH, LETA S.
The Psychology of the Adolescent. New York: Partridge. 1928.

TAYLOR, K. W.
Do Adolescents Need Parents? New York: D. Appleton Century Incorporated. 1938.

FLEMING, C. M.
Adolescence: Its Social Psychology. London: Routledge & Kegan Paul, Ltd. 1948.

BIBLIOGRAPHY OF RELEVANT STUDIES OF FRIENDSHIP AMONG CHILDREN

BLANCHARD, B. EVERARD
'Social Acceptance Studies of Pupils in Public Schools', *Journal of Educational Research*, XL, 7, 1947, pp. 503–512.

BONNEY, M. E.
'A Sociometric Study of the Relationship of some Factors to Mutual Friendships in the Elementary, Secondary and College Levels', *Sociometry*, IX, 1946, pp. 21–47.

CATTELL, R. B.
'Friends and Enemies: A Psychological Study of Character and Temperament', *Character and Personality*, III, 1934, pp. 55–63.

CHALLMAN, R. C.
'Factors Influencing Friendships among Pre-school Children', *Child Development*, III, 1932, pp. 146–158.

ELLIOTT, MERLE H.
'Patterns of Friendship in the Classroom', *Progressive Education*, XVIII, 1941, pp. 383–390.

FLEMMING, E. G.
'Best Friends', *The Journal of Social Psychology*, VIII, 1932, pp. 385–390.

FURFEY, P. H.
'Some Factors Influencing the Selection of Boys' Chums', *The Journal of Applied Psychology*, XI, 1927, pp. 47–51.

GREEN, E. H.
'Friendships and Quarrels among Pre-school Children', *Child Development*, IV, 1933, pp. 237–252.

HAGMAN, E. P.
'The Companionships of Pre-school Children', University of Iowa, *Studies in Child Welfare*, VII, 4, 1933.

HORROCKS, J. E., AND THOMPSON, G. G.
'A Study of the Friendship Fluctuations of Rural Boys and Girls', *The Pedagogical Seminar and The Journal of Genetic Psychology*, LXIX, December, 1946, pp. 189–198.

IOVETZ-TERESCHENKO, N. M.
Friendship-Love in Adolescence. London: George Allen & Unwin, Ltd. 1936.

JENKINS, G. G.
'Factors involved in Children's Friendships', *The Journal of Educational Psychology*, XXII, 1931, pp. 440–448.

JENNINGS, H. H.
'A Sociometric Study of Emotional and Social Expansiveness', in Barker, R. G., *et alia*, *Child Behavior and Development*. New York and London: McGraw-Hill Book Co. Inc. 1943.

NORTHWAY, M. L.
'Children with Few Friends', *The School*, XXXII, January 1944, pp. 380–384.

PARTRIDGE, E. D.
'A Study of Friendships among Adolescent Boys', *The Journal of Genetic Psychology*, XLIII, 1933, pp. 472–477.

PINTNER, R., FORLANO, G., AND FREEDMAN, H.
'Personality and Attitudinal Similarity among Classroom Friends', *The Journal of Applied Psychology*, XXI, 1937, pp. 48–65.

POTASHIN, R.
'A Sociometric Study of Children's Friendships', *Sociometry*, IX, 1, 1946, pp. 48–70.

POTASHIN, R., AND FRANKEL, E. B.
'A Survey of Sociometric and Pre-sociometric Literature on Friendship and Social Acceptance among Children', *Sociometry*, VII, 1944, pp. 422–431.

SEAGOE, M. V.
'Factors Influencing the Selection of Associates', *The Journal of Educational Research*, XXVII, 1933, pp. 32–40.

SHUKLA, J. K.
'A Study of Friendship among Adolescents.' Unpublished M.A. Thesis. University of London. 1948.

SMITH, M.
'Some Factors in Friendship Selection of High School Students', *Sociometry*, VII, 1944, pp. 303–310.

VREELAND, F. M., AND COREY, S. M.
'A Study of College Friendships', *The Journal of Abnormal and Social Psychology*, XXX, 1935, pp. 229–236.

WELLMAN, BETH
'The School Child's Choice of Companions', *The Journal of Educational Research*, XIV, 1926, pp. 126–132.

WILLIAMS, P. E.
'A Study of Adolescent Friendships', *Pedagogical Seminar*, **XXX**, 1923, pp. 342–346.

WINSLOW, C. N.
'A Study of the Extent of Agreement between Friends' Opinions and their Ability to Estimate the Opinions of Each Other', *The Journal of Social Psychology*, VIII, 1937, pp. 433–441.

CHAPTER TEN

LEADERLESS DISCUSSIONS BY TWO GROUPS OF ADOLESCENTS

THIS experiment was inspired by the work done by the British Army psychologists with leaderless groups both in officer selection[1] and in group therapy[2] and also by the later investigations of the Tavistock Institute of Human Relations into certain of the intellectual and emotional factors which determine group behaviour.[3]

Its purpose was to study groups of adolescent girls over a period of time with the prerequisite that the experiment should not be purely diagnostic or of interest to the experimenter but that it should meet the conscious needs of the group.

In planning the investigation several tentative hypotheses with reference both to diagnosis and to therapy were suggested, and these are listed below.

(*a*) *Diagnosis*. It was hoped that recordings of group discussions and behaviour would reveal the development of certain trends within the group: (i) the transference of leadership between different members of the group, (ii) the pattern of aggressive and constructive tendencies within the group, (iii) the mechanism used by the group to deal with difficult situations and with obstreperous and dominant members, (iv) and last, the different stages in the formation of what it was hoped would become a cohesive group.

(*b*) *Therapy*. It was also hoped both that the existence of the group would satisfy the girls' conscious wish for group discussion and also that they would achieve a greater awareness of their relationships within group situations. Morris[4] has claimed that the Army psychiatrists made use of the discovery that the function of discussion is the communication of emotions as well as ideas. It was hoped that through being allowed complete freedom of action and being therefore forced to examine their own actions, the individual members of the group might themselves become aware of some of these under-lying forces. Finally it was hoped that this awareness would include a recognition and acceptance of their own social interdependence as members of a group. Lewin[5] in describing adolescence as a period in which there occurs a change of 'group belongingness' claimed that the behaviour of a person depends on the momentary situation, and that the 'space of free movement' for the adolescent is both uncertain and unreliable. It was hoped that the members of these groups would come to use the discussion meetings as a 'space' in which to adjust themselves freely to the developing situation.

The experiment was originally carried out with a group of adolescent girls in the sixth form of a Secondary Grammar School in the London area during the months of May, June and July, 1948. It was then repeated with a group of girls of similar age from a residential Approved School in the same area. Each group discussed a series of topics of its own choice and under the chairmanship of one of its own members over a period of ten to twelve weeks; and the observer functioned only as a recorder, except when her help was really required.

Since discussion was to be the medium, the relation of the experiment to the group had to be considered. Their needs could be met in two ways. The first alternative was to base the topics selected on some issue related to a specific school problem, such as, for example, the strong desire of the school for a house system. This, it was felt, could have been developed into a comprehensive series of discussions as readily as the alternative—the wish to link the activities of the school with those of the community into which pupils were to enter on leaving school. Both issues were important in the eyes of the first group chosen; they were, however, specifically related to that group and might quite possibly have been unsuitable for the other group. The House problem was one which had arisen at a specific period and it might quickly have become meaningless if the needs of the school had altered. It was therefore decided to make use of the second suggestion—to base the discussion on 'topics of importance to the individual and to the community'. It was felt that adolescents with their developing sense of responsibility towards the world in which they lived would find this relevant to their interests.

Individuals in the first group had expressed on several occasions a wish for such discussions; and this, it was hoped, supplied a suffi-ciently conscious need for the experiment to be genuinely 'operational'. This was believed to be of importance. Therapy is as essential as diagnosis; therapy was therefore regarded as an essential constituent of this research, as was the enthusiasm necessary if the group was to function without the direction or encouragement of a leader.

CHOICE OF GROUPS

Since the groups were to be organised on discussion lines and left dependent on their own initiative for action, the choice of groups became important. It was felt that this type of work required a fairly mature approach both intellectually and in the realm of human relations if it was to be of use. The sixth form of sixteen and seventeen-year-old girls was therefore asked to co-operate in the experiment. It was suggested that the discussions would serve the two-fold purpose of supplying an answer to their own demand for discussion and of giving the experimenter an opportunity to observe and to examine group discussions as an educational instrument. Volunteers were therefore called for to attend a series of such groups during their current-events period, each week. Though only nine or ten were desired, fifteen volunteered.

Later, in order to include the study of a group of girls with different social backgrounds and different personal histories, the experiment was repeated with a group of nine to ten girls from a residential Approved School containing in all sixteen to twenty girls. These girls had been attending a current-events class run by a visiting lecturer. The discussions therefore filled a useful gap in the timetable and, though attendance was not voluntary in the same sense as in the Grammar School group, any girl not wishing to attend had perfect liberty to relinquish her place in favour of another. Allocation to the group was from the promotion list, and relieved the participants from housework on Saturday morning. The frustration necessary for a member to leave the group would therefore have had to be great.

DEVELOPMENT AND CONSTRUCTION OF TOPIC LIST

When the group began to meet it was intended to allow them freedom to discuss whatever they wished, if they proved willing to organise their own scheme. It was felt, however, that some direction into which the discussion could be canalised was probably desirable. Topics of importance related to the self and the community were therefore sought for. Students from an Emergency Teachers' Training College were approached and asked to submit lists of topics which they would consider suitable and of interest for the given type of group. These students themselves met and discussed the problems in groups ranging from three to eight in number, the average being six. Eleven groups in all submitted lists of topics, several of which overlapped. The most popular ones on group choice were noted.

Fifty-five topics were then classified under four headings:

(1 and 2) responsibility of the individual to the self and to the State;

(3 and 4) responsibility of the State to the individual and the State.

These were then re-classified on a broader basis of topics related to:

(*a*) individual interests and problems;

(*b*) society including (i) family and school problems, (ii) local community interests;

(*c*) topics related to the State;

(*d*) topics related to Work;

(*e*) topics related to International problems.

From these sub-groups the most popular topics were chosen, so that each contained four or five suggestions making the final list of forty-four topics.

At the first group meeting, each individual received a topic list and voting paper on which they recorded their first ten or twelve choices (in order of preference), a suggestion being given that at least one should come from each group. The observer then analysed these, listing the final choice in order of popularity and returning it to the girls. It was made clear that this in no way tied them to a set plan: they were free to choose, and in fact did choose other topics from the list, or occasionally selected entirely different subjects. The differences between the original choice of topics, and those actually discussed may be attributed to the working of three possible factors —the effect of emotional tensions, the lack of intellectual capacity to cope with the problems chosen, or the inefficiency of a voting system to satisfy the needs of a group, which because it was small always had a large minority. It is more than probable that all three factors had some effect on this lack of agreement between choice and practice.

DEVELOPMENT OF RECORDING TECHNIQUE

Once the groups were convened the problem of how and what to record became a pressing factor. Techniques for recording group sessions were used in early group experiments by Shaw, and later by Potashin, Anderson, Hartley and Lippitt and White. Research at the Western Electric Company also involved the recording of informal interview sessions.[6] Shaw used observers to record as far as possible interesting behaviour and talk within the group sessions, but in the other researches interview forms and observation blanks were evolved which succeeded in categorising various forms of behaviour, action, and discussion; in this way an attempt was made to reduce the errors due to changeability in observers and to counteract the subjective element by more objective procedures. Anderson and Brewer evolved a highly differentiated set of categories. Concerning themselves chiefly with integrative and dominative factors, they achieved a high degree of reliability, but recorded only specific acts of individuals towards each other, and since no effort was made to show the way in which these situations developed or to record the continuous field situation, they sacrificed a complete picture for the sake of examining separate factors. At the Western Electric, although an effort was made to record details, nevertheless what was recorded sprang from the spontaneous discussion and was not dictated by any preconceived idea. Lippitt and White, however, concerning themselves with the whole group situation, used a far more comprehensive technique: using several observers they obtained (i) a quantitative running account of the social interaction, (ii) a minute-by-minute group structure analysis, (iii) an interpretative running account of actions, (iv) a continuous stenographic record, (v) interpretative action of inter-club relations, (vi) an impressionistic write-up by leaders, and (vii) more records of several segments of club life. This, although ideally satisfactory, was totally impracticable in the present experiment, besides removing the observer completely from the field of the experiment, instead of including her as a necessary factor in the group. (It should be explained here that although the observer did not act as an interpreter, nevertheless the presence of the recorder influenced the discussion continually, and produced a certain tension in the group which made its members anxious to know what was going on and critical of their own behaviour.)

Faced with the necessity for recording, the observer felt it imperative to formulate fully the principles underlying her decision to observe the groups rather than the individuals within them. In the first place, the analysis was concerned with the factors and trends within the whole group rather than with the effects of the discussion on individual personality (though obviously the interaction of the two had to be considered); in the second place, the method of recording had to be designed in such a way as to avoid, if possible, the danger of reducing the dynamic situation to a static picture. In the third place, the intra-group relationships, as they revealed themselves in the discussions, were to be examined rather than the changes in attitude which these inter-actions might bring about.

In this respect experience gained by the observer in attempting to record verbatim a series of seminars on Group Dynamics at the Institute of Human Relations showed the value of these reports as a means of describing the group atmosphere. The words might be constructive or aggressive, but the context in which they came could completely alter their meaning. An antagonistic remark could, by the addition of even a few insignificant words, be changed into an encouraging one. It was felt that this atmosphere was the most valuable for considering group behaviour and therefore, at the expense of accuracy and complete records, an effort was made to obtain a verbatim report of each discussion. This method is, of course, open to the criticism that it is subjective. That assessments based on these observations are even more subjective is also true: yet what was finally recorded did provide a wealth of material in a live setting and indicated certain trends within the group. The possibility of validating such a technique or obtaining the reliability of the observations was carefully considered but finally discarded. The changing behaviour in each group session and the fact that the observer was a part of the group made any attempt at developing a split-half or test-re-test reliability impossible. Several techniques including those developed by Barker, Dembo and Lewin, were, however, considered. All that can be stressed here is that errors due to the variability in the record did exist, but in the overall picture of the situations certain factors were felt to be worth considering. As a sequel of the original reports a more systematised analysis was developed, again dependent on individual assessment. This can best be understood in relation to a sample verbatim report taken from the discussions of the second group.

KEY TO VERBATIM REPORTS AND CHARTS

Symbols		Words abbreviated	
→	through, towards	v	very
|·|	between	gp	group
∴	therefore	ag, ag^n	aggression
∵	because	+ve	positive
i.e.	that is	−ve	negative
⊤	under	const^n	construction
⊥	over	thro'	through
⇥	overt aggression	def.	definite
⋲	overt construction	w.i.	with
†	disagree	d—	dominant
PJH.	observer		

VERBATIM REPORT WEEK TWO

(Symbols excluded)

TOPIC:

(i) 'Education of German Youth should be along English lines and methods.'

(ii) 'Parents should have the final influence in the choice of their children's careers.'

JO.: What do you think, Jc.?

JC.: Well, I don't think it should be carried out along German lines in England. . . .

Silence (1)

JO.: Well—why not?

JC.: I thought it was German Methods in England—well, I do think so . . . I don't know. . . .

Silence (2)

JC.: I don't know anything about the subject.

JC. TO JO.: What do you think—you're in the chair, Jo?

EL.: Yes, what do you think, Jo.?

JO.: I don't know . . . Elsie?

Silence (3). *Murmurs—gossip*

EL.: I don't know.

VA. TO JA.: Hitler Youth methods before the war.

JC.: I thought the subject was the other way round.

VA.: Jc.! (scornful).

SH.: They were taught to worship Hitler.

Subject peters out. Silence (4)

JO.: Jc.?

VA. TO JO.: You are supposed to set it going—to express your opinion. Then we can argue against it.

Silence (5)

213

J.—S.—discuss shorthand

JO.: I don't know anything about it.

PJH.: *Well, what are you going to do about it? Change subject?* (sticky— PJH. compelled to direct.)

EL.: Get rid of it.

VA.: Go on to next on list.

VA.: Follow what we've already got—what we've picked.

JA.: Or shall we just pick it out anywhere?

Gp. discussion.—All at once—active aggressive. (*Sh. teaching Jo. shorthand*)

JC.: What is next one?

JO.: No. 12.

PJH.: *Look—quite welcome to scrap everything.*

EL.: No. 16?

JC.: What about number 1 and 19?

VA.: What about a subject we can really talk about?

JO.: No. 16.

GP.: Well, what can we say about it?

MA.: No. 8?

JO.: Ja., what nos. do you say?

JA.: No. 16.

JO.: All right.

JC.: No. 18?

VA.: Well, let's pick a subject for heaven's sake.

JO.: We'll start with No. 18.

JA.: Better than sitting here and saying nothing.

GP.: Don't know gambling.

VA.: Well, it means dog tracks and racing, etc.

GP.: What do we know about it? (Defensive.)

Silence (6)

JA.: What about No. 28?

VA.: Vote for the subject. Come on, Jo.

JA.: You pick. You're chairman.

VA.: Jo., pick out the subject. Last week was one we knew something about and could talk of.

JO.: What about No. 11? (*Parents again.*) Jo., do you agree? If so, we'll start. Ja.? Je.? El.?

JE.: I don't know (Sounded No.)

JC.: Well, we all agree except one.

JE.: Who is the one? I didn't! (Indignant.)

('Parents should have the final influence in the choice of their children's careers.')

JO.: Well, I don't think so, because if the child wasn't happy in her job. . . .

JC.: I agree, too. Parents choose and child definitely wouldn't be happy.

JC.: Mother should have some say in it. Girls choose and mother sees what it's like.

JO.: Child not happy—throws it up in parent's face.

(*Dog barks—Gp. shout 'Jane, shut up'.*)

214

MA.: Supposing girl wanted to do nursing. Well, if mother didn't agree, daughter would be unhappy. Same as Jo. is really.

JA.: Girl or boy wouldn't do a job so well if they weren't interested.

EL.: Some girls like mothers to choose it.

JO.: But if you didn't want to do it.

JC.: Supposing you had wanted to do a job of shorthand and had been made to go in a factory.

JO.: Start you off on wrong road.

JC.: All have choice.

JC.: Mother should have some say in it. Girl could choose and mother see what it is like.

Silence (7)

JO.: What do you think, Va.?

VA.: I don't! Most young people of to-day not interested in what parents think.

JO.: Well if parents' choice they stay away for ever and may get into bad company.

Silence (8). (*Gp. embarrassed.*)

JO.: Je., what?

JE.: I don't know.

JA.: You haven't said anything.

EL.: It's good for the mother as well.

JA.: Mother and father should go for the interview with them.

VA.: Mother can help—encourage you to go to evening schools. It's natural for the mother to want to help you. Both can have an equal say in it.

PJH.: *What happens when girls or boys don't know what they want?*

JC.: Well, parents could suggest.

EL.: They could go to Labour Exchange.

SH.: What about training?

JO.: There are evening classes.

(*Gp. feeling this is what I want.*)

VA.: Well, if you want to go in for Art or Dramatics you have to go to college!

SH.: Agree.

Silence (9). (*Murmurs—Feeling of inadequacy.*)

JO.: Possible for parents to choose. (Va. cross.)

EL.: Many girls change first job.

PJH.: *Yes, easy to change job, but the same kind because trained, e.g. laundress, secretary.*

SH.: Child could save for her career, but if father is a doctor and wanted son to be one and he didn't want to, then it's wrong.

Silence (10)

JC.: I agree with you, Sh., partly, but if you're set on job, parents should let you do it.

SH.: Yes, but who is going to pay?

JC.: (Explains to El.) Go out and do any job of work.

JC.: If a girl is very interested in a career, she does anything to get it.

EL.: She puts it away in savings.

PJH.: *Do you think parents have right to dictate?*

JC.: Yes, to a certain extent.

PJH.: *Why, Jc.?*

Silence (11)

SH.: Parents have brought up child and ought to do so out of respect.

JO.: Disagree.

JC.: No, they shouldn't domineer.

SH.: But if interested girl will save up and get own career.

Gp. discussion

SH.: Factory work is not a career.

EL.: I've enjoyed factory work. Wouldn't do anything else.

MA.: Depends, El.

SH.: Go to factory and never get anywhere—doesn't require anything of you.

Gp.: Forewomen in factory.

JC.: Yes, but forewomen have been there many years.

JO.: They know job thoroughly.

VA.: Don't you think too much choosing of people's jobs in past? Elder son pushed into being a lawyer. Younger son . . . clergy or army.

SH.: Disagree. Younger son would have to go to college for clergy.

VA.: And it doesn't happen now.

VA.: But in those days.

SH.: We're talking about now.

EL.: Well, she's trying to give you a point . . .

JE.: And show what was wrong in past.

SH.: I'm well aware, Je. I'm trying to help.

Laughter

EL.: Come on, Ja. . . .

JE.: She can't say anything if she doesn't think.

Giggles

JO.: Well, I agree with statement.

Silence (12)

JO.: Do you think when girl is fifteen she is old enough to know her own mind?

JC.: No.

Gp. splits up and argues

MA.: Girls do pick own careers now! Well, now they're called up for service like W.A.A.F. and at seventeen, go in for. . . .

SH.: Parents don't care.

EL.: Go in for what, Ma.?

Laugh

JO.: What do you mean, Ma.?

MA.: . . .

Discussion breaks up

SH.: When fifteen they may have an idea of what they want to do. And somebody may give them an idea and they might like it.

EL.: Yes, somebody might suggest being a nurse or doctor.

Gp. giggles (at El. not fully repeating).

EL.: Do you have to pay to train to be a doctor?

EL.: You do learn something with home nursing.

Gp. gets excited.

SH.: Can soon find out whether young girl wants to be·a nurse.

JO.: Yes, they have certain unpleasant jobs to do to begin with, which soon tests their interest.

JO.: When interested you have to take the rough with the smooth.

JO.: Got to take dirty jobs as well.

Gp. breaks up—discusses.

PJH. feels must say something.

Silence (13)

EL.: I'm just saying anything. What do you think, Va.?

VA.: Jo., what do you say?

VA.: Well, I think they should talk with parents.

MA.: Mother usually helps child.

SH.: Disagree.

Uproar

SH.: I'm talking with experience.

VA.: I find it happens in 'poor class' with many children. It's natural for parents to do so.

MA.: I agree.

SH.: Yes, but the same wage all way up.

VA.: But in salary earners, they take interest in their careers—send them to Art Schools, etc.

JA.: Don't know what they want to do.

PJH.: *Two classes with same problem really. Explains.*

Silence (14)

SH.: If parents wanted them to do so and child no feelings, all right.

PJH.: *Time nearly up—settle next week. Bad to chop and change. Choose and make notes beforehand; next one is 44 on your choice.*

VA.: Not 44, I should think Nos. 6 or 27 better.

JA.: No. 17.

VA.: I think it's quite good, or No. 15.

PJH.: *What do you think?*

GP.: 27.

PJH.: *Chair. Ma. Vote, don't argue.*

GP. VOTE: Jc., 5. Ja., 2. El., 2.

Group behaviour was first analysed under the following six headings:

(1) Person.

(2) Type of response.

(3) To whom.

(4) Dominative, aggressive or constructive action.

(5) Leader rôle.

(6) New ideas.

Week: 2. Group: II			Type: Initiate Agree Contradict Repeat	Behaviour of Individuals				Feelings		Topic Attitude	Number of Responses	Participant Rating	New Ideas	Comparison with Last Week
Person	Response	To Whom		Constructive Dominant Aggressive	Leader Rôle	Respond to Silence	Individual to Group	Individual to Individual	Group to Individual					
Va.	+ve −ve	Topic Gp. and Jo.	Leader still dominant	Const.: Ideas but very aggressive	9	1	Gp. aggn. sullen	to aggn. Jc. El. Jo.	+ve Tries to placate	1. Nothing 2. Pro. co-opn. with parents	17	4	5	Less active
Jc.	+ve −ve	Jn. and Gp. El. Ma.	Tried to take initiative	Const. some aggn.	2	4	+ve	Je. aggn. Ma. El. Jc. +ve Sh.	Dependent on her ∴ aggn.	1–2. Mother should have some say	21	4+	5	Same
Jo.	+ve dependent	Gp. Val.	Lack of initiative	+ve Const. in attitude	8	7	+ve	aggn. El. but +ve on whole	+ve but aggn.	1. Nothing 2. Must be interested in job	30	5	3	More active
Sh.	+ve Gave up taking notes	Val.	Critical	Const. but dominant	3+2	2	Dominant	aggn. Val and El. but also +ve Val.	+ve somewhat aggn.	1. Nothing 2. Mother some say	18	4	4	More active
El.	−ve	Jc.	Amplifn. agree	Some const. defensive		3	Antagonistic	aggn. Jo. Jc.	Aggressive	1. Nothing 2. Parents have say (strong)	15	4	3	More active
Ma.	+ve	Va.	Repetitive amplified	Tried to be const.			Defensive Va.	aggn. Je. Sh.	Tolerate but not v. patient	1. Nothing 2. Agrees with Val.	8	3	2	Less active
Je.	−ve	—	Incidental	Const. gp. some aggn.	—	1	+ve	+ve Va. −ve Sh. Jc.	+ve Accept	1. Nothing 2. Nothing	5	2	—	Same
Ja.	+ve	Va.	Repetitive	Some const. action where knowledge and intelligence not needed	—	1	+ve More dominant	+ve Va.	+ve Accept	1. Nothing 2. Parents take part	8	3	2	Same
En.							AWAY							
Gl.							AWAY							
P.J.H.								26 + 5 Includes responses to P.J.H.			122 7		11 22	

218

The complete discussion was re-written under these headings, thus giving the position of the various acts in response to the general situation and indicating whether an individual's action within the group was spasmodic or continual, whilst allowing separate behaviour to be analysed. From this first analysis each individual's behaviour was summarised in an Analysis Chart under the headings:

  (1) Person.
  (2) Response.
  (3) To whom.
  (4) Type constructive or aggressive.
  (5) Responses to silence.
  (6) Leader rôle.
  (7) Feelings of (*a*) individual to individual;
                (*b*) individual towards the group;
                (*c*) the group towards the individual.
  (8) Topic attitude.
  (9) Number of responses.
 (10) Participant rating.
 (11) New ideas and comparison of behaviour.

Numbers 5, 6, 9 and 11 were the sum of an individual's performance in these respects obtained from the first analysis. Two final analyses were then made, firstly of the chairman's behaviour, and secondly of the total group behaviour in terms of

  (1) Number of silences.
  (2) Noticeable laughter, uproar and break-up of the group.
  (3) Changes of subject.
  (4) and (5) Noticeable aggressive and constructive acts.
  (6) and (7) Numbers of leaders and dominators.
  (8) Numbers of participants on a 5-point scale, very active, active, less active, spoke rarely and non-participant.
  (9) and (10) General comments on group feelings and behaviour of the chairman.

After each session the observer also recorded some form of criticism of the group.

INTERPRETATION OF ANALYSIS CHARTS

In the first analysis each person's response was assessed in terms of her positive or negative attitude towards the person or group to

GROUP II   **GROUP BEHAVIOUR**   Analysis Chart II

Week	Silences	Noticeable laughter, etc.	Change of Subject	Noticeable Ag. Act.	Noticeable Constn. Act.	Nos. of Leaders	Dominators	VA	A	LA	SO	NP
										Participators		
I	13	Uproars 2 P.J.H. −4	(4) 26	(13) 15	(9) 42	2	Va. Ma. — 2	1	2	1	3	2
II	14	Breakups 5 Laughs, giggles 4 P.J.H. 6	Uproar (19) 2 22	(17) 18	(11) 27	4	Va. Sh. — 2	2	3	2	1	—
III	20	Breakups 0 Laughs 3 P.J.H. 14	(26) 31	(11) 14	(11) 38	5 (2)	Va. — 1	2	1	3	0	1
IV	14	Breakups 1 Laughs 3 P.J.H. 4	(34) 59	(41) 55	(16) 61	5 (3)	Gl. — 1	3	2	1	0	0
V	21 24 3	Breakups 6 Laughs 7 P.J.H. 14	(21) 40	(24) 40	(15) 42	7 (3)	Va. Gl. El. — 3	2	1	5	0	0
VI	12	Breakups 4 Laughs 2 P.J.H. 5	(16) 34	(34) 28	(14) 30	6 (4)	Va. Ma. Ja, Jc, Gl. — 5	1	2	4	0	0
VII	11	Uproars 8 Laughs 6+ P.J.H. 4	(15) 4046	(40) 48	(22) 40	Whole gp. 8 (4)	Sh., Va. Ja., El. En, Jo. — 6	2	2	4	0	0
VIII	8	Uproars 7 Laughs 4 P.J.H. 8	(18) 3650	(22) 30	(19) 37	4 (+ 1)14	El. Ma. Sh. — 3	(1)2	1	2	(1)	0
IX	7	Uproars 3 Laughs 3 P.J.H. 6	(29) 3877	(43) 47	(28) 53	8 (Chief 4)	Sh. Gl. Va., Jo, Ma. — 5	3	4	1	0	
X	9+	Uproars 2+2 Laughs 6 P.J.H. 6	(22) 4185	(38) 48	(28) 45	Whole gp. 8 (4 main)	Va. (vd.) 1 Jc., Jo. }4 En. (once), Ja.	1	4	1	1	0
XI	N.B. 2 20 mins. only	Uproars 9 Laughs 5 P.J.H. 3	—	(21) 24	(16) 19	5 (2 main)	El. Jo. Va. — 3	1	1	2	3	1
XII	2	Uproars 5 Laughs 9 P.J.H. 8	—	(21) 21	(15) 35	5 (2n)	Va. Jo. Ma. — 3	2	2	2	1	1
XIII	6	Uproars 1 Laughs 3 or 4 P.J.H. 8	(18) 34	(15) 16	(13) 19	3 (1)	Va. — 1	1	1	2	2	—
		P.J.H 8	( ) Complete change of subject	( ) Overt aggn.	( ) Overt constn.							

Participant Ratings

VA—Very active.
A—Active.

LA—Less active.
SO—Spoke rarely

NP—Non-participant.

whom she was speaking. The response was then considered more fully as to whether it was that of a supporting rôle, or one in which the individual assumed the initiative, contradicted or disagreed with the other person. The emotional content of the response was then considered at two levels—conscious and unconscious. On interpretation, if it showed constructive or aggressive action this was recorded, in the fifth column; if, however, the observer, whilst collecting the verbatim report, was at the time conscious of aggressive or constructive acts, this was recorded symbolically on the verbatim report by the side of a person's name as follows:

$\rightarrow$ or $agg^n.$ signifying aggression (overt level).

$\in$ constructive act (overt level).

These admittedly were assessed partly on the atmosphere at the time of recording, and to distinguish them from those assessed for the first analysis of the verbatim report they were classified as overt, constructive or aggressive acts. In deciding whether any individual had assumed the rôle of Leader, the observer considered both the nature of her contribution and the response of the group to that contribution. An effort to guide the discussion into more worthwhile channels, or a remark calling the group to order would be considered, for example, an act of leadership. The fact that many of the new ideas and amplifications of old ones were valuable contributions to the group effort, though often not solely constructive, decided the observer to include a final category, New Ideas.

The second analysis was an attempt to take a cross-section for each individual of this longitudinal study, besides making a general assessment of behaviour on each of the categories referred to in the first analysis. An effort was made to gauge the attitude of each individual towards the group and towards other individuals in the group, where this showed in discussion. Responses to periods of silences and efforts to continue conversation in these circumstances were regarded as worthy of recording. The sum totals of the individual responses to new ideas and the assumption of leader rôles were also noted, in the hope that they would indicate the general behaviour of the individual. Since the total number of the responses for the whole group and for individuals varied considerably from week to week a participant rating on a 5-point scale was also introduced, and general comments were made on each individual's behaviour from week to week. This rating had five categories: (1) 'Very active', (2) 'Active', (3) 'Less active', (4) 'Spoke rarely' and (5) 'Non-participant'. Girls were allocated to these according to the degree and quality of their activity, the points 5, 4, 3, 2, 1 representing the given categories.

Once each individual's behaviour had been analysed, the chart of generalised group behaviour was obtained, each result being based on the sum total of group behaviour in each category. See Graphs I and II. It is true that these summations were based on subjective assessments which under another observer would have been different, but the actual numerical result was not considered important; what was emphasised was the general level of behaviour reached and this the observer felt was indicated by the numbers. It did not matter whether there were thirteen or fifteen silences one week and only eight or nine the next week. What did matter was that a considerable change in behaviour had occurred and this, it was felt, was recorded by these numbers with a fair degree of accuracy. Finally, comments on Group and Chairman behaviour were also assessed by the observer.

The Chairman's behaviour report, whilst embodying the second analysis, was concerned with the rôle of chairman from week to week as well as with the individual performing it. Such aspects as (1) whether the chairman was participant or withdrawn, (2) whether she was constructive, dominant, or laissez-faire, (3) what direct responses were made to the rôle, were all considered and assessed. From these analyses and from the observer's report a wealth of material was obtained, which, it must once more be stressed, was used always in the knowledge of the possible errors due to recording and to subjective assessment.

In this way both individual and group behaviour was represented from week to week. For each individual, frequency graphs showing the New Ideas, Responses to Silence and to Leadership, and the total number of responses per week were constructed. For the group, frequency curves showing the different types of participant ratings, group behaviour and Chairman behaviour were also made.

Actiongrams. From the overt aggressive and constructive acts recorded, actiongrams were planned—one for each discussion period for each group. The individuals were represented symbolically as in the sociograms, in their circular seating order of the given week. A line with one arrow from A to B indicated an act of aggression from A towards B. The total number of arrows indicated the total number of aggressive acts occurring during the discussion. A similar method

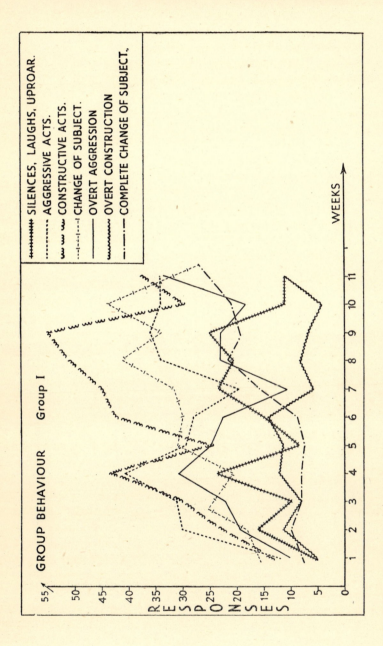

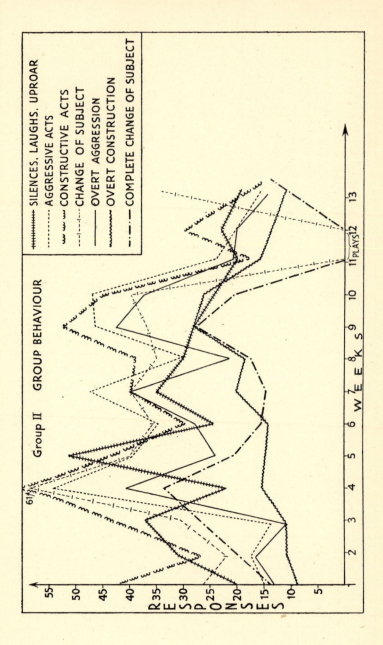

CHAIRMAN BEHAVIOUR

Analysis Chart III

GROUP II

Week	Chairman	Nos. of Responses	New Ideas	Constructive Laissez Faire Dominant	Participant Withdrawn	Direct Responses to Rôle	Summing up	Attitude to Group	Group to Chair	Comments
I	Va.	50	15	Constructive; v. dominant	Participant (very)	15	Attempts	+ve underlying superiority	Follow; +ve	V(a) as +ve and made definite efforts to take gp. with her. Sulked when attacked at end.
II	Jo.	30	2+1=3	Laissez faire; some attempt at constn.	Participant	(Some v. weak) 9	Definite act, but weak	Desire to direct; lack capacity	Follow; required more of her	Jo. did not take initiative till urged by gp. Seemed dependent on Va. and sensitive to her sullenness. Was quick to say do this and that when suggested.
III	Jc.	28	9	Fairly construc-tive	Willing parti-cipant; lacked ability	8	No attempt, but P.J.i.H. re-sponses	Desired to direct and express own views	Agreed with	Took Initiative as long as had own views to express. 'Was killed by observer'.
IV	Gl.	52	11	Dominant; not very const.	Participant	Many but poor	Tried, but lacked ability	Aggressive (in-stance)	Became agg. as result of attack	Directed gp. by attacking members; used Ma. as scapegoat to hide own lack of ability to express self.
V	En.	16	2	Laissez faire; tried	Participant; lacked ideas	11	None to begin with; vague effort when urged	Lacked effort	Aggressive; en-joyed discom-fort	En. lacked completely power to lead and group took advan-tage of this.
VI	El.	23	4+	Laissez faire, except to boss	Participant; lacked ideas	8	Vague attempt after Ja. had done it	-ve; dominant	Tolerated	El.'s thinking weak. Unsure of her own authority. Unwilling to act in silences.
VII	Ja.	25	6	Dictator, leader; const. when forgot	Participant; too hurried to think to begin with	12	Summed in mid-dle not at end	+ve on whole	+ve; but lacked control	Ja. lacked ability to begin with, but in due course became const., then ceased to lead and direct; unable to do both.
VIII	Jc.	27	2	Attempted to direct, but was not supported	Participant	10	No attempt, but asked question	-ve; agg. when prompted	Group react in end	Lacked ability to take initiative when no ideas. Made no attempt to control uproar.
IX	Je.	25	4	Fairly laissez faire; const.	Participant	6	No attempt though asked	-ve	Lack of ideas; otherwise re-sponded	Je. was willing to express own views, but not willing to take initiative otherwise.
X	Ma.	28	11	Const.; initiative	Participant; produced ideas	11	No opportunity; no attempt	+ve, but very defensive	Tended to bully, lacked respect	Ma. was quick and willing to assume lead. Inability to express herself clearly resulted in self-inferiority, made for aggres-sion.
XI	Va.	11	2	Laissez faire	-ve	2	None	-ve; aggressive	-ve; irritated with lack of guidance	N.B.—Probably personal relations outside gp. affected her; not keen on play. Took no part or resp. in. gp. Did not exert herself.
XII	En.	13	4	Const.; not leader	Participant	2	—	+ve; interested	—	Took part willingly, but did not lead.
XIII	Va.	26	15	Const.; at-tempted to lead	Participant	10	Summing up ex-pressing own view	+ve; directed	Followed, but unwilling to ex-press feelings	1. Gp. not prepared to face issue at all. Thus quibbled over words.

with dotted lines and arrows was used to indicate constructive acts. Since several acts of aggression were directed towards the group as a whole and towards the observer, the latter in her seating position was represented by the symbols P.J.H. in a circle or square, whilst the former was represented by the symbol GP.

In Group II a tendency for individuals to band together in attacking, or for one person to show aggression towards two or more group members at once, occurred in the later sessions. This was represented on the actiongrams by thicker lines joined together, arrows at the junctions indicating the direction of behaviour. Furthermore, as the observer was obliged to aid this group occasionally in its discussions these acts of direction were represented by a line and arrow towards the group (see Actiongram I).

It was hoped that these pictorial representations would give a more dynamic picture than a sociogram concerned purely with expressed desires. Inability to show the sequence of events, however, does reduce it to a somewhat static picture. Where one girl A attacked another girl B and was at a later date attacked by this same girl B, the sequence of events was indicated by the numbers 1, 2 as follows in Fig. 1. If, however, the action seemed to be mutual or

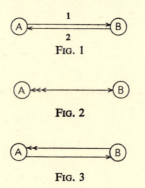

Fig. 1

Fig. 2

Fig. 3

the period between the actions was not long, then either single or double lines without suffixes were used (see Figs. 2 and 3).

A table of distribution of overt aggressive acts and one showing the total number of overt constructive acts were also prepared. (It should be stressed that the overt aggressive and constructive acts assessed were those which the observer consciously recorded at the

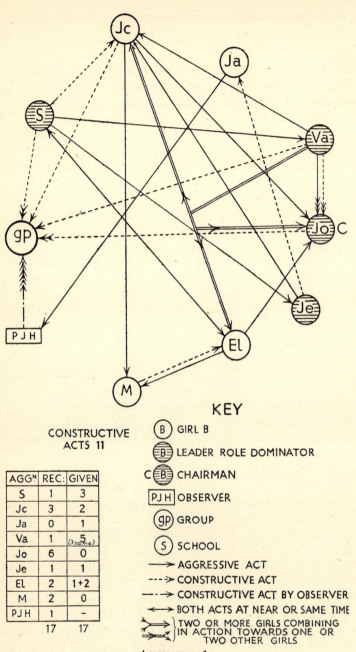

KEY

CONSTRUCTIVE
ACTS 11

AGGⁿ	REC:	GIVEN
S	1	3
Jc	3	2
Ja	0	1
Va	1	5 (3 same)
Jo	6	0
Je	1	1
El	2	1+2
M	2	0
PJH	1	-
	17	17

Ⓑ GIRL B

Ⓑ LEADER ROLE DOMINATOR

C Ⓑ CHAIRMAN

[PJH] OBSERVER

⑨℗ GROUP

Ⓢ SCHOOL

⟶ AGGRESSIVE ACT

----→ CONSTRUCTIVE ACT

—·—·→ CONSTRUCTIVE ACT BY OBSERVER

⟵⟶ BOTH ACTS AT NEAR OR SAME TIME

⟹ } TWO OR MORE GIRLS COMBINING
⟹ } IN ACTION TOWARDS ONE OR
       TWO OTHER GIRLS

ACTIONGRAM 1

Group II, Week 2. Topic 1. Re-education of German youth: Topic 2. Parents
should choose their children's careers

227

time of the discussion and not those which were determined afterwards.)

A Sociometric Test was also given to both groups based on ten criteria, all chosen in an attempt to determine the social structure of each group. It was hoped that these sociograms with the records of behaviour would make up a clear picture of each individual's social status within the group, as well as give an overall picture of the structure and social maturity of both groups—the extent to which each group showed a differentiation between the psychegroup and the sociogroup being taken as a sign of the degree of social integration within the group.

The ultimate form of each test satisfied only one of Moreno's two conditions for a Sociometric Test,[8] and they can be interpreted only in the light of this fact. The tests were constructed in relation to particular criteria with a view to determining the feelings of the individuals towards each other in connection with each criterion. They were therefore asked to choose associates for a particular task or occupation, and no choice was invited purely in respect of friendships.

Moreno also stipulates that the criteria should have meaning for the subject. To the extent that all the criteria chosen were from real life situations well within the possible experience of each girl, this condition was satisfied; but, nevertheless, since it was known that no actual attempt would be made to alter their environment as a result of their answers, a certain reality and incentive was missing. The purpose of the Test in the eyes of the group was weakened, and a certain lack of interest due to this had to be considered when examining the results obtained. Both groups did, however, respond well; Group II in particular finding the 'reality' of the situation greater than Group I.

The choice of criteria was based on an analysis of the social situations in which the subject might find himself, the factors considered being study, leisure, sociability, leadership, difficulty and co-operation. As far as possible the school environment was used, and each individual was asked to choose three people with whom she would like to (a) work, (b) organise a school activity, (c) organise a social activity, (d) go on a holiday, (e) take with her when visiting strangers, (f) go to in case of danger, (g) go to when in difficulty for help and advice, (h) and (i) work under when organising in-school and out-of-school activities, and (j) keep in touch with outside of school. The last criterion was taken to indicate a choice of more lasting friend-

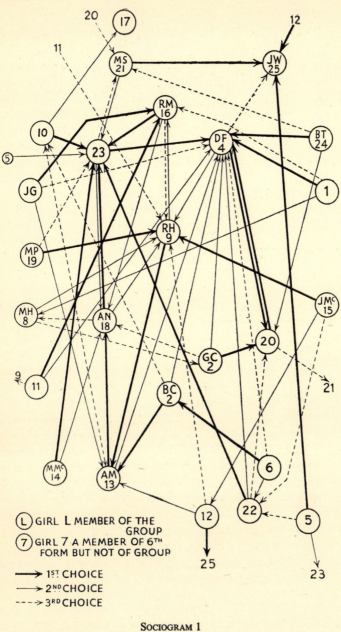

GIRL L MEMBER OF THE GROUP

GIRL 7 A MEMBER OF 6ᵀᴴ FORM BUT NOT OF GROUP

→ 1ˢᵀ CHOICE

→ 2ᴺᴰ CHOICE

---→ 3ᴿᴰ CHOICE

SOCIOGRAM 1

Group I, Criterion 2 (1). Co-operation in school activities

229

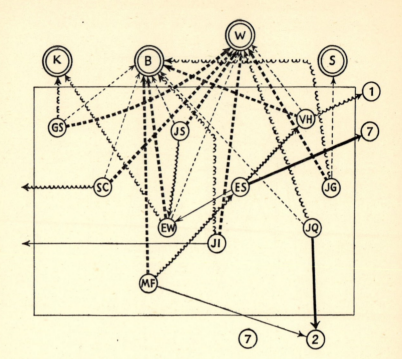

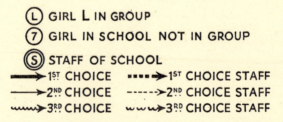

(L) GIRL **L** IN GROUP
(7) GIRL IN SCHOOL NOT IN GROUP
(S) STAFF OF SCHOOL

━━━━▶1ST CHOICE   ■■■■▶1ST CHOICE STAFF
━━━▶2ND CHOICE   -----▶2ND CHOICE STAFF
ᴡᴡᴡ▶3RD CHOICE   ᴡᴡᴡ▶3RD CHOICE STAFF

CHOICES OUTSIDE	2
CHOICES OUTSIDE GROUP	4
CHOICES IN GROUP	4
CHOICES TO STAFF	20

SOCIOGRAM II
Group II, Criterion 2 (1). Co-operation in School Activities

230

ship. The girls of Group I had, through youth clubs and community groups outside school, opportunities to lead a completely separate life if they so wished. In Group II, on the other hand, the girls came from all over the country and only genuine friendship would make them keep in touch with one another; moreover, such acquaintanceship as might have developed between them would probably be less permanent as a result of being associated in their minds with a period of control.

Group I was composed of girls who were already members of several overlapping, well-defined units, whereas Group II belonged to no such clearly defined structures: unlike Group I it had no previous knowledge of the observer, and was not free to take part in the life of the local community. Group I as a group felt able to depend on its contemporaries for most of the relationships which might affect the lives of its members, and had an average I.Q. above normal. Group II, on the other hand, had little trust in its peers and tended to lean on staff for guidance and support, its average I.Q. being below that of average intelligence.

Two charts, one for each group, were constructed to show as far as possible the factors which could have influenced the different discussions. In Group I these were divided into four sections, two dealing with the school and home structures of which this group was a cross-section, and two with the permanent and momentary factors which might have influenced the discussion. Where tension and, to a certain extent, antagonism were known to exist between the different groupings, these were indicated by lines and arrows. Three factors listed in this last section need comment: they refer to (a) the recorder's relationship with several of the girls who had been in her form the previous year; (b) the recorder's relationship with two of the girls to whom she taught mathematics; and (c) the automatic division of the group before the meeting into those who had been to swimming and those who had not. The chart shows clearly the multiplicity of groupings within the group and its position within the school and the local community; at the same time it represents diagrammatically some of the factors which were affecting the overt level of the discussion.

In Group II the division was somewhat different: since in their conversation the girls distinguished clearly between their in- and out-of-school lives, the factors influencing the discussion were first divided under these two headings and then subdivided into momentary

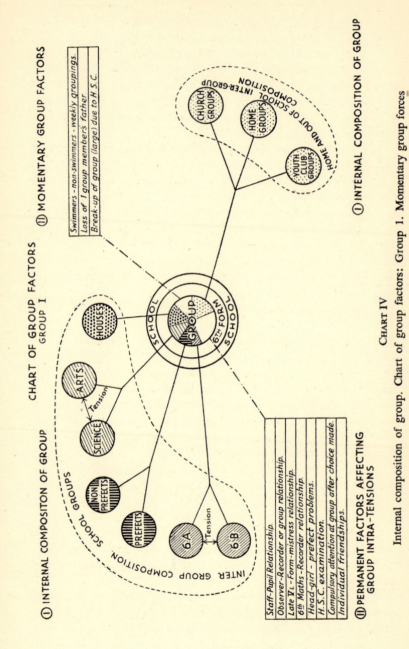

CHART OF GROUP FACTORS
GROUP I

① INTERNAL COMPOSITION OF GROUP

② MOMENTARY GROUP FACTORS

Swimmers – non-swimmers – weekly groupings.
Loss of 1 group member's father.
Break-up of group (large) due to H.S.C.

① INTERNAL COMPOSITION OF GROUP

② PERMANENT FACTORS AFFECTING
GROUP INTRA-TENSIONS

Staff-Pupil Relationship.
Observer-Recorder or group relationship.
Late VI. -Form-mistress relationship.
6th Maths -Recorder relationship.
Head-girl - prefect problems.
H.S.C. examination.
Compulsory attention at group after choice made.
Individual friendships.

CHART IV

Internal composition of group. Chart of group factors: Group 1. Momentary group forces

232

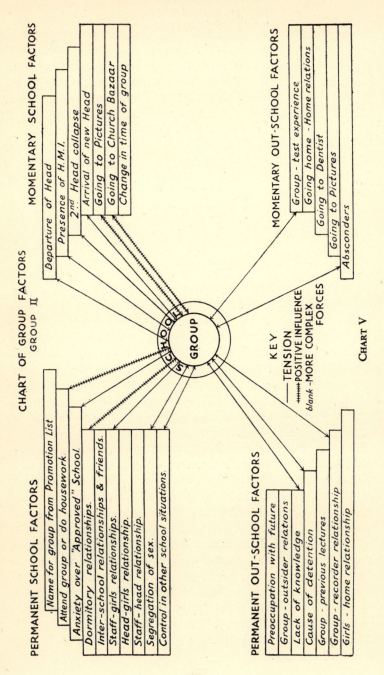

CHART OF GROUP FACTORS
GROUP II

MOMENTARY SCHOOL FACTORS

Departure of Head
Presence of H.M.I.
2ⁿᵈ Head collapse
Arrival of new Head
Going to Pictures
Going to Church Bazaar
Change in time of group

PERMANENT SCHOOL FACTORS

Name for group from Promotion List
Attend group or do housework
Anxiety over "Approved" School.
Dormitory relationships.
Inter-school relationships & friends.
Staff-girls relationships.
Head-girls relationship.
Staff-head relationship.
Segregation of sex.
Control in other school situations.

SCHOOL

GROUP

MOMENTARY OUT-SCHOOL FACTORS

Group - test experience
Going home - Home relations
Going to Dentist
Going to Pictures
Absconders

KEY
———— TENSION
+++++ POSITIVE INFLUENCE
blank - MORE COMPLEX
FORCES

PERMANENT OUT-SCHOOL FACTORS

Preoccupation with future
Group - outsider relations
Lack of knowledge
Cause of detention
Group - previous lectures
Group - recorder relationship
Girls - home relationship

CHART V

233

and permanent factors. Those which were permanent were regarded as existing during the whole experiment, and those which were momentary, only at certain periods of the discussion. It will be seen that those producing tension were numerous, and as the meetings proceeded the observer became more and more aware of the existence of these factors behind the scenes. It was for this reason that the discussion that developed on the 'Ideal Approved School' was felt to be of value to the girls, since in it they were able to make conscious their thoughts and opinions on several issues, such as detentions, absconders, the departure of the Head and their own anxiety over being in school.

COMPARISON OF ACTIONGRAMS FOR GROUPS I AND II

GROUP I

In the early sessions of this group the charts show comparatively little overt aggression or construction. In *Week* 1 several individuals neither gave nor received any such acts: all the five constructive efforts were directed towards the group as a whole. In *Week* 2 this positive action was increased and, while the pattern on the whole was similar to that of the previous week, MMc. was at the same time more aggressive herself and more frequently the victim of aggression than anybody else in the group. She still remained the focal point for this hostility during the following meeting, and was herself attacking one individual fairly consistently. More girls were by then involved in these intra-group relationships and only three girls did not participate. In *Week* 4 the activity increased still further, and attacks on the observer were recorded for the first time. MMc. met less opposition, but she herself was more belligerent. JW. in particular suffered from her attack, and also received as chairman marked attacks from the rest of the group. Neither of these girls contributed in a constructive way to the discussion. A number of other girls began to dominate the group and, moreover, made all the constructive efforts towards the group which were recorded for that session. *Week* 5 showed a decline in the number of girls involved in these interactions; JW. met less antagonism, and the group as a whole continued to receive constructive efforts and help. RH. and RM. formed with MMc. a triangular group structure which showed both aggression and excited hostility.

In *Week* 6 there was an increase in both types of reaction: four constructive acts were directed towards RM.; on the other hand, she and MMc. suffered more aggression than anybody else. The group activity seemed to be centred on these two girls and on RH. and JW., and attacks on the observer were again noticeable. In *Week* 7 both types of reaction decreased again and the group split into two factions.* In the *following week* MS. received a concentrated attack from the group, and from JW. in particular, but this was tempered by the constructive efforts of several other girls. The group in general was more active, and with this keener participation came an increase in both constructive and aggressive behaviour, the first now being directed towards individual girls as well as the group. In *Week* 9 the girls again divided into small groups which left RH. isolated in spite of her active participation. MMc. after her absence again became the centre of aggression and was victimised more frequently than she had formerly been. MS. on the other hand, after the group's reaction the previous week, was no longer the object of attack, while DF., in spite of being chairman, maintained a similar inactive rôle. For the *final two weeks*, when the membership was reduced to six, the pattern of behaviour differed considerably. In the first of these meetings there was much aggression and constructiveness between MS., RM. and JW. Two of the remaining three took no part in this activity: the third, JMc., interacted with MS., and so participated to some extent in the activity. In the last meeting complete interaction occurred for almost the first time in the series between all members of the group.

GROUP II[1]

As in Group I, constructive acts in the early meetings were mostly directed towards the group. From *Week* 2 onwards the girls tended to combine in joint acts of aggression towards one or more individuals, and such acts became very marked in *Weeks* 6, 7, 8 and 13. Both the number and distribution of both kinds of action varied from week to week, as did the number of observer contributions. *Week* 3 was noticeable for the large number of constructive acts compared with aggressive acts; yet its actiongram revealed less activity than the previous ones. In *Week* 4 more individuals attacked

---

* This lack of positive and negative reaction is interesting when it is remembered that the group when discussing the topic on marriage appeared to be avoiding all emotional issues.

each other—not once but many times—and the resulting pattern was close-knit and resembled that of *Week* 11 in Group I. Constructive acts radiated towards the group in *Week* 5, but the girls on the whole showed fewer reactions to one another. In *Week* 6 several girls were particularly constructive towards the group, but there was a marked increase in aggression especially towards Va. and El. The action pattern for *Week* 7 was similar to that of *Week* 6. More girls combined in pairs to attack one another; and more constructive acts were directed towards the observer than in previous meetings. Va. was attacked only once, but there was an obvious antagonism between El. and Sh. In *Week* 8 Jc. as chairman was victimised and the aggressive influence of both Sl. (one of the visitors) and El. was shown by the number of paired actions in which they participated. The *ninth* discussion brought about a higher degree of interaction between the girls than any other of the series: many constructive acts towards the group were recorded; there was some indication of hostility towards the school and to the observer, but no individual in the group was made the object of excessive aggression. In *Week* 10, when still discussing the same subject, Va. became very aggressive towards Jo. and Ma., and was herself attacked by the rest of the group; the school, on the other hand, received support and approval in the course of the discussion. The charts for *Weeks* 11 and 12 show a decrease in both types of reaction: in the eleventh week Jo. acted constructively and Va. was attacked; in the twelfth, Jo. was attacked and both Va. and Ma. individually and the group as a whole were constructive towards Ja. Finally, in *Week* 13, there was a reversion to paired acts of aggression and a sudden increase in the observer's participation.

Compared with that of Group I, the behaviour of this group formed more complicated and inter-related patterns, and all the girls reacted more frequently to one another and to the group. When the subject of discussion was of real interest and the girls felt free to discuss it (as in Group I Week 11, Group II Week 9) the actiongrams revealed a very even distribution of activity, but when discussion appeared inhibited by other factors (as in Group I Week 7 and Group II Week 3) there was little interaction. When compared with one another the charts indicate that in spite of weekly variations there is a general tendency for the patterns to increase in complexity and for the actions to become more evenly distributed amongst the girls as the time goes on.

SUMMARY OF GROUP INTERPRETATIONS

The members of Group I were well acquainted with the observer before the meetings began, and this probably affected their anxiety over her note taking and lack of participation. Earlier experiences in discussions had also led them to expect guidance and staff help, so that to begin with certain behaviour patterns had to be modified, and this produced tension within the group. As time went on, techniques were developed for dealing with difficulties and opportunities for testing out the observer and group members occurred: different individuals, such as MMc., attempted to manipulate the group, which reacted to these efforts in such a way that both aggressive and constructive acts became more frequent. The increase in such acts, the greater speed of discussion and the variety of aspects considered, also showed the steady development of internal group relationships and suggested that individuals were beginning to respond more naturally. This was especially noticeable later when the group was reduced in size. The reactions both of the girls and observer in any one group session were felt to be affected by the incidents which had occurred the week before, and by the absence of certain individuals: the observer's frustration at certain periods might have been a reflection of the group's anxiety to make her take part in the discussions. The ability of any one chairman to produce fresh ideas and direct the group, and the manner in which the group responded to her action, were found to have an important bearing on the development of the discussion.

The topics themselves often presented difficulties which individuals had not considered when originally choosing them. Thus certain subjects might require more factual knowledge than the members had, and nobody would appear willing to assume responsibility for acquiring it. At other times when the topics were related to personal issues the girls seemed unwilling to discuss them and so failed to probe into them deeply.

The behaviour appeared to be affected on the one hand by the group structure shown in the sociograms, and on the other by the relationships existing outside the group.

In Group II the discussions as a whole were centred on the immediate experiences of the group, and tended to fail or disintegrate when attempts at generalising or considering deeper issues were made. The group was very concerned with the influence of parents on their children, and this subject cropped up in many of the earlier discussions. Dogmatic statements on the right behaviour for parents and a general emphasis on the parents' responsibility seemed to suggest an underlying concern with their own lack of satisfactory home relationships. During the earlier discussions the group was concerned with saying the 'right thing' and creating the 'right impression', and anxiety showed every time a member 'let them down'. As time went on the girls became more sure of themselves and began to test the observer and to show concern over the recording. This often took the form of questions after the discussion, about the observer's reasons for coming and the purpose of her note taking. Their concern with their own position still showed in the refusal to refer directly to their own school and in their veiled queries about that of the observer. This testing out of her and the aggressive behaviour towards her reached a climax in one week when a new Principal arrived and appeared to be partly influenced by this outside insecurity.

The behaviour of the group was felt to be decidedly influenced by the day-to-day relationships which occurred outside the group. On arrival the observer invariably sensed an atmosphere of co-operation or lethargy: some individuals would be active and others would take no interest. During the discussion the unco-operative girls would sometimes begin to respond, so that at the end the group would appear more united and active. It was evident in the group meetings that emotional feelings were always near the surface and ready to be released: whilst repetition and amplifying of ideas was developed by the girls as a technique for prolonging and maintaining discussion.

The discussion of the subject of Approved Schools developed at an interesting stage in the life of the group. It was held, not as was usual on Saturday morning, but on a Sunday evening at the end of a comparatively free day, which probably influenced the ensuing discussion. Similarly, certain happenings in the school had caused the girls a great deal of concern and anxiety. This was released in the discussion in which the girls gave an immediate constructive response to the school. Finally, their appreciation of the efforts made on their behalf by the observer on this day was probably partly responsible for their willingness to co-operate in the unfinished plays during the last two weeks of the session. These two plays provided the group with fresh difficulties at a period when they were beginning to develop cohesion, but this cohesion itself probably helped them to tackle the acting of the plays and to adjust themselves to this new situation.

The final discussion showed an end of group feeling. Members were unwilling to get down to the subject and reverted to old techniques for dealing with difficulties. The personal element in this topic, as in the earlier discussion on marriage, caused some anxiety.

In general, two kinds of participation appeared—the regular steady participation of Jc., Je., Ja. and Ma., and the very active but spasmodic participation of Sh., Va., Jo., Gl., and El. The group quickly made the chairman play a specific rôle, and cheerfully transferred responsibility for the discussion to her. Yet in these very situations each individual learnt to some extent to depend on her own reaction and came to realise that the group, too, was dependent on each of its members.

Details of the verbatim report, actiongrams and chart for the ninth week of Group II are given below for comparison with those shown earlier.

GROUP II

VERBATIM REPORT. WEEK NINE

TOPIC:

    (i) Coal should not be used for luxury purposes when it is mined under such conditions of danger and discomfort.

    (ii) The Ideal Approved School.

GP. *in an excited giggly mood.*
PJH.: *Well, will you act as Chairman? (To Je.)*
JE.: Yes, but I don't know anything about subject.
JA.: What does luxury mean?
SH.: Well, you need coal for household purposes.
JA.: What does luxury mean?
JC.: Doesn't it mean . . .
MA. (dominant—rowdy): Well . . .
JE.: Definitely people need it in the home.
JA. (giggly): Well, a luxury to have it in three rooms, I suppose.
Group laugh (1)
GL. (dominant): Not much use.
JE.: What do you think about it, Ma.?
MA.: I like to feel a good fire.
JO. (dominant): I don't think it should be used for luxury.
JE.: I do.
JO.: I don't. Come on, Gl. Let's fight.
GL.: While sitting round fire.
JA.: Oh, I disagree (aggressive).
JO. (excited and dominant). (*Sh. taps pencil.*)

239

JC.: Sh., don't; I don't like it.

JO.: After all: should use it for output.

MA.: Same thing. Oh, I wish . . .

JC.: In country they can't use other things, except for cooking.

MA.: Oh, you silly little thing!

JO.: I disagree, should only use it for output.

MA.: Same thing. Oh, I wish . . .

JC.: In country they can't use other things, except for cooking.

MA.: Lots of people use kitchen ranges.

JE.: Not on subject.

JC.: Well, you often see people going to wharfs to get their own coal.

Semi-silence (1)

Gp. semi-embarrassed by this ('sign of class').

JO.: Ain't somebody going to argue?

GL.: What do you really call a luxury.

JE.: Here! I'm not chairman. Well, Va., what do you think?

VA.: Well, they have to go down mines for the coal.

Gp. uproar and laugh (2)

Gl. scorn.

VA. (defiant): Always something to say.

TH.: Oh well, I shall say anything.

JE.: Some like it—going down mines.

JO.: Cost of coal.

Gp. discusses.

GL.: They pay 4s. 8d. cwt.

SH.: Oh! Oh dear! (*Giggles*)

MA.: Well, they get 5 cwt. a month.

Gp.: That's a lot . . .

MA.: Houses down our way are large anyway.

VA.: I thought yours was a prefab.

JA.: One person talk at a time. I suppose fires in cafés—call that a luxury.

SH. (facetiously): Well, you need a fire in a café. I do.

Laugh (3)

JC.: I don't think that should be allowed.

SH.: Well, what also do they use coal for?

JO.: Puff-puffs!

Gp.: Shut up

Silence (2)

JC.: They use them in copper works.

MA.: They use coal in factories, too.

PJH.: *I think by luxury they mean, should one use coal in private homes when we could use electricity, etc., which can be got without such discomfort and danger.*

JC.: Well, what about cuts in electricity?

SH.: That only comes with warning.

VA.: Well, it is usually in paper.

JE.: We were not warned last night.

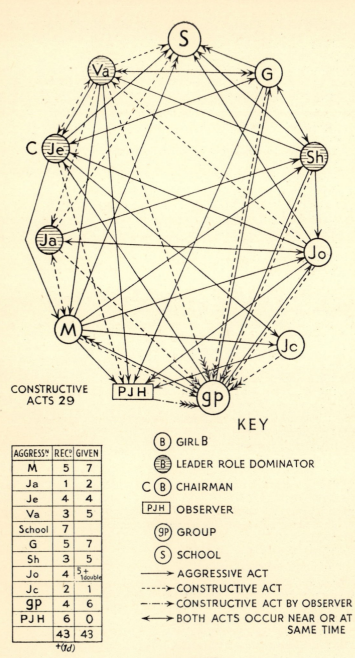

CONSTRUCTIVE
ACTS 29

AGGRESS^N	REC^D	GIVEN
M	5	7
Ja	1	2
Je	4	4
Va	3	5
School	7	
G	5	7
Sh	3	5
Jo	4	5 + 1double
Jc	2	1
gp	4	6
PJH	6	0
	43	43
+(1d)		

KEY

Ⓑ GIRL B

Ⓑ LEADER ROLE DOMINATOR

C Ⓑ CHAIRMAN

[PJH] OBSERVER

ⓖⓟ GROUP

Ⓢ SCHOOL

⟶ AGGRESSIVE ACT

----⟶ CONSTRUCTIVE ACT

—·—⟶ CONSTRUCTIVE ACT BY OBSERVER

⟷ BOTH ACTS OCCUR NEAR OR AT
SAME TIME

ACTIONGRAM II

Group 11, Weekly, Sunday Evening: Topic 1. Coal should not be used for
luxury purposes; Topic 2. Ideal Approved School

241

VA.: It wasn't a cut but a fuse.

JE.: Oh, I didn't know.

GL.: We'll be singing carols soon.

Silence (3)

MA.: That is what I was thinking.

Gp. giggles.

JE.: Anyone else anything to say?

Gp. argues.

JO.: *Laughs* and argues loudly off subject of coal.

JC.: Jo., stop it.

JE.: That's nothing to do with the subject.

VA.: Well, why don't you say your own point of view?

JE.: I haven't got one; I don't know anything about it.

MA. (dominant): Talks about glasses.

JE.: Who is talking about glasses?

JA.: Look, Ma., be silent.

JO.: Jc. hasn't said much.

MA.: What about Sl.?

Silence (4)

MA.: She don't know anything about it. Men get called up for mines.

JA.: What about those six women working in mines now?

VA. (sulkily): Not half so dangerous nowadays, and with colleges, and they do get paid for it.

SH.: Yes, they have proper trained men and machinery.

Silence (5)

MA.: Some mines still dangerous.

SH.: Besides, they don't think about danger, and it is voluntary.

Enter Subwarden. Silence (6)

PJH.: *What about scrapping List and discussing subject of your own?*

GP.: Yes (*agree quickly*).

JC.: C. Lodge. *Laugh* (4)

GL. (dominant): Oh, let's keep right away from that. Wonder why we can discuss freely in dormitory and not here?

VA: Well, you can say exactly what you think in dormitory.

Gp. smiles, look at PJH.

PJH.: *Meaning you cannot discuss here openly?* (*Attempt to put unspoken thoughts into words, but no attempt to deny it.*)

JO.: Well . . .

MA.: What subject shall we have?

JE.: Approved schools.

GP.: C. Lodge.

MA.: What people could do. What about this school?

JO.: No, don't whatever we do talk about this school.

JA.: What about school leaving age?

GL.: We've had that, haven't we?

PJH.: *It did come into one discussion.*

VA.: Yes, somebody stood on it.

JE.: Well, what subject?

GP.: You're chairman.

GLA. (but dominant): Should people under eighteen be allowed in public houses?

Gp. disagree. Laugh (5)

VA.: They are at sixteen, but cannot drink anything.

GLA. (*laughing*): What do they drink? Lemonade.

VA.: Should think you'd know.

JE.: Keep away from that subject. Let's pick something.

MA.: Talk about knitting! *Laugh* (6)

VA.: Should small children mix in remand homes with older ones?

GP.: No.

GL. (dominant): School. You learn more in a remand home than anywhere else.

VA.: Girl of seven in ours (the one with all the fuss—she was removed).

MA. (dominant): There was a girl of eight at Stanford.

JC. and VA. discuss and argue.

SH.: Oh, forget remand home.

PJH.: *Why not plan your Ideal Remand Home. How it should be run— discipline, freedom, activities, length of stay, etc.*

GP.: Oh yes—do you mean home or approved school?

PJH. *Approved School.*

JE.: That's a good one!

SH.: No uniform in school.

GP.: *Agree strongly.*

JC.: Well, not for girls over fourteen—not in Senior School.

GL.: Girls were up to fourteen years at Kilken house.

JO.: How was it run?

SH.: Young people should be looked after by young people.

MA. (misunderstands).

SH. (explains about staff).

VA.: I think there ought to be a school for older girls than us, not sent to prison after eighteen years.

JA.: Should you be looked after, after you leave here?

GP.: No.

VA.: But the thing is, if I do what I like I'd be back here, so perhaps we ought to have after-care.

SH.: Yes, but before you go from here they shove you around anywhere.

MA.: I think there should be younger staff.

JO.: Only grannies here! (*Laugh* (7))

VA.: But if you get young and inexperienced, girls won't respect them.

GL.: Yes, think they're a lot of saps.

SH.: For head they should be older but not for matrons.

JC.: Agree with Va.

VA.: We had Miss M., and she had to resign in end. Only twenty-two.

JC.: Yes, all the girls would not take much notice.

JO.: Should be about middle age—thirty.

Gp. laugh (8). Query middle age thirty!

JC.: Senior girls should be allowed home once a week.

SH.: Do you think seniority a good thing?

VA. (dominant): I don't think any girl should deal out punishments. Promotion is a good thing.

JA.: Do you think detention is a good thing?

Uproar. Group discuss one girl in school at present.

VA.: You've got to have some sort of a place. It is not a luxury home.

VA.: Miss W. wouldn't have had her here.

GL.: You can't just pat them on the back.

JC.: They wouldn't stay.

VA.: Oh, they're not daft.

SH.: Well, we're talking about the ideal approved school.

VA.: A swimming pool in each home.

MA.: A race course for the girls.

VA.: A what—half bets?

Gp. laugh (9). May explains.

JA.: What about tennis courts?

Uproar.

JC.: I think a swimming bath nice here.

JO.: We're not talking about here.

VA.: I think a girl ought to have a chance of going out to school or college.

JC.: I agree.

JE.: What, to school?

VA.: Lots of girls can't even read.

JC.: Yes, Sl.

VA.: Well, I thought it ought to be compulsory.

SH.: It is no good if you have the best education and don't want to learn.

Silence (7)

JA.: Can't just learn nothing.

VA.: I expect Sh. would be willing to learn.

SH.: Va. doesn't think much of people.

VA.: People just expect them to do it. They look at them twice if they don't.

JE.: Anyway, you can go on learning till the day you die.

PJH.: *Even school teachers could learn more.*

MA.: Like Miss A. said.

VA.: Yes.

MA.: It would be good if one could have education.

JA.: We do have quite a lot of classes.

VA.: Yes, we do have dressmaking, etc., and don't have to be educated to do that.

GL.: Sh. will have a couple of maids.

SH.: I'm not going to marry.

VA.: My old man will have fish and chips. *Laugh* (10)

Silence (8)

SH.: All I want is a parrot. *Group*—Why?

244

VA.: Let's get back on the subject. (*Semi-silence.*) Perhaps a girl could have her own pets. (*Roar of laughter* (11).) Tell you what they should have—a gymnasium.

(*Gp. agree.*)

JE.: I think girls should go out more.

JA.: Well, Dramatics Monday, Wednesday, Thursday, Friday, Saturday. Hardly time.

JC.: What about those who abscond?

VA.: Perhaps time *should* be made longer for absconders.

GL.: Don't look at me.

JC.: Some schools the girls bash the girls up who abscond.

GP.: Don't agree with that.

Silence (9)

JO.: What's a good punishment for absconders?

GP.: ——

MA.: Ignore them for a while.

GP.: Disagree. No.

GL. When I came in they used to do that here. Some wouldn't like it.

VA.: Well, that's a reason for doing it.

GL.: Wouldn't worry me (Va.–Gl. argue).

SH.: Would worry me.

MA.: Promotion list good.

SH.: Yes, if girls rude or insolent can put it in book.

VA. (Agrees).

JO.: Some girls don't mind about it (Gp. argue).

VA.: I tell you what should be taken into consideration—for girls who do go home when it comes to going to the pictures.

GL.: I know a girl with name in book four times and still goes home.

GP. discuss Stella.

VA.: Well, I think it was jolly mean.

JC.: I think girls should be stopped going to flicks as well as going home.

VA.: If a girl doesn't go home she should have special place in going to pictures.

JC.: I've done it myself, but I agree.

MA.: Here, here.

MA.: Look at Janet.

JE.: Girls should go home Sat. Then couldn't go to flicks as well.

VA.: Oh, that's not fair.

JC.: Yes, mayn't be convenient.

JA.: Girls who don't have parents just don't know.

MA.: Gp. (talks) (cuts her out. Reference to Je.)

JE.: I've had visitors twice.

VA.: Yes, but do get parcels. Ja's home far away.

SH.: Why not put her in a school near home.

JE.: Yes, I don't think that's right.

JC.: It's what magistrates do.

VA.: I don't think it's fair. Where I was in Wales one Welsh girl; all rest came from London.

MA.: You know, I think voting for promotion wrong, still that's gone now.

JE.: It's silly now because girl went to flicks and her name was in book.

VA.: But she didn't own up. (Group splits.)

MA.: Netball girls—(Stella issue comes up again) will they go to flicks.

JA.: They would soon have gone against May if it had been her.

VA.: You know what it is. St. is in a clique and she shouts them down.

SH.: How long to stay in approved school?

GL.: 18 months.

GP.: No.

JC.: Six months here.

VA.: Six months in hostel.

JC.: Not as though a discipline school.

JE.: Those who don't behave should be sent away.

SH.: Shouldn't mix types of girls.

VA.: But you can't not do that.

MA.: We've given Miss H. something to talk about.

JC.: Every girl's a different type.

(PJH.: *Interested—Next Week ?*)

JC.: Do you think it's right to be in dormitories or cubicles?

MA.: Both.

VA.: Every girl should be allowed privacy.

GL.: Yes, popping under curtains pinching clothes.

SH.: Even bathrooms not private.

(GP. discuss.)

VA.: Sh. never allowed in approved school.

PJH.: *Finish next week. Or would you rather think of something fresh ?*

GP.: We'll think.

JC.: And will you too?

The sociograms of this group, as illustrated by that on co-operation in school activities, revealed a surprising dependence on their adult teachers, many of the choices going to the staff of their school; a fact which did not once occur in the Grammar School group. (See pages 229, 230 above.)

Answers to an attitude questionnaire on social responsibility also showed a high range of scores, practically identical with that of the Grammar School. (On the record card filled in by the Approved School authorities, some of these girls were not assessed as having such a sense of responsibility.) This dual attitude was also noted in several discussions and led the observer to conclude tentatively that the members of this group were very conscious of what was a correct approach to life and verbally convinced themselves of their belief in it. By a process of reconciliation unknown to the observer they also accepted other standards and feelings in relation to themselves in

CHART VI

Week 9, Group II			Type: Initiate Agree Contradict Repeat	Behaviour of Individuals				Feelings		Topic Attitude	Number of Responses	Participant Rating	New Ideas	Comparison with last Week
Person	Response	To Whom		Constructive Dominant Aggressive	Leader Rôle	Respond to Silence	Individual to Group	Individual to Individual	Group to Individual					
Sh.	+ve −ve	Gp.	Facetious	Constructive at times	7	0	Unhelpful then helpful	agg^n. Jc.	−ve		26	4	12	Abs.
Va.	+ve	Gp.	Initiative	Constructive leader	10+1	1	−ve 1st topic +ve 2nd topic	+ve Ja. agg^n. Jn.	+ve		48	5+	21+	Abs.
Jc.	+ve −ve	Gl gp. P.J.H.	Repeat	Constructive towards end	2	2	Excitable and facetious	−	agg^n.		22	4	3	Abs.
Je.	+ve	Gp. Ja.	Constructive amplifier	Leader	5	1	+ve but unwilling to lead	−	+ve but agg^n.		25	4	4	Abs.
Ja.	+ve +ve	Gp. Ma.	Constructive	Constructive	4	2	+ve	+ve	+ve gp.		16	3	9	Less, but more thoughtful
El.							ABSENT							
Ma.	+ve +ve	Gp. Ja.	Dominant	Constructive	2	0	+ve but dominant	−	agg^n.	−	33	5	6	Same
Gl.	−ve	Gp.	Loud Vulgar	Disruptive Dominant Aggressive	3	−	Negative Facetious Dominant	agg^n. Je.	agg^n.	−	26	4	6	Less
En.							ABSENT							
Jc.	+ve	Va. En.	−	Constructive	2	1	+ve C. Constructive	+ve Val.	+ve	−	30	4+	11	More active
					3 39	7							3 75+2 77	Gp.

NO INTEREST IN 1ST TOPIC VITALLY INTERESTED IN 2ND TOPIC

practical out-of-school situations. As the meetings progressed discussion showed that members gradually became conscious of these conflicting attitudes in themselves, and finally faced up to them and acknowledged their own difficulties.

SUMMARY AND CONCLUSIONS

Statistical analysis of the data confirmed the conclusions drawn from verbatim records and diagrams, etc. Raw scores of the number of New Ideas, Responses, acceptances of Leadership Rôles and responses to silence were obtained by averaging weekly scores. These were compared with Sociometric, Attitude and Intelligence test scores. Rank correlations were determined and the probability levels for these results were found from normal probability tables. A contingency test was also used, based on the Null hypothesis that there was no connection between the two factors compared, χ^2 tables being used to find the significance levels.

In the graphical analysis individual weekly responses were plotted for each girl on the four scores, and these all showed marked similarities in the girls' weekly behaviour. These similarities increased towards the end of the experiment in both groups, but new ideas appeared to circulate more rapidly in Group II where there was also a greater range of total responses than in Group I. The slight U shape of these curves supports the suggestion that the groups experienced a period of insecurity and negative reaction to the observer during the middle phase of the experiment.

Finally, graphs showing the weekly behaviour of the group, the weekly silences, and the behaviour of the chairmen were also constructed.

The conclusions which follow are based on consideration of all this evidence.

This experiment developed into an examination of group and of individual behaviour under certain controlled conditions. The extent of this control was theoretically not great, and was implied in the three facts: each group was presented with a list of topics, and the girls were told that they were free to choose their own subject and to organise themselves as they wished: both groups met for between thirty and forty minutes, though Group II sessions were usually a few minutes longer than Group I; and both experienced the recording of the observer. Practically, the experiment was controlled even more by the acceptance of the form of behaviour and topic list suggested by the observer, though Group I was more willing to take the initiative in deciding its future behaviour than was Group II, who relied continually on the observer for direction. As the experiment proceeded the study of the group behaviour was found to go hand in hand with the study of the individual girl's behaviour and needs, and most especially in Group II it was felt that therapy was going hand in hand with diagnosis. This therapy was itself a function of the group behaviour and was related to the observer only in the fact that girls came to feel that the discussions were worth while.

Certain trends in group behaviour were noted for both groups: the first sessions appeared as a period of anxiety in which the members of the group were not altogether happy with their freedom from the direction and guidance of the observer. This was followed by a period of less activity and of dissatisfaction with the discussion, but the activity soon increased again. (The phenomenon referred to here is indicated by the slight U-shaped appearance of the sets of graphs showing individual weekly behaviour.) During the discussions, aggressiveness and constructiveness towards each other and the observer varied, but tended to increase when the discussion was active and satisfying. Both individual and group activity changed considerably from week to week, and the response to any topic was felt to depend not only on the subject chosen, but on the external and emotional factors influencing the girls' lives. In Group II the effect of the departure of their old Principal and the arrival of the new one, of permission to visit the cinema or a church bazaar, of the return of three absconders, and of the girls' daily relationships with other girls and staff was plainly noticeable in the moods of the members themselves and of the group as a whole. Group I also reflected this, though to a lesser extent, probably because the school community did not form such a big factor in their lives. Although several girls made very poor responses as chairmen, yet the graphs of their behaviour show that every girl did increase her number of responses on these occasions; this signifies that an effort (often not noted and recognised by the observer) was made. Topics directly related to the experiences of the girls proved the most fruitful, and the meetings appeared to be used by both groups to discuss their own problems (Group I, Week 11, Group II, Weeks 9 and 10), and towards the end of the sessions each group constructively helped individual girls;

thus Group II responded to Ja. and Je. in Week 10, and Group I to RM. in Week 11.

At different periods in the discussions both groups focused their attention on scapegoats (RM. Group I, Week 1; Ma. Group II, Week 4); several girls tended to dominate the group, and these appeared capable of affecting the atmosphere; thus MMc. in Group I and Va. in Group II had a marked influence, and on occasions they received considerable aggression. The group sometimes divided into smaller units which gossiped and rebelled against the larger unit, but this was more noticeable in Group II. The leadership of both groups was often transferred from one girl to another as the discussion progressed, and four types of chairman behaviour were found: Laissez Faire, Dominant and Constructive, Aggressive, and Constructive but not Active.

Several techniques were developed for dealing with difficulties, and the girls continually used silences and gossiping and often related personal experiences as a means of dominating the discussion. On the other hand, they also avoided those issues in a topic which might have a personal relevance to themselves: thus Group I pointedly stressed the legal aspect in a discussion on marriage, and would not consider responsibilities within the school when discussing Responsibility and Moral Standards; in several discussions Group II talked about the rights and responsibilities of parents, but never once with respect to their own parents. Repetition of statements in different words and often by means of a particular example was used by individual girls, especially in Group II to prolong conversation, and neither group was willing to prepare beforehand for the discussion. They both appeared perturbed by the presence and activities of the recorder, but this anxiety occurred at a later stage in Group II than in Group I. The democratic system of voting did not satisfy any of the girls: Group I twice continued to discuss a problem after a vote or expression of group opinion, while Group II openly criticised the system although it continued to use it.

It was noted that in discussing the same topics the two groups showed certain similarities and certain differences: in discussing marriage, they both concentrated mainly on the legal aspect; in discussing the education of German Youth, each found that it lacked sufficient information to tackle the question fully: on the topic of Sunday Cinemas Group I stressed the religious aspect and Group II the social aspect; whilst on the question of Domestic Science each group emphasised the factor which concerned it personally (Group I the examination issue and Group II the problem of compulsion). Both postponed raising the important topics until the end of the experimental period: Group I, who wanted to discuss Sex Education, unfortunately was unable to meet; Group II discussed the Church, but without much thoroughness. (This, the observer felt, was probably due to an 'end of the group' feeling.)

Finally because Group II was smaller than Group I all its members participated: at the same time the active participation of the observer was more frequent in that group than in Group I, because, though the quantity of discussion here was greater, the girls had more difficulty in dealing with intellectual problems. The statistical analysis of the different responses indicated that all forms of verbal activity and participation showed positive correlations which were significant.

THE USES OF THIS RESEARCH

These groups were 'leaderless' only in the sense that they were not directed by someone outside the group, but the leadership did rotate from person to person within it and they could therefore be used in diagnosis and in the training of both pupils and teachers.

As a diagnostic instrument the group discussion technique reveals very clearly a person's relationships to the rest of the group, her popularity, her ability to co-operate and to get on well with others, her capacity for organising and assuming the leadership of the group at different times and her willingness to assume responsibility; furthermore, the response of the group to the leadership and direction of the individual is also shown. The graphs plotted also give a continuous analysis of an individual's behaviour over a period of time and in changing conditions. The actual discussions were found to be of use in amplifying the record card, especially on such questions as co-operation, sociability and relationships to others, and also revealed differences in attitude which were often not conscious.

In the analysis of group behaviour, the recordings give a continuous picture from week to week. Actiongrams show activity within the group, and these could be extended to record other types of responses besides construction and aggression. Thus initiative and repetition could also be symbolised on charts, though it would be advisable to have separate charts for the different pairs of factors.

In the training of pupils the value of these groups was threefold: they offered a medium in which co-operation and working with others was a necessity and where individuals were placed in such a position that the majority had to take action. Nearly every girl as chairman was sooner or later forced to deal with others, to attempt to direct the group and to assume responsibility for its functioning. Finally, the difficulties which were encountered in these discussions had to be dealt with by the group and not by the observer, and this situation seemed to develop a keener awareness of these difficulties and to force individuals to make decisions.

For the training of teachers it is suggested that the technique could be used in two ways—through observation of a group and through participation in a group. The investigator found that observing the activity without participating in it provided a vivid experience, in which the right moment for direction and help was clearly seen; in contrast to this, the teacher, when participating in corporate action, is often too busy to realise and to note this time objectively, with the result that guidance and direction may be given too often or not often enough. Secondly, if students themselves participated in such a group, with no specific leader on whom to depend, and if at intervals they were to try to determine what was happening within the group, they would through this experience become aware of the extraneous forces which influence group behaviour and so become better prepared to consider them when participating in other groups. The emphasis in such training would be on the experience gained rather than on explanation and description. Both these techniques could be tried out in training colleges, by groups of students observing and participating in such projects.

FUTURE RESEARCH

Underlying this experiment has been the question of accurate recording. The observer felt that the recorder should be a part of the group, since in this way the atmosphere was experienced, even though as a group member in particular situations she was compelled to participate with resulting inaccuracy in the records. Assessments of constructiveness and aggressiveness were also based on the actual situation, and certainly if an attempt is made to consider the unconscious forces influencing a group, then the recording must be made by people and not by machines alone. This does not belittle the use of dictaphones or the Interaction Recorder[9] but stresses the need for supplementing these records. Moreover, such machines are not always available to those doing research, and the suggestion is made that where possible two people, and not one, should be responsible for the records: that whereas one should remain within the group the other should be removed from it though able to observe it, and that final assessments of the different types of behaviour should be based on their joint decision. In this way errors in recording could be reduced if not fully removed.

As a result of the difficulties which both of the groups experienced in dealing with some discussions, it is suggested that a similar examination of group behaviour could be carried out with practical situations. These would have to be clearly defined and limited: thus, for example, 'The making of a doll's house' could form the basis of a group activity, provided the materials—a wooden box, nails, tools and other necessary requisites—were made available, or the planning of a party or visit to some place of interest. Such projects would have to be carried through to completion, and the whole series of meetings should be planned to have some relation to each other. These two factors are of importance if the group is to achieve any feeling of group-belonging and continuity.

Whatever the medium used, there are certain issues arising from this research which could be enquired into more closely—for example, the transference of the rôle of leader to different group members in any one discussion, the influence of out-group forces and emotional factors on group behaviour, the development of aggression and construction and the different rôles (such as the scapegoat) within the group. Many of the trends and techniques observed in this experiment need to be carefully and fully analysed for several groups, drawn from different communities, from different age ranges and from both sexes. The task of observing several groups could be dealt with by a team of research students, working in pairs, and planning, as a group itself, the scope of the research; after the data were assembled, each individual could himself concentrate on one particular aspect of group behaviour, and so at one and the same time participate in real group research and provide his own specific contribution.

In this new field of research different types of tools are useful only as data on which to base interpretation of a complete picture. The investigator must recognise the fact that he cannot remain outside this picture: his activity is influenced by the group he studies as the group is influenced by him. Spontaneous interaction between people is an essential part of such an experiment and thus places a greater responsibility on the research worker, who must ensure that each person gains something from the experiment. The possibilities of research into these fields of human life are numerous and fascinating, and the results should enable communities to understand better how to live in harmony.

REFERENCES

1. SUTHERLAND, J. D.
   'Some Sociatric Lessons from Officer Selection', *Report to the General Meeting of the British Psychological Society*, December 6th, 1945.

2. BION, W. R., AND RICKMAN, J.
   'Intra-Group Tensions in Therapy', Abstract from *The Lancet*, November, 1943, p. 678.

   BION, W. R.
   'Experiences in Groups', *Journal of Human Relations*, Vol. I, Nos. 3 and 4, 1948. Vol. II, Nos. 1 and 3, 1949.

3. JACQUES, E. (Ed.)
   Journal of Social Issues, Vol. III, No. 2. 'Interpretive Group Discussions as a Method of facilitating Social Change', *Journal of Human Relations*, Vol. I, No. 4, 1948.

4. MORRIS, B.
   'The Psychology of Group Discussion', in the *Speech Fellowship News Letter*, No. 38, 1948.

5. LEWIN, K.
   'Field Theory in Social Psychology', *American Journal of Sociology*, XLIV, May, 1939.

6. For these references see bibliography below, pp. 255–261.

7. BARKER, R. G., DEMBO, T., LEWIN, K.
   'Frustration and Regression', in Barker, R., Kounin, T. S., and Wright, H. F. (Ed.), *Child Behavior and Development*. New York: McGraw-Hill Book Co. 1943.

8. MORENO, J. L.
   'Who Shall Survive? A New Approach to the Problem of Human Inter-relations', *Nervous and Mental Disease Monograph Series*, No. 58. Washington, D.C.: Nervous and Mental Disease Publishing Co. 1934.

9. BALES, R. F., AND GERBRANDS, H.
   'The Interaction Recorder', *Journal of Human Relations*, Vol. 1, No. 4, 1948.

SHORT BIBLIOGRAPHY RELEVANT TO GROUP DISCUSSION

(*a*) MONOGRAPHS

ANDERSON, H. H., AND BREWER, H. M.
'Dominative and Socially Integrative Behavior of Kindergarten Teachers, *Applied Psychology Monograph*, No. 6, June 1945.

ANDERSON, H. H., AND BREWER, J. E.
'Effects of Teachers' Dominative and Integrative Contacts on Children's Classroom Behavior', *Applied Psychology Monograph*, No. 8, July 1946.

ANDERSON, H. H., AND BREWER, J. E., AND REED, M. F.
'Follow-up Studies of the Effects of Dominative and Integrative Contacts on Children's Behavior', *Applied Psychology Monograph*, No. 11, December 1946.
'Studies of Teachers' Classroom Personalities, I, II and III', *Applied Psychology Monographs of the American Association for Applied Psychology*. Stamford University Press. 1945–46.

BRONFENBRENNER, U.
'The Measurement of Sociometric Status, Structure and Development', *Sociometry Monograph*, No. 6. Beacon House Press. 1945.

JENNINGS, H. H.
'Sociometry of Leadership: based on the Differentiation of Psyche-Group and Sociogroup', *Sociometry Monograph*, No. 14. Beacon House Press. 1947.

MORENO, J. L.
'Psychodramatic Treatment of Performance Neurosis', *Psychodrama Monograph*, No. 2. New York: Beacon House Press.
'Spontaneity Test and Spontaneity Training', *Psychodrama Monograph*, No. 4. New York: Beacon House Press.
'The Theatre for Spontaneity', *Psychodrama Monograph*, No. 3. New York: Beacon House Press.
'Mental Catharsis and Psychodrama', *Psychodrama Monograph*, No. 6. New York: Beacon House Press.
'Psychodrama and Therapeutic Motion Pictures', *Psychodrama Monograph*, No. 11. New York: Beacon House Press.
'Psychodrama and the Psychopathology of Inter-Personal Relations', *Psychodrama Monograph*, No. 1. New York: Beacon House Press.
'Live Situation Test', *Psychodrama Monograph*, No. 20. New York: Beacon House Press.
'Sociometry and the Cultural Order', *Sociometry Monograph*, No. 2. New York: Beacon House Press.
'Group Method and Group Psychotherapy', *Sociometry Monograph*, No. 5. New York: Beacon House Press.
'Psychological Organisation of Groups in the Community', *Sociometry Monograph*, No. 12. New York: Beacon House Press.

MORENO, J. L., AND MORENO, F. B.
'Spontaneity Theory of Child Development', *Psychodrama Monograph*, No. 8. New York: Beacon House Press.

MORENO, J. L., AND JENNINGS, H.
'Sociometric Measurement of Social Configurations', *Sociometry Monograph*, No. 3. New York: Beacon House Press.
'Sociometric Control Studies of Grouping and Re-Grouping', *Sociometry Monograph*, No. 7. New York: Beacon House Press.

NORTHWAY, M. L., FRANKEL, E. B., AND POTASHIN, R.
'Personality and Sociometric Status', *Sociometry Monograph*, No. 11. New York: Beacon House Press.

SCHMIDT, B. G.
'Changes in Personal, Social and Intellectual Behavior of Children originally classified as Feeble-Minded', *Psychological Monograph*, Vol. 60, No. 5. Washington: The American Psychological Association. 1946.

TOEMAN, Z.
'Role Analysis and Audience Structure', *Psychodrama Monograph*, No. 12. New York: Beacon House Press.

(*b*) EXTRACTS FROM JOURNALS AND BOOKS

ALLPORT, F. H.:
'The Influence of the Group upon Association and Thought', *Journal of Experimental Psychology*, III, 1920.

BALES, R. F., AND GERBRANDS, H.
'The Interaction Recorder', *Journal of Human Relations*, Vol. I, No. 4, 1948.

BARKER, R. G., DEMBO, T., AND LEWIN, K.
'Frustration and Regression', in Barker, R., Kounin, J., and Wright, H. (Eds.), *Child Development and Behavior*. New York: McGraw-Hill Book Co. 1943.

BION, W. R.
'Advances in Group Therapy', *International Congress on Medical Psychotherapy*. London: August 1948.
'Experiences in Groups', *Journal of Human Relations*, Vol. I, Nos. 3 and 4, 1948.

BION, W. R., AND RICKMAN, J. See Rickman, J.

BLATZ, W. E.
'The Individual and the Group', *American Journal of Sociology*, XLIV, May 1939.

BONNEY, M. E.
Editorial to 'Sociometry and Education', *Sociometry*, X, No. 2, 1947.

BONNEY, M. E.
Values of Sociometric Studies in the Classroom, Vol. VI, No. 3, 1943.
Sociometric Study of Agreement between Teacher Judgments and Student Choices, Vol. X, No. 2, 1947.

BROWN, J. F.
'The Individual Group and Social Field', *Journal of Sociology*, XLIV, May, 1939.

DASHIELL, J. F.
'An Experimental Analysis of some Group Effects', *Journal of Abnormal and Social Psychology*, XXV, 1930. (Also in Newcomb, T. N., and Hartley, E. L., *Readings in Social Psychology*, Henry Holt, 1947.)
'Experimental Studies of the Influence of Social Situations on the Behavior of Individual Human Adults', Murchison, C. (Ed.), *Handbook of Social Psychology*. Worcester, Mass.: Clark University Press. 1935.

FESTINGER, L.
'The Role of Group Belongingness in a Voting Situation', *The Journal of Human Relations*, Vol. I, No. 2.

FRASER, J. M.
'New Type Selection Boards in Industry', *Journal of Occupational Psychology*, October 1947. (Reprint.)

GABRIEL, B.
'An Experiment in Group Treatment', *American Journal of Auto Psychiatry*, IX, 1939.

GILLILAND, A. R., AND BURKE, R. S.
'A Measurement of Sociability', *Journal of Applied Psychology*, 1926.

HAMLEY, H. R.
'The Project Method in the Secondary School', *The Schoolmaster and Women Teachers' Chronicle*, December 1st and 21st, 1944.

HARTLEY, R. E.
Sociality in Pre-Adolescent Boys. New York: Columbia University Press. 1946.

HUTTE, H. A. (ED.)
Mental Health in Industry and Industrial Relations. Edited Summary of Reports from the Preparatory Commissions of the International Congress on Mental Health, London, 1948.

JACQUES, E.
'Principles of Organisation of a Social Therapeutic Institution' and 'Social Therapy; Technocracy or Collaboration?', *Journal of Social Issues*, Vol. III, No. 2, 1947.
'Interpretive Group Discussion as a Method of Facilitating Social Change', *Journal of Human Relations*, Vol. I, No. 4, 1948.

JENNESS, A.
'Social Influences in the Change of Opinion and the Role of Discussion in Changing Opinion regarding a matter of fact', *Journal of Abnormal and Social Psychology*, XXVII, 1932.

JENNINGS, H. H.
'Structure of Leadership', *Sociometry*, I, No. 1, 1937. (Also see Monograph).

JORDAN, D. (ED.)
'Group Methods of Education', *English New Educational Fellowship Bulletin* 34, 1946.
'Report of the E.N.E.F. Conference on Human Relations', *English New Educational Fellowship Bulletin*, No. 39, 1946.

KATZ, D., AND HYMAN, H.
'Industrial Morale', in Newcomb, T. M., and Hartley, E. L. (Ed.), *Readings in Social Psychology*. New York: Henry Holt & Co. 1947.

KELNAR, J.
'Treatment of Inter-Personal Relations in Groups', *The Journal of Social Issues*, III, No. 2, 1947.

KING, P.
'Task Perception and Interpersonal Relations in Industrial Training', *Journal of Human Relations*, I, Nos. 1 and 13, 1947, 1948.

LEWIN, K.
'Group Decision and Social Change', in Newcomb, T. M., and Hartley, E. L. (Eds.), *Readings in Social Psychology*. New York: Henry Holt. 1943.
'Psychology and the Process of Group Living', *Journal of Psychology*, XVII, 1943.
'The Research Centre for Group Dynamics at Massachusetts Institute of Technology', *Sociometry*, VIII, No. 2, 1945.
'Field Theory in Social Psychology', *American Journal of Sociology*, XLIV, May 1939.
'Frontiers in Group Dynamics', *Journal of Human Relations*, I, Nos. 1 and 2, 1947.

LEWIN, K., AND GRABBE, P.
'Conduct, Knowledge and Acceptance of New Values', *Journal of Social Issues*, I, No. 3, August 1945.

LEWIN, K., AND LIPPITT, R.
'An Experimental Approach to the Study of Autocracy and Democracy', *Sociometry*, I, No. 1.

LEWIN, K., LIPPITT, R., AND WHITE, R. K.
'Patterns of Aggressive Behavior in Experimentally created "Social Climates"', *Journal of Social Psychology*, X, 1939.

LIPPITT, R.
'Field Theory and Experiment in Social Psychology: Authoritarian and Democratic Group Atmospheres', *American Journal of Sociology*, XLV, 1939.
'Techniques for Research in Group Living', *Journal of Social Issues*, II, No. 4, November 1946.

LIPPITT, R., AND WHITE, R. K.
'An Experimental Study of Leadership and Group Life', in Newcomb, T. M., and Hartley, E. L. (Ed.), *Readings in Social Psychology*. New York: Henry Holt & Co. 1947.
'The "Social Climate" of Children's Groups', in Barker, R., Kounin, J., and Wright (Ed.), *Child Development and Behavior*. New York: McGraw-Hill Book Co. 1943.

JONES, M.
'Group Psychotherapy', *British Medical Journal*, 1942, pp. 276–278.
'Rehabilitation of Forces Neurotic Patients in Civilian Life', *British Medical Journal*, April 1946, pp. 533–535.

MERCER, E. O.
'Psychological Methods of Personnel Selection in a Women's Service', *Journal of Occupational Psychology*, XIX, No. 4, 1945.

MORRIS, B. S.
'The Psychology of Group Discussion', *The Speech Fellowship News Letter*, No. 38, January 1948.
'Education and Human Relations', *Journal of Social Issues*, III, No. 2, 1947.
'Education and Human Relations', *The New Era in Home and School*, XXIX, No. 6, 1948.

MILLER, C., AND SLAVSON, S. R.
'Integration of Individual and Group Therapy in the Treatment of a Problem Boy', *American Journal of Orthopsychiatry*, IX, 1939.

MORENO, J. L.
'Interpersonal Therapy and Psychopathology of Interpersonal Relations', *Sociometry*, I, No. 1, 1937.
'The Philosophy of the Moment and the Spontaneity Theatre', *Sociometry*, IV, No. 2, 1941.

MORENO, J. L., AND JENNINGS, H. H.
'Sociometric Control Studies of Grouping and Regrouping', *Sociometry*, VII, No. 4, 1944. (Also see *Sociometry Monograph*, No. 7.)

MORENO, J. L., AND TOEMAN, Z.
'The Group Approach in Psychodrama', *Sociometry*, V, No. 2, 1942.

MOWRER, O. H.
'Authoritarianism versus "Self-Government" in the Management of Children's Aggressive (anti-social) reactions as a preparation of Citizenship in Democracy', *Journal of Social Psychology*, X, 1939.

NEWCOMB, T. M.
'Some Patterned Consequences of Membership in a College Community', in Newcomb, T. M., and Hartley, E. L. (Ed.), *Readings in Social Psychology*. New York: Henry Holt & Co. 1947.

NORTHWAY, M.
'A Study of the Personality Patterns of Children Least Acceptable to their Age Mates', *Sociometry*, VII, No. 1.

PARTRIDGE, E. D.
'The Sociometric Approach to Adolescent Groupings', *Sociometry*, VI, No. 3, 1943.

POTASHIN, R.
'A Sociometric Study of Children's Friendships', *Sociometry*, IX, No. 1, 1946, and also in *Sociometry Monograph*, No. 11, 1947.

RAPHAEL, W.
'A Study of Some Stresses and Strains within the Working Group', *Journal of Occupational Psychology*, XXI, No. 2, 1947.

RICKMAN, J., AND BION, R.
'Intra-Group Tensions in Therapy: their Study as the Work of the Group', *The Lancet*, November 27th, 1943, p. 678.

REDL, F.
'Resistance in Therapy Groups', *Journal of Human Relations*, I, No. 3, 1948.

SHAW, M. E.
'A Comparison of Individuals and Small Groups in the Rational Solution of Complex Problems', *American Journal of Psychology*, XLIV, 1932. Also in Newcomb, T. M., and Hartley, E. L. (Ed.), *Readings in Social Psychology*. New York: Henry Holt & Co. 1947.

SMUCKER, O.
'Measurements of Group Tensions through the Use of Negative Sociometric Data', *Sociometry*, X, Nov. 1947.

SOUTH, E. B.
'Some Psychological Aspects of Committee Work', *Journal of Social Issues*, III, No. 2, 1947.

SUTHERLAND, J. D.
'Some Sociatric Lessons from Officer Selection', Report to the General Meeting, *British Journal of Psychology*, December 6th, 1945.

SUTHERLAND, J. D., AND FITZPATRICK, G. A.
'Some Approaches to Group Problems in the British Army', in Moreno, J. L. (Ed.), *Group Psychotherapy: A Symposium*. New York: Beacon House Press. 1945.

SUTHERLAND, J. D., AND MENZIES, I. E.
'Two Industrial Projects', *Journal of Social Issues*, III, No. 2, 1947.

WALLEN, R.
'Individual Estimates of Group Opinion', *Journal of Social Psychology*, XVII, 1943 (experiment performed in 1941).

WATSON, G. B.
'Do Groups think more effectively than Individuals?', *Journal of Abnormal and Social Psychology*, XXIII, 1928.

WHEELER, R. D., AND JORDAN, H.
'Changes of Individual Opinion to accord with Group Opinion', *Journal of Abnormal and Social Psychology*, XXIV, 1929.

WILSON, A. T. M.
'Implications of Medical Practice and Social Case Work for Action Research', *Journal of Social Issues*, III, No. 2.

WOODWORTH, R. S.
'Individual and Group Behavior', *American Journal of Sociology*, XLIV, May 1939.

ZELENY, L. D.
'Sociometry in the Classroom', *Sociometry*, III, No. 1, 1940.
'The Value of Sociometry in Education', *Sociometry*, VI, No. 3, 1943.

ZNANIECKI, F.
'Social Groups as products of Participating Individuals', *American Journal of Sociology*, XLIV, May 1939.

See also:

HIGGINBOTHAM, P. J.
'An Investigation into the use of Leaderless Group Discussion on Topics of Importance to the Self and to the Community with a Group of Adolescents.' Unpublished M.A. Thesis.   University of London. 1949.

ROETHLISBERGER, F. J., AND DICKSON, W. J.
Management and the Worker. Cambridge, Mass.: Harvard University Press.

INDEX TO TEXT

263

The International Library of
SOCIOLOGY AND SOCIAL RECONSTRUCTION

Editor: KARL MANNHEIM

Late Professor of Education in the University of London

ADVISORY BOARD: SIR HAROLD BUTLER, K.C.M.G., C.B.; SIR ALEXANDER CARR-SAUNDERS, M.A., Director of the London School of Economics; SIR FRED CLARKE, M.A. (Oxon), formerly Chairman of the Central Advisory Council for Education; LORD LINDSAY OF BIRKER, C.B.E.

PLAN OF THE LIBRARY
Sections

ROUTLEDGE & KEGAN PAUL LTD
68-74 Carter Lane, London, E.C.4

SOCIOLOGY OF EDUCATION

Education after School
by C. STIMSON   *15s.*

Mission of the University
by ORTEGA Y GASSET. Translated and introduced by HOWARD LEE
NOSTRAND   *7s. 6d.*

Total Education: A Plea for Synthesis
by M. L. JACKS, Director, Department of Education, Oxford University
Third Impression. 12s. 6d.

Education in Transition
A Sociological Analysis of the Impact of the War on English Education
by H. C. DENT   *Fifth Impression. 12s. 6d.*

The Social Psychology of Education: A Sociological Study
by C. M. FLEMING, Ed.B., Ph.D., University of London Institute of
Education   *Sixth Impression. 7s. 6d.*

German Youth: Bond or Free
by HOWARD BECKER, Professor of Sociology, University of Wisconsin
Illustrated. 18s.

Education and Society in Modern Germany
by R. H. SAMUEL of the Department of Germanic Languages, Melbourne
University and R. HINTON THOMAS   *12s. 6d.*

The Museum: Its History and Its Tasks in Education
by ALMA S. WITTLIN, Dr. Phil.   *Illustrated. 25s.*

Comparative Education
A Study of Educational Facts and Traditions
by NICHOLAS HANS, Reader in Comparative Education at the University
of London, King's College   *Second Impression. 21s.*

Educational Thought and Influence of Matthew Arnold
by Dr. W. F. CONNELL, with an Introduction by SIR FRED CLARKE
21s.

2

Modern Education in England in the 18th Century

by NICHOLAS HANS, Reader in Comparative Education at the University of London, King's College *About 15s.*

SOCIOLOGY OF RELIGION

Sociology of Religion

by JOACHIM WACH *30s.*

The Economic Order and Religion

by FRANK KNIGHT, Prof. of Social Sciences, University of Chicago, and THORNTON W. MERRIAM, Director of U.S.O. Training, Nat. Council of the Y.M.C.A. *15s.*

SOCIOLOGY OF ART AND LITERATURE

Sociology of the Renaissance

by ALFRED VON MARTIN, translated by W. L. LUETKENS
Second Impression. 8s. 6d.

Chekhov and His Russia: A Sociological Study

by W. H. BRUFORD, M.A., Professor of German in the University of Edinburgh *16s.*

The Sociology of Literary Taste

by LEVIN L. SCHÜCKING, Dr. Phil. *Second Impression. 7s. 6d.*

Men of Letters and the English Public in the 18th Century, 1660-1744, Dryden, Addison, Pope

by ALEXANDRE BELJAME, Edited with an Introduction and Notes by Prof. BONAMY DOBREE. Translated by E. O. LORIMER *25s.*

SOCIOLOGICAL APPROACH TO THE STUDY OF HISTORY

The Aftermath of the Napoleonic Wars: The Concert of Europe—An Experiment

by H. G. SCHENK, D.Phil. (Oxon) *Illustrated. 16s.*

Sociology of Law

by GEORGES GURVITCH, Ph.D., LL.D., Prof. of Sociology, University of Strassbourg, France. With an Introduction by ROSCOE POUND, Prof. of Jurisprudence, late Dean of the Faculty of Law, Harvard University
18s.

The Institutions of Private Law and Their Social Functions

by KARL RENNER, President of the Austrian Republic. Edited with an Introduction and Notes by O. KAHN-FREUND, Ll.M., Dr. Jur., Lecturer in Law, University of London
25s.

Legal Aid

by ROBERT EGERTON, Hon. Sec. Legal Sub-committee Cambridge House, Solicitor of the Supreme Court. With an Introduction by D. L. GOODHART, K.C., D.C.L., Ll.D., Prof. of Jurisprudence, Oxford
Second Impression. 10s. 6d.

Soviet Legal Theory: Its Social Background and Development

by RUDOLF SCHLESINGER, Ph.D., London   *Third Impression. 16s.*

CRIMINOLOGY AND THE SOCIAL SERVICES

Juvenile Delinquency in an English Middletown

by HERMANN MANNHEIM, Reader in Criminology in the University of London
12s. 6d.

Criminal Justice and Social Reconstruction

by HERMANN MANNHEIM, Dr. Jur., Reader in Criminology in the University of London   *Second Impression. 15s.*

The Psycho-Analytical Approach to Juvenile Delinquency: Theory, Case Studies, Treatment

by KATE FRIEDLANDER, M.D., L.R.C.P. (Edin.), D.P.M. (Lond.), Hon. Psychiatrist, Inst. for the Scientific Treatment of Delinquency; Clinical Dir., W. Sussex Child Guidance Service   *Second Impression. 18s.*

Voluntary Social Services since 1918

by HENRY A. MESS, late Reader in Social Science in the University of London in collaboration with Constance Braithwaite, Violet Creech-Jones, Hilda Jennings, Pearl Jephcott, Harold King, Nora Milnes, John Morgan, Gertrude Williams and W. E. Williams. Edited by GERTRUDE WILLIAMS, Lecturer in Economics, University of London   *21s.*

A Textbook of Penology

by HERMANN MANNHEIM   *In preparation. About 25s.*

A Textbook of Criminology

by HERMANN MANNHEIM   *In preparation. About 25s.*

Drink: An Economic and Social Survey

by HERMANN LEVY   *About 21s.*

SOCIOLOGY AND POLITICS

Social-Economic Movements: A Handbook to the Understanding of the Modern Political Scene

by H. W. LAIDLER   *Illustrated. 35s.*

The Analysis of Political Behaviour: An Empirical Approach

by HAROLD D. LASSWELL, Professor of Law, Yale University School of Law   *Third Impression. 21s.*

Dictatorship and Political Police

The Technique of Control by Fear by E. K. BRAMSTEDT, Ph.D. (London)   *15s.*

Nationality in History and Politics

by FREDERICK HERTZ, Author of "Race and Civilisation"   *Third Impression. 25s.*

The Logic of Liberty: Reflections and Rejoiners

by MICHAEL POLANYI, F.R.S., Professor of Social Studies at Victoria University, Manchester   *About 15s.*

5

FOREIGN AFFAIRS, THEIR SOCIAL, POLITICAL AND ECONOMIC FOUNDATIONS

Patterns of Peacemaking

by DAVID THOMSON, Ph.D., Cantab., Research Fellow of Sidney Sussex Coll., Cambridge; E. MEYER, Dr. rer. pol., and A. BRIGGS, B.A., Cantab *21s.*

French Canada in Transition

by EVERETT C. HUGHES, Professor of Sociology, University of Chicago *15s.*

State and Economics in the Middle East

by A. BONNE, Dr. œc. publ., Director, Economic Research Institute of Palestine *30s.*

Economic Development of the Middle East

An Outline of Planned Reconstruction by A. BONNE, Dr. œc. publ., Director, Economic Research Institute of Palestine

Second Impression. 12s. 6d.

The Danube Basin and the German Economic Sphere

by ANTONIN BASCH, Dr. Phil., Columbia University *18s.*

The Regions of Germany

by R. E. DICKINSON, Reader in Geography, University College, London

Second Impression. 10s. 6d.

Political Thought in France from the Revolution to the Fourth Republic

by J. P. MAYER *12s. 6d.*

MIGRATION AND RE-SETTLEMENT

Economics of Migration

by JULIUS ISAAC, Ph.D., London. With an Introduction by Sir ALEXANDER CARR-SAUNDERS, Director of the London School of Economics *18s.*

Co-operative Communities at Work

by HENRIK INFIELD, Director, Rural Settlement Inst., New York

15s.

ECONOMIC PLANNING

Retail Trade Associations
A New Form of Monopolist Organisation in Britain, by HERMANN LEVY, Author of "The New Industrial System" *Second Impression. 15s.*

The Shops of Britain: A Study in Retail Trade Distribution
by HERMANN LEVY   *Second Impression. 21s.*

The Price of Social Security—The Problem of Labour Mobility
by GERTRUDE WILLIAMS, Lecturer in Economics, University of London
                    Second Impression. 12s. 6d.

Private Corporations and their Control
by A. B. LEVY   *Two volumes. 70s. the set.*

SOCIOLOGY OF THE FAMILY AND ALLIED TOPICS

The Family and Democratic Society
by J. K. FOLSOM, Professor of Sociology, Vassar College   *30s.*

Nation and Family
The Swedish Experiment in Democratic Family and Population Policy
by ALVA MYRDAL   *Second Impression. 21s.*

Adolescence
Its Social Psychology: With an Introduction to recent findings from the fields of Anthropology, Physiology, Medicine, Psychometrics and Sociometry
by C. M. FLEMING, Ed.B., Ph.D., University of London Institute of Education   *Second Impression. 16s.*

Studies in the Social Psychology of Adolescence
by C. M. FLEMING, Ed.B., Ph.D., University of London Institute of Education   *About 16s.*

7

TOWN AND COUNTRY PLANNING.
HUMAN ECOLOGY

The Social Background of a Plan: A Study of Middlesbrough
Edited by RUTH GLASS. Illustrated with Maps and Plans   *42s.*

City, Region and Regionalism
by ROBERT E. DICKINSON, Reader in Geography, University College, London. With Maps and Plans   *21s.*

The West European City: A Study in Urban Geography
by ROBERT E. DICKINSON, Reader in Geography, University College, London. Illustrated with Maps and Plans.   *In preparation. About 42s.*

Revolution of Environment
by E. A. GUTKIND, D.Ing.   *Illustrated. 30s.*

The Journey to Work
by K. LIEPMANN, Ph.D., London. With an Introduction by Sir Alexander Carr-Saunders, Director of the London School of Economics
Second Impression. 15s.

SOCIOLOGICAL STUDIES OF MODERN COMMUNITIES

Negroes in Britain
A Study of Racial Relations in English Society
by K. L. LITTLE, Ph.D., London   *25s.*

Co-operative Living in Palestine
by HENRIK F. INFIELD, Director, Rural Settlement Inst., New York
Illustrated. 7s. 6d.

ANTHROPOLOGY AND COLONIAL POLICY

The Sociology of Colonies: An Introduction to the Study of Race Contact
by RENÉ MAUNIER. Translated from the French by E. O. Lorimer

Two volumes. 63s. the set

Malay Fishermen: Their Peasant Economy
by RAYMOND FIRTH, Prof. of Anthropology, University of London

Illustrated. 25s.

Peasant Life in China
by HSIAO TUNG FEI, Ph.D., London

Fourth Impression. Illustrated. 15s.

A Chinese Village: Taitou, Shantung Province
by MARTIN C. YANG
18s.

A Japanese Village: Suye Mura
by JOHN P. EMBREE, Visiting Assoc. Prof. of Anthropology, University of Chicago. With an Introduction by a A. R. RADCLIFFE-BROWN, Professor of Social Anthropology, Oxford University *Illustrated. 18s.*

The Golden Wing: A Sociological Study of Chinese Familism
by LIN HUEH-HWA, with an Introduction by RAYMOND FIRTH

16s.

Earthbound China: A Study of Rural Economy in Yunnan
by HSIAO-TUNG FEI and CHIH-I CHANG *Illustrated. 18s.*

Under the Ancestors' Shadow: Chinese Culture and Personality
by FRANCIS L. K. HSU *Illustrated. 16s.*

The Mende: A West African People in Transition
by K. L. LITTLE, Ph.D., London *About 25s.*

9

SOCIOLOGY AND PSYCHOLOGY OF THE PRESENT CRISIS

Diagnosis of Our Time
by KARL MANNHEIM   *Fifth Impression. 10s. 6d.*

Farewell to European History or the Conquest of Nihilism
by ALFRED WEBER   *16s.*

The Fear of Freedom
by Dr. ERICH FROMM   *Fifth Impression. 15s.*

Freedom, Power, and Democratic Planning
by KARL MANNHEIM   *About 18s.*

SOCIAL PSYCHOLOGY AND PSYCHO-ANALYSIS

Psychology and the Social Pattern
by JULIAN BLACKBURN, Ph.D., B.Sc., (Econ.), Lecturer on Social Psychology, London School of Economics   *Fourth Impression. 10s. 6d.*

The Framework of Human Behaviour
by JULIAN BLACKBURN, Ph.D., B.Sc. (Econ.), Lecturer on Social Psychology, London School of Economics   *12s. 6d.*

A Handbook of Social Psychology
by KIMBALL YOUNG, Professor of Sociology, Northwestern University
Fourth Impression. 21s.

Sigmund Freud—An Introduction
A Presentation of his Theories and a discussion of the Relationship between Psycho-analysis and Sociology by WALTER HOLLITSCHER, Dr. Phil.   *Second Impression. 8s. 6d.*

The Social Problems of an Industrial Civilisation
by ELTON MAYO, Professor of Industrial Research   *12s. 6d.*

APPROACHES TO THE PROBLEM OF PERSONALITY

The Cultural Background of Personality
by RALPH LINTON, Professor of Anthropology, Columbia University
Second Impression. 10s. 6d.

The Feminine Character. History of an Ideology
by VIOLA KLEIN, Ph.D., London. With an Introduction by KARL MANNHEIM   *12s. 6d.*

A History of Autobiography in Antiquity
by GEORGE MISCH. Translated by E. W. Dickes
Two volumes. 42s. the set.

Personality and Problems of Adjustment
by KIMBALL YOUNG   *35s.*

PHILOSOPHICAL AND SOCIAL FOUNDATIONS OF THOUGHT

Homo Ludens: A Study of the Play Element in Culture
by Professor J. HUIZINGA   *18s.*

The Ideal Foundations of Economic Thought
by W. STARK, Dr. rer. pol., Dr. Jur.   *Third Impression. 15s.*

The History of Economics in its Relation to Social Development
by W. STARK, Dr. rer. pol., Dr. Jur.   *Second Impression. 7s. 6d*

America: Ideal and Reality
The United States of 1776 in Contemporary European Philosophy by W. STARK, Dr. rer. pol., Dr. Jur.   *10s. 6d.*

The Decline of Liberalism as an Ideology
by J. H. HALLOWELL   *12s. 6d.*

Society and Nature: A Sociological Inquiry
by HANS KELSEN, Formerly Prof. of Law, Vienna and Geneva, Department of Political Science, University of California   *21s.*

Marx: His Time and Ours
by R. SCHLESINGER, Ph.D., London   *30s.*

The Philosophy of Wilhelm Dilthey
by H. A. HODGES, Prof. of Philosophy, University of Reading
About 12s. 6d.

GENERAL SOCIOLOGY

A Handbook of Sociology
by W. F. OGBURN, Professor of Sociology, University of Chicago, and M. F. NIMKOFF, Professor of Sociology, Bucknell University
Second Edition (Revised). *25s.*

Social Organization
by ROBERT H. LOWIE, Professor of Anthropology, University of California
25s.

FOREIGN CLASSICS OF SOCIOLOGY

Wilhelm Dilthey: Selected Readings from his Works and an Introduction to his Sociological and Philosophical Work
by H. A. HODGES, Prof. of Philosophy, University of Reading
Second Impression. *10s. 6d.*

From Max Weber: Essays in Sociology
Translated, Edited, and with an Introduction by H. H. GERTH and C. W. MILLS
21s.

DOCUMENTARY

Changing Attitudes in Soviet Russia
Documents and Readings concerning the *Family*
Edited by R. SCHLESINGER, Ph.D., London
25s.

Changing Attitudes in Soviet Russia
Documents and Readings concerning *National Autonomy and Experiments in Administrative Devolution*
Edited by R. SCHLESINGER, Ph.D., London
In preparation. About 21s.

Changing Attitudes in Soviet Russia
Documents and Readings concerning *Foreign Policy*
Edited by R. SCHLESINGER, Ph.D., London   *In preparation. About 21s.*

All prices are net

THE WESTMINSTER PRESS, LONDON, W.9